ferrari testa rossa V-12

by JOEL E. FINN

illustrations by Frank Campione

MOTORBOOKS
INTERNATIONAL

This edition published in 2003 by Motorbooks International, an imprint of
MBI Publishing Company, Galtier Plaza, Suite 200, 380 Jackson Street,
St. Paul, MN 55101-3885 USA

First published in 1979 by The Newport Press, 1001 West 18th Street, Costa
Mesa, California 92627

Motorbooks International titles are also available at discounts in bulk quantity
for industrial or sales-promotional use. For details write to Special Sales
Manager at Motorbooks International Wholesalers & Distributors,
Galtier Plaza, Suite 200, 380 Jackson Street, St. Paul, MN 55101-3885 USA.

ISBN 0-7603-1735-6

Printed in China

TABLE OF CONTENTS

ACKNOWLEDGMENTS

Chapter 1
Kurt Worner: 3, 12 (bottom)
Jesse L. Alexander: 4, 5, 8, 9, 10, 11
Joel E. Finn: 6
Gordon Wilkins: 12, 13 (bottom)
G. Mantovani: 13 (top)

Chapter 2
Alexander: 26, 29, 31
Diana Bartley: 27
Worner: 28, 29, 30, 32
Bahamas News Bureau: 32

Chapter 3
Finn: 37
Dr. Vicente Alvarez: 38, 39
Ernie Weil: 40, 44, 45
Peter Dechert: 41, 42, 43
Bartley: 43 (top)
Alexander: 46, 48, 56
Bernard Cahier: 47, 49
MOTORSPORT: 51, 53, 54
Peter Coltrin: 52
Worner: 55
Geoffrey Goddard: 58, 59, 60, 61, 62, 72
Gordon Wilkins: 63
Chuck Magin: 66
Lester Nehamkin: 67
Warren Ballard: 68
Bahamas News Bureau: 70
Leo Cummings: 71

Chapter 4
Finn: 74 (top), 87 (center)
Alexander: 74, 75, 76, 77, 90 (right), 91, 92,
        93, 94, 95, 99, 100, 102 (bottom),
        105, 106 , 107 (bottom)
Worner: 78, 102 (top)
Alice Bixler: 79, 84, 85, 87 (bottom), 114
        (right)
Bartley: 79 (bottom), 80 (top)
Weil: 81, 87 (top)
Irving Dolin: 88
Cahier: 90 (center & bottom)
MOTORSPORT: 96 (top), 110
Gunther Molter: 96 (bottom)
Associated Press: 98
Goddard: 107, 108
Henry Manney: 109 (bottom)
Gus Vignole: 112, 113 (center), 115
Robert Johnson: 113 (top)
Nehamkin: 113 (center)
Robert Tronolone: 114 (left)
Nassau Tourist Bureau: 116

Chapter 5
Bartley: 149 (bottom)
Benno Muller: 119
Alvarez: 121
Dan Rubin: 123
Finn: 136 (bottom), 149 (top)
Coltrin: 125, 126
Alexander: 126 (top right), 127, 128, 131, 132,
        135, 136 (top), 137, 138, 141, 143,
        145, 146
CAR & DRIVER: 134 (top)
MOTORSPORT: 139
Nehamkin: 148 (center), 150 (bottom)
Tronolone: 148, 150 (center)

Chapter 6
Coltrin: 154, 162, 175, 178 (top & center)
Alexander: 155, 172, 173
Bixler: 156, 158 (top), 159, 160 (center), 180,
        183 (top & bottom), 184, 189
Finn: 158
Rubin: 157, 160 (top and bottom)
MOTORSPORT: 161, 165 (top)
Worner: 164, 165 (bottom)
Lynn Sloniger: 166
Goddard: 168, 170, 171, 172 (inset), 174

Didier Dorot: 167
Julius Weitmann: 173 (inset), 177
United Press International: 178 (bottom)
Larry Tomaras: 182
Phillip Haub: 182 (inset)
Bahamas News Bureau: 183 (center)

Chapter 7
Bixler: 189, 209
Dave Allen: 190, 192
Martin Cross: 194
Worner: 197, 198
Armand Poule: 199
Alexander: 201, 202
MOTORSPORT: 204, 205
Weil: 206
Rubin: 207, 208

Chapter 8
Bixler 212
Allen: 213
Goddard: 215, 216, 217
Alessandro Stefananini: 222

APPENDIX II
Finn: 235, 238
Alexander: 236

APPENDIX III
Pierre Perrin: 246, 247
Lionel Birnbom: 248
Road America: 250
CAR & DRIVER: 250 (bottom)

INTRODUCTION

It is always a pleasure to write about a winner. The mere fact that a racing machine became a winner is an indication that all the necessary facets of the endeavor were successfully carried out. These include the initial assessment of what was needed to win, the basic design, the constructor's skill at making the design a working reality, the drivers, crew, team manager and others who fought the race battles, and continual effort to resolve problems or make the machine more competitive over time. The machine is only a reflection of the people involved, and its goodness a measure of their ability.

This book is an attempt to present a balanced account of the background, development, and racing activity of one of the most successful competition cars of all time, the Ferrari V-12 Testa Rossa. I have chosen to structure the work as a racing history to more concisely relate the roles and interactions of the people who made the car a winner. My goal has been a narrative that accurately describes all the facets of the Testa Rossa years.

Many people have assisted me during the long process of researching and writing this book and to all of them go my thanks. In particular I would like to acknowledge the efforts of Jesse Alexander, Denis Jenkinson, Geoffrey Goddard, Pete Coltrin, and Dr. Vicente Alvarez.

I hope you will find this book not only interesting to read, but also informative on providing insights into the circumstances surrounding the success of the Testa Rossa.

CHAPTER 1
The Prototypes

THE ORIGIN OF FERRARI's introduction of the V-12 3.0-liter Testa Rossa series for the 1958 World Sports Car Championship is rooted in the nature of racing in the immediate preceding years.

After capturing the championship in 1955, Mercedes-Benz retired its all-conquering 300 SLRs, leaving only Maserati and Ferrari to contest the entire series the following year with factory-sponsored teams. Ferrari won the championship in 1956, and the 1957 series promised to be another battle between the two Italian concerns, with engine displacements growing steadily larger.

This state of affairs aroused serious concern among those who controlled the sport, as they wished to reduce speeds and foster more competition by encouraging a wider base of participation. Other makes competed, such as Jaguar, always a top contender at Le Mans, but seemingly with little interest or incentive to compete in the other races, as the live-axle D-Type was basically unsuitable for anything other than a smooth, fast course. Porsche continually lurked in the shadows, ready to pounce if the primary contestants fell out on any given occasion. Normally, Porsche could not be considered contenders for outright wins excepting tight courses such as the Targa Florio, where their handling prowess might overcome a serious horsepower disadvantage. The remaining major competitor, Aston Martin, only infrequently made an appearance, and though the equipment was certainly capable of winning, their race organization often left a lot to be desired.

Maserati and Ferrari went all out to win in 1957, both firms resting their hopes on 400 bhp-or-more 4-camshaft engine designs. In the case of Maserati, their 4.5-liter 450S V-8 model had a clear superiority over any rival that year, but they failed to capture the championship for a host of reasons. Ferrari's 4-camshaft V-12 design began the season in 3.8-liter size, designated the 315 S, but later became enlarged to slightly over 4.0-liters, known as the 335 S, in an effort to keep up with Maserati's more potent machine. The two rivals waged a close battle all season, with the outcome not decided in Ferrari's favor until the last event of the year at Caracas, when almost all the Maseratis were destroyed in accidents and fires. Contributing to the closeness of the struggle and delaying the outcome were the victories of Jaguar at Le Mans, and Aston Martin at the Nürburgring, neither of which could otherwise be counted as consistent competitors.

While Ferrari proceeded to garner the championship for the second consecutive year, the wind of change was already at work. In early 1957, discussions began among the CSI (Commission Sportive Internationale), the car constructors and the promoters which suggested a 3.0- to 3.5-liter displacement limitation beginning in 1958 as a means of lowering speeds and fostering increased competition. They hoped Mercedes-Benz might reenter the fray, as the 300 SLR already met the proposed displacement limit, and that Aston Martin and Jaguar would become more consistent competitors, creating additional international interest in the series and enhancing its prestige and importance. Though the issue remained undecided well into mid-1957, Ferrari very astutely took advantage of the long lead time to begin preparation in earnest for the projected new formula.

Sizing Up The Situation

Ferrari's assessment of the potential caliber of 3.0-liter competition for 1958 yielded the conclusion that it would be necessary to have a solid 300 horsepower in hand, with an all-up completed car weight in the 1800-1900 pound range, or less. This was based mostly on the characteristics of one of the potential primary contenders, Aston Martin, whose DBR1 already seemed to meet this set of criteria. The other manufacturers faced more serious problems insofar as 1958 could be discerned. If the D-Type Jaguar were not redesigned, then it would likely have even less power in 3.0-liter form. Its greater weight would also be a handicap, though possibly negated by the very aerodynamic body permitting high speeds on circuits such as Le Mans. The Maserati 300S seemed incapable of significant further development, but the advantages of several hundred pounds less weight and excellent handling partly offset the lack of power. Mercedes-Benz had to be considered an unknown quantity, though wishful thinking rumors suggested that an updated 300 SLR might be produced.

Enzo Ferrari had to be concerned not only about the potentials and problems of 1958 international racing, but also what course of action should be taken relative to his competition customer sales program. The primary and continually expanding market seemed to be the United States, enjoying a boom period in sports car racing. The Sports Car Club of America (SCCA) racing structure operated along displacement size lines with the "modifieds," i.e., anything other than production street cars, in groupings of 1100 to 1500 cc, 1500 to 2000 cc, 2000 to 3000 cc, 3000 to 5000 cc, etc. Unfortunately, actual races for the modifieds were usually split into two events,

under 1500 cc in one and over 1500 cc in another, the latter considered to be the "feature" attraction. This meant that the very popular, four-cylinder, 2.0-liter, Testa Rossas might win their particular class within the over-1500 cc race, but had little hope for outright victories and the resulting publicity.

Though many successes had been achieved, Ferrari was now disenchanted with the capabilities of 4- and 6-cylinder engine designs. Consequently, most of the factory development activity was directed toward replacement of the 2.0-liter Testa Rossa with a new model suitable for both the team and customers. As the SCCA tended to follow the international rules, Ferrari reasoned that if the new formula called for a 3.0-liter limit, then that appropriate American class (2000 cc to 3000 cc) would become the most prestigious. It could also mean a substantial number of sales to 2.0-liter owners upgrading their equipment, as well as sales for replacement of the aging 4-cylinder Monza series, formerly top contenders for victories in that class.

The Ferrari engineering team, led by Andrea Fraschetti, had a choice of three engine possibilities. First, they might pursue development of a new 3.0-liter 4-camshaft motor based on the 315 S-335 S type, but this approach would probably result in a heavy and bulky design. In addition, such an engine might be unsuitable for customer usage because of its complexity and high maintenance cost. A further problem would be the difficulty in making it reliable in time for the beginning of 1958 racing season.

Ferrari's second option would be to speed up development of the Dino V-6 family, originally intended partly as a 2.0-liter replacement for the 4-cylinder Testa Rossa series. However, like the 4-camshaft design, it also might not be available for the start of the 1958 racing.

The third possibility was to extract more power out of the production 3.0-liter 250 GT engine. The design was sound, well proven and featured excellent reliability characteristics, and thus it became the basis for starting experimentation. Development work continued on the other approaches and though eventually appearing in one form or another, they do not constitute a fundamental part of the V-12 Testa Rossa series story from this point on.

The 250 GT Gets Hot

In 1956, Ferrari had produced a small run of Berlinettas utilizing modified 250 GT engines and aimed at capturing the Tour de France. They had given good accounts of themselves at that event as well as other Gran Turismo races throughout the season. Before starting to make really drastic modifications to the basic 250 GT engine, an attempt was made to determine how much more power could be gained while retaining the basic design concept. The result of these experiments became installed in a very light new Berlinetta (chassis 0677) and entrusted to the impassive Belgian, Olivier Gendebien, then Ferrari's leading Gran Turismo driver, who proceeded to win the Circuit of Sicily with it in early April, 1957.

Encouraged by this success, Ferrari rebuilt the engine once again in an even more powerful form with 290 MM camshaft timing, installed it in the coupe, and entered the car for Gendebien in the Mille Miglia held on May 11, 1957. While the motor retained its inside spark plugs and three downdraft Weber carburetors, contemporary journals universally refer to it being in a "wild state of tune." Output was estimated to be in the 250 to 260 bhp range, possibly an understatement. Gendebien, who had finished 5th overall and 1st in class with a Ferrari Gran Turismo in the 1956 Mille Miglia, was accompanied in 1957 by his cousin, Jacques Wascher, as navigator. Gendebien not only always remained calm, but could drive very rapidly while preserving the machinery at the same time, always endearing attributes to a racing car manufacturer.

The combination of Gendebien/Wascher and Berlinetta proved to be a brilliant choice, as an outstanding performance resulted. The car finished the grueling 1000-mile grind 3rd overall, only eight minutes behind the winner, at an average speed of 93.63 mph—only one mph slower than Taruffi managed in his victory with the 335 S Ferrari. Reports indicated that Gendebien drove flat out all the time, and one writer suggested the accelerator pedal must have been nailed to the floor. The other Ferrari team drivers reported they could only pass Gendebien with difficulty, even on the long, straight Northern Italian stretches. This must indicate something significant about the power of the Berlinetta, not to mention Gendebien's skill. In addition to capturing 3rd overall, Gendebien also won the Gran Premio Nuvolari, awarded to the fastest car on the homebound stretch from Cremona to Mantua (Tazio Nuvolari's hometown) to Brescia, a distance of 82 miles. Gendebien averaged 123.91 mph for this leg, beating Wolfgang Von Trips' time of 122.52 mph in a 315 S, and Taruffi's mark of 121.47 mph in the 335 S, though it must be admitted that both of the larger machines were suffering from transaxle problems likely causing their chauffeurs to slow down to make the finish. Still, the performance more than met Ferrari's hopes and encouraged the engineering team, now under Carlo Chiti's direction, to press on with more drastic experiments to the 250 GT engine.

The Mille Miglia coupe appeared next at the Nürburgring to contest the 1000-kilometer race held on May 26, 1957. Most of the Ferrari team drivers tried it out during practice, turning in times only 10 to 12 seconds slower than its bigger brothers and more than 30 seconds faster than anything else in the Gran Turismo class, primarily a horde of Mercedes-Benz 300SL coupes. Unfortunately, Von Trips crashed the Berlinetta on the day before the race at Wehrseifen, about halfway around the circuit. He momentarily forgot the coupe was equipped as a production machine with a right-hand accelerator pedal, unlike the sports racers with their central go button, and hit the firewall instead of the brake. Unable to recover quickly enough, he shot straight off the road and down a steep bank, coming to rest in some substantial shrubbery. The front end was damaged sufficiently to keep it out of the race, and Von Trips had the misfortune to suffer a broken vertebrae in his back, not a particularly serious injury, but one so painful that it would keep him out of action for a month.

The Berlinetta was eventually rebuilt and competed in a number of other Gran Turismo events in 1957, such as Reims, but never played any further significant role in the development of the Testa Rossa. However, it certainly influenced the design of the 1958 Tour de France series of Berlinettas, and in that context must be considered their direct prototype.

The First V-12 Testa Rossa Prototype

Also appearing at the Nürburgring was a new prototype, constructed on chassis number 0666 and destined to become the direct predecessor of the 1958 V-12 Testa Rossa team cars. It was based on the 1956 style right-hand drive 290 MM chassis, a ladder-type frame design on a 92.5-inch wheelbase. The 290 MM normally used a De Dion tube, transverse leaf rear suspension with coil springs in front. In 1956 guise, it carried a 3.5-liter V-12 engine with four distributors denoted as the Type 130 S. The 290 MM was not exactly sylphlike, weighing in at just over 2100 pounds, courtesy of the substantial frame and rear suspension layout. In 1957, the 290 MM became updated with 4-camshaft engines and other modifications, in concert with the model's nomenclature changing to 315 S (3.8-liter) and 335 S (4.0 liter). This particular method of naming model types followed the standard Ferrari policy throughout the period of using the cylinder capacity in cubic centimeters as the identification. For instance, 335 cc (335 S model) times 12 cylinders equals 4020 cc, except for rounding off, the actual total displacement.

Installed for the Nürburgring venture was the 250 GT engine/transmission combination, essentially in Mille Miglia form. The whole car had been slapped together in great haste as the bodywork and general detailing were crude and not well finished, quite unlike normal Ferrari practice. The bodywork had been somewhat modified for the experiment, and even the most casual observer could spot the several different shades of red paint employed in the reworked sections. Whatever the case with the bodywork, mechanically it seemed to be in fine fettle, emitting a peculiar rasping and very biting exhaust note indicative of really radical timing.

Though Ferrari claimed the engines in the coupe and roadster were identical, the difference in sound alone proved the new prototype had undergone further development.

During practice for the Nürburgring, the prototype got a thorough workout from all the Ferrari team drivers, with Gendebien eventually establishing 6th fastest time overall, only some 5 seconds slower than the larger displacement Astons and Ferraris. Everyone seemed pleased with its handling, particularly Phil Hill, then in his first full season of campaigning team Ferraris.

Masten Gregory, the bespectacled young Kansan, had been hired by Ferrari specifically for this event to drive the prototype, partnered by Gendebien. Unfortunately, the Von Trips accident required some driver assignment reshuffling, with Gendebien being selected to take the German's vacated seat in a 335 S. This left Gregory without a co-driver for the prototype. Romolo Tavoni, the Ferrari team manager, seemed unable to find another suitable chauffeur, and as it was already late in the final day before the event, he decided to tentatively scratch the entry.

Gregory was furious at Tavoni's apparent lack of action, and argued vehemently in a futile attempt to change the team manager's mind. Tavoni did agree to continue looking for a replacement, but as time was short, the sop to Gregory looked rather feeble. Gregory stormed off to his hotel, convinced he would only be a spectator at the following morning's 9:00 o'clock race start.

Masten Gregory in the prototype at the 'Ring. Externally, the car appears identical to the 290 MM.

Roused from sleep and rushed to the 'Ring only moments before the start, Gregory nonetheless gave a good account of himself and the prototype TR (wearing No. 7).

Tavoni was true to his word, however, and late Saturday night engaged the services of Carlo Marolli, nominally an OSCA pilot, to co-drive the prototype with Gregory. Poor Marolli had no opportunity to try out the Testa Rossa on the track due to the short time remaining, and had to be content with a few blasts up and down the pit lane. He would obviously have to learn as he went along during the race. As can readily be imagined, Marolli likely spent rather a sleepless night in anticipation of the morrow's uncertainties.

Gregory had not bothered to set his alarm clock that night, figuring there was no necessity to arise early and prepare to drive. The race was to commence at 9:00 a.m., and when Gregory didn't appear by 8:30, a worried Tavoni sent a mechanic to search out his errant driver. Gregory was still asleep when the mechanic pounded on his door with barely 20 minutes to go before the race was to commence. He made the Le Mans style start with only seconds to spare, unshaven, uncombed, half dressed and probably only half awake, without ever meeting Marolli.

Gregory got off to a slow start, hardly surprising considering the circumstances, but within a few laps he powered his way up into a secure 4th place, essentially achieved by some very aggressive driving. His progress through the Karussel on each lap was something to behold, the curve being negotiated in a series of opposite lock power slides. No one could ever accuse Gregory of not being a charger.

He retained his grip on 4th place throughout the remainder of his initial drive, before turning over the chores to Marolli. He proved to be an unwise choice as co-driver, seeming very uncomfortable in the car, probably the first powerful racing machine he had ever driven. A measure of the discomfort were his lap times, as much as 3 minutes slower than Gregory's. The prototype lost position steadily, partly due to some rear end stability problems in the final laps, and eventually finished the race a somewhat discouraging 10th overall. However, the point had been established—the concept had potential; it only needed additional development.

Gregory hoists himself from the cockpit while Marolli begins refueling during a driver changeover.

Testa Rossa Engine Development

While this prototype activity was taking place, discussions were going on as to the future of sports car racing, particularly in view of De Portago's tragic accident in the Mille Miglia, resulting directly in its demise forever, as well as causing the cancellation of that year's Targa Florio race. The idea of a 3.5-liter formula seemed readily acceptable to many manufacturers such as Jaguar, already at 3.4-liters, and Aston Martin, which could easily produce any size from 3.0 to 3.7-liters for their DBR1. Maserati concluded that no further substantial power gains could be achieved with the unfashionable long-stroke 300S, which could not be bored out further, and so began work on a 3.5-liter V-12 derived from their 250F Grand Prix program.

Ferrari's engineering team finished constructing their initial pair of redesigned 250 GT engines shortly after the Nürburgring, and the changes from the street configuration were numerous. The engines both used the same block assemblies and displacement dimensions of 75.0 x 58.8-mm bore and stroke totaling 3117 cc. They differed in cylinder head configuration as one had a twin-camshaft layout (one per bank) like the 250 GT, while the other featured 4-camshaft construction (two per bank) such as fitted to the 290 MM-315 S-335 S family.

Revisions to the block included enlarging the crankshaft main journals from 55 to 60 mm, with the center main now having a 4-bolt cap for greater bottom end rigidity. The other major change was a modification to provide a 4-bolt head tightening pattern around the cylinders, rather than the three utilized on the 250 GT, the purpose being to provide a better gasket seal for the higher revs required in a racing engine.

The single camshaft-per-bank engine utilized 250 GT-based cylinder heads but altered rather substantially. It now had outside spark plugs located near the exhaust valves, where formerly there were inside plugs located by the Siamesed intake ports. This arrangement allowed the installation of six twin-throat, downdraft Weber 38 DCN carburetors in the valley between the heads, each throat feeding a separate cylinder. Larger valves were fitted, as were specially forged and machined connecting rods and lightweight aluminum pistons. Most other 250 GT engine components remained basically

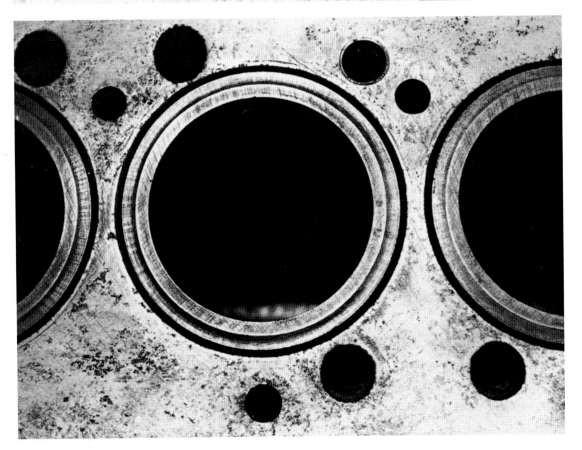

Bodied by Scaglietti, this pontoon-fender chassis, No. 0704, was the second TR prototype. It is shown here at the Le Mans weigh in. The supporting struts for the fenders were removed later.

the same, including the hairpin valve springs and the wet sump oiling systems.

The twin camshaft per bank derivation, known as the Type 312 LM, was a Fraschetti initiated effort to attempt a marriage of the lighter 250 GT block assembly with a scaled down version of the more efficient 290 MM- 315 S-335 S family cylinder head layout. During initial testing, it is purported to have produced approximately 320 bhp at 8000 rpm, though possessing a relatively narrow power band. Both Solex and Weber carburetors were fitted, though it is believed that six of the latter became the final choice.

Pontoon Fenders For Le Mans

For the 1957 Le Mans on June 23/24, the single-camshaft engine and a companion 250 GT reinforced 4-speed transmission were installed in a lengthened and strengthened 4-cylinder Testa Rossa right-hand-drive chassis (0704). This second prototype became the direct progenitor of the 1958 customers series of

V-12 sports racers. The wheelbase of the very light 4-cylinder ladder-type frame chassis was lengthened from 88.5 to 92.5 inches, but retained its original suspension organization of coil spring front and live rear axle incorporating coil springs and radius rods.

The distinctive body style of this prototype caused something of a sensation at Le Mans, being a fresh new design by Sergio Scaglietti. It had a long sloping nose extending as a seemingly separate unit from the cutaway front fenders. The object of the exercise was to increase the flow of cool air to the front brakes, reducing fade problems due to over-heating in the long distance races. The design, at first unnamed, soon became known as sponson or pontoon fenders, and remains one of the more striking and visually exciting race car shapes ever produced. At the official Le Mans weigh-in the new car tipped the scales at just slightly over 1700 pounds, even with some fuel in the tank, a figure more than 300 pounds lighter than its 4-camshaft brothers, and no doubt stirring competitive interest.

Competitors became much more intrigued with the new prototype's performance in practice, where it turned consistent lap times in the 4-minute and small change area, only a few seconds slower than the best 3.8-, 4.0-liter Ferrari, or 4.5 Maserati speeds. Gendebien and Maurice Trintignant were assigned to drive the car for the race and both were extremely pleased with its potential, believing they had a good chance of finishing in a top spot.

The Nürburgring prototype had also been brought to Le Mans, bodied as before with the 4-camshaft engine installed, but did not run because of suspected piston failure while being warmed up in the pits prior to the start of practice. All the Ferraris at Le Mans that year were using a new piston design, giving trouble even in practice and making life thoroughly difficult for the mechanics. As they had their hands full, no attempt was made to repair the Nürburgring prototype for the race, it being left on the transporter for the duration.

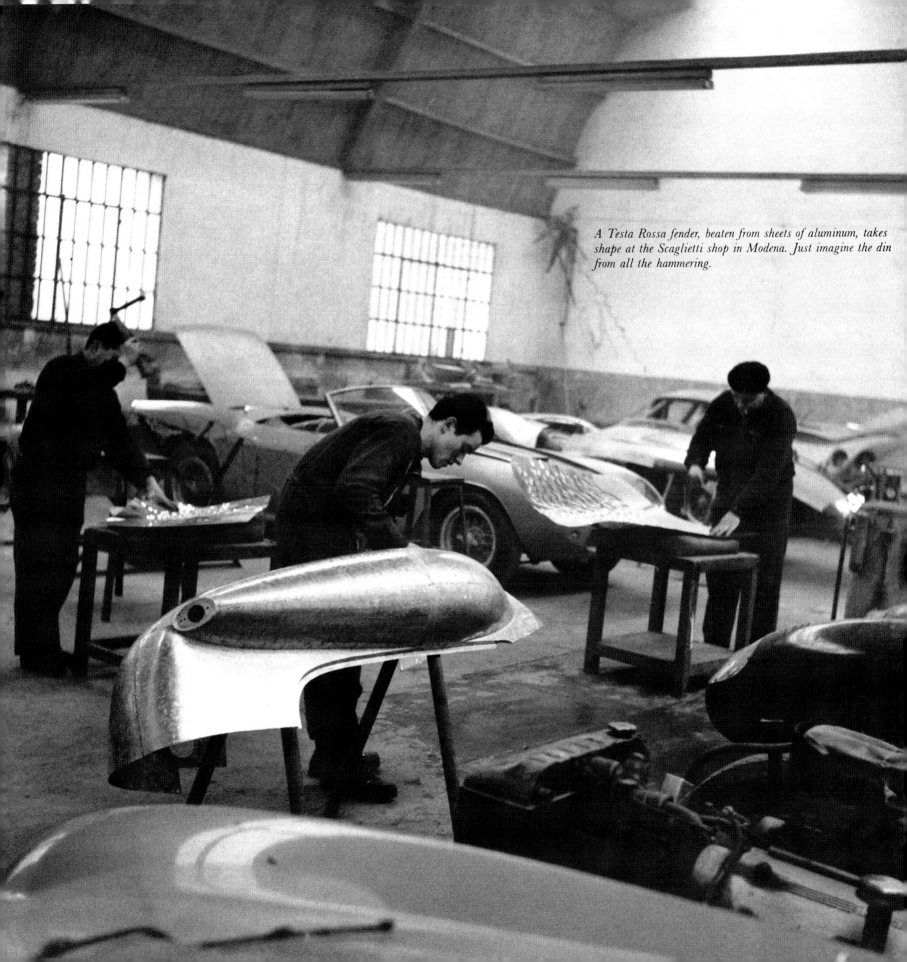

A Testa Rossa fender, beaten from sheets of aluminum, takes shape at the Scaglietti shop in Modena. Just imagine the din from all the hammering.

The second prototype at Le Mans, in second place by the third hour.

During the race, starting at 4:00 p.m., the second prototype performed magnificently, moving into 2nd place by the third hour before slipping back one spot during the early evening hours. It held that position until dropping out just past midnight with a burned piston. This same problem eliminated all the other team Ferraris but one, and is believed to have been a case of too-high compression coupled with gasoline of too-low an octane. While running flat-out on the Mulsanne Straight, the combination produced excessive leanness and pre-ignition pinging, evidently not audible to the driver over the wind and mechanical noise.

Eventually the pistons would burn through. The one Ferrari that survived the 24 hours, the Lewis-Evans/Severi 3.8-liter machine, was very conservatively driven, evidently a necessity to escape the problem.

In spite of not finishing, the second prototype had certainly given a good account of itself. Another encouraging performance and once more indicative that Ferrari was on the right track for 1958.

Subsequent to Le Mans, a clearer picture of 1958 regulations began to emerge, with general concurrence on a 3.0-liter limit imposition by the CSI. There were still two more races left on the 1957 calendar, Sweden and Venezuela, that would allow Ferrari to complete his experimentation, finalize the design and enter the 1958 campaign with proven equipment.

A decision made just after Le Mans was to drop further immediate attempts to refine the 312 LM engine and concentrate all attention on producing a finalized derivation of the single-camshaft-per-bank configuration. The decision was based on Chiti's expectation that the revised outside plug cylinder head would be almost as efficient as the 4-camshaft layout, less complex, easier to maintain, and lighter. He predicted a safe and reliable 300 to 310 bhp could be realized with the single camshaft design, only 10 to 20 bhp less than the much more complicated 312 LM. To him, the effort and expense to gain such a negligible difference in power was not worth the bother. The 312 LM engine was removed from the Nürburgring prototype and put on the shelf for future work. It would not be seen again in competition until early 1958.

Teething Problems At Sweden

Both prototypes were further reworked over the summer and next appeared at Kristianstad, for the 6-hour Swedish Grand Prix for Sports Cars held August 11, 1957, on the bumpy Rabelovsbana 3.8-mile circuit.

The Nürburgring prototype (0666) now had the second prototype's 3.1-liter Le Mans engine/transmission combination installed, but retained its De Dion rear end. The second prototype (0704) was fitted with what can be considered the final derivation of the 1957-58

Left: *The engine of 0704 at Sweden, compared with 0666 at* **Right.**

Gendebien in 0666 at Sweden. The air duct to the rear brakes was apparently used only on this car, but both prototypes had the short exhaust pipes. **Inset:** *Shows 0666 cockpit.*

V-12 Testa Rossa engine. It displaced 2953 cc using a 73.0x58.8-mm bore and stroke combination identical to the original 250 GT dimensions, but with revised camshaft timing, larger carburetor chokes, and other internal modifications raising output to 300 bhp at 7200 rpm. Installed in conjunction with the engine was a new style transmission, still a front mounted 4-speed unit but now containing stronger shafts and gears in a reinforced case. The shift lever assembly had been moved farther back and higher than on the 250 GT predecessor, and the quadrant contained a lock-out lever for reverse.

As usual, both cars were tried out in practice by most of the Ferrari team drivers, but the results were somewhat inconclusive, as the Nürburgring prototype's engine didn't want to rev as high as it should, and the Le Mans version suffered a broken gearbox. The gearbox problem turned out to be a cracked mainshaft that could not be repaired perfectly in time for the race. Gendebien/Trintignant were assigned the original car, assumed to be in better condition, while Gregory/Seidel drew the short straw and were handed the questionable condition second prototype.

Neither entry performed well in the race, which began at noon. The Gendebien/ Trintignant mount suffered from various engine ailments before being withdrawn at 1:50 p.m. Engine failure was given as the very simple, official reason for its retirement, though one observer noted that the car had been "withdrawn as being out of breath, lacking pistons, rings, valves, or a combination of the lot." Poor Trintignant never even got to drive.

The Gregory/Seidel car ran as high as 5th before succumbing once again to transmission problems only a little more than an hour into

The second prototype underway at Sweden, Masten Gregory up.

the grind. Seidel, like Trintignant, never had a chance to race.

Sweden was certainly a poor performance for the Testa Rossa, and teething problems obviously remained, though there was plenty of time to resolve them as the season finale, to be held at Caracas, Venezuela, was not scheduled until November 3.

In early September the CSI confirmed the 1958 3.0-liter limit as a reality, spurring Ferrari to finish testing the new model and begin volume production of the finalized version. The second prototype (0704) was utilized as the test car and logged countless practice laps at the Modena Autodrome to prove the reliability of the package. During the same period the first prototype was completely stripped and rebodied to the pontoon-fender design with inside door hinges, a feature shared by most of the production examples well into 1958.

Reliability Comes At Caracas

For the crucial Venezuelan race, the 1957 championship decider, Ferrari sent both prototypes as backup to a pair of 335 S models entered as the primary candidates to achieve victory. At Caracas, Von Trips/Seidel were assigned to the original prototype (0666) with Trintignant/ Gendebien sharing the newer machine (0704) which seemed to be somewhat slower than had been expected, though the cause remained unknown. They finished 3rd and 4th respectively behind their larger teammates, after all the Maserati opposition had been literally destroyed. Both cars had a trouble-free run, providing proof that the needed reliability had been achieved.

Testa Rossa Announcement

Ferrari announced his 1958 Sports Car racing plans to the public at his annual press conference held in Modena on November 22, 1957. He officially introduced the V-12 Testa Rossa series and stated it would be his primary entry for the 1958 International races. In Ferrari terminology the new series was denoted as the 250 TR, the 250 referring to individual cylinder capacity in cubic centimeters. The sobriquet of Testa Rossa, meaning "Red Head" in Italian, was also carried forward to the new model, though red had been the normal color of all sports racing Ferrari's camshaft covers beginning with the Mondial-Monza types in 1954, and the name of Testa Rossa for a model designation was already being used for the 4-cylinder 500 TRC series. As seen on the prototypes, the Scaglietti pontoon fender body design would be the standard coachwork.

The partially completed chassis of a customer's TR.

Ferrari stated that there would be two versions of the new series, one for the team and a slightly differing model for customers. Both would utilize the same engine, said to produce 300 bhp at 7200 rpm, coupled with the revised 4-speed transmission. The 92.5-inch wheelbase chassis would be basically identical, both ladder-type frames with coil spring front suspensions and drum brakes based on the 4-cylinder Testa Rossa, but differing in rear end design. The factory cars would employ either the 290 MM style De Dion-transverse leaf spring or a live axle, while customer cars used only the latter. The other major area of difference would be that factory cars might be produced with right- or left-hand drive, while customers' cars would always be built with left-hand drive.

At the press conference, the discontinuance of the 4-cylinder series became official, though it was stated that many of that model's features, such as the live axle, lightweight frame, and general suspension design, had been retained for the customer's version of the V-12 Testa Rossa,

as they had proven to be reliable and easily maintainable by privateers and therefore more suitable for their use than the complicated De Dion setup. Also manifested was the belief that the customer's version should be the car to beat in American races, enhancing its sales appeal in Ferrari's most important market.

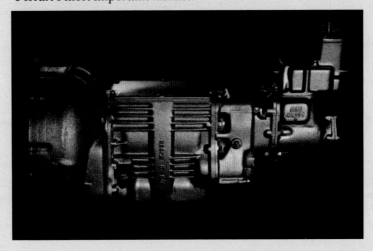

The V-12 TR transmission is identifiable by the stiffening ribs on the side of the case and a raised, offset gearshift lever.

Part of the rationale for the demise of the 2.0-liter sports racing series was unspoken at the time, though work was known to be well underway on a V-6 engine for that class. Observers expected a new model using such an engine in a shortened V-12 TR chassis, to be announced in early 1958, as a replacement for the aging 4-cylinder Testa Rossa.

Also unmentioned during the press conference were any references to the 4-camshaft cylinder head conversion for the V-12 Testa Rossa motor, a dry sump system, and the 5-speed transmission, experiments all known to be actively pursued during that time frame.

On display at the press conference was the first example built of a customer's car (0710), constructed for John Von Neumann, Ferrari's west coast U.S. distributor. No team cars were on exhibit, as both the Caracas veterans had been left in Venezuela in care of Carlos Kaufman, the Ferrari South American distributor, where they would be shipped from there to Buenos Aires, Argentina, for the opening event of the new championship season.

Comments by journalists about the new Testa Rossas were very interesting. There was some concern about the effectiveness of the body shape and several Italian correspondents questioned the reality of a stylist such as Scaglietti trying to interpret aerodynamics. After all, Scaglietti was a body builder, not an engineer. They hinted that perhaps it was about time that Ferrari secured the services of an aerodynamicist, and did the job more realistically. While the pontoon fender design was beautiful, the Testa Rossa was bulky overall when compared to some of the English competitors such as Jaguar. In addition, the frontal area was enormous and needed paring down.

The English journalists of course raised the same issues in even more detail, but reserved their most biting comments for the engine. They argued that the V-12 Testa Rossa power plant was outmoded because it was based on a 10-year-old design. To them, Ferrari could have done much better than to utilize such a bulky and heavy engine. Of course the English writers had a field day criticizing the retention of drum brakes instead of discs, and the (to them) overly substantial chassis.

Top: *The first customer's TR (0710) at press conference.*
Center: *A TR engine being assembled at Maranello.* **Bottom:** *The cockpit of 0716.*

The Ferrari Design Philosophy

What some of the detractors failed to fully understand was that the Testa Rossa, like its predecessors, had been designed and constructed exclusively to meet the demands imposed by endurance racing, not sprints. Reliability and durability were of paramount importance in finishing the long-distance grinds, each of which exacted a unique set of taxing requirements. As examples, Sebring was hard on chassis components and brakes, the Targa Florio on transmissions and rear ends, the Nürburgring on suspensions, and Le Mans on engines (though very easy on everything else). A competitor had to complete one of these races to win or score points, a fact uppermost in the Ferrari order of importance. His cars rarely fell by the wayside due to mechanical problems, as the Ferrari solution was to over-engineer and over-design all components to preclude as much as possible the potential for failure. This meant, in practice, using a conservative approach by fitting only tried and true components coupled with rigorous testing procedures.

This is not to imply that Ferrari did not keep abreast of the latest developments, as the organization continuously experimented with new ideas. In fact, at any point in time an almost bewildering variety of experiments might be in process, and only those that met Ferrari reliability and durability goals would be finally employed. Ferrari tended to let others be the pioneers and prove new concepts in actual racing, before installation on his cars. Often this gave competitors a momentary advantage, but many times it was nullified by frequent breakdowns. When he felt a concept to have been proven worthwhile and reliable, then it would be installed on his machines. Ferrari racing cars were always noted for their toughness and the ability to keep on slogging around long after the pioneers or sprinters had dropped out, a direct result of this kind of approach.

None of this is meant to imply that a Ferrari was sluggard by any means in the shorter races, but sturdiness exacts a toll in heavier construction, a handicap often difficult to overcome, particularly at the more sinuous tracks. The English constructors during the mid-fifties, primarily Cooper and Lotus, were pioneering the concepts that would lead inexorably to a new generation of rear-engine, lightweight, and better handling machinery. While difficult to beat in sprint events of the period, they rarely competed successfully in the long and tough endurance races, as lasting reliability was yet to be attained. Suspension components habitually seemed to fall off or apart, a distressing occurrence at best and more often downright dangerous.

The Ferrari legend is to a great extent based on the durability of his machines, coupled with a dedication to achieving success that few competitors have brought to bear on the sport over a comparable period of time. The Ferrari planning process was oriented toward winning in the future as well as currently. The Testa Rossa was a complete embodiment of this approach and the model's success over its competitive lifetime would be a significant factor in enhancing the Ferrari legend.

250 testa rossa

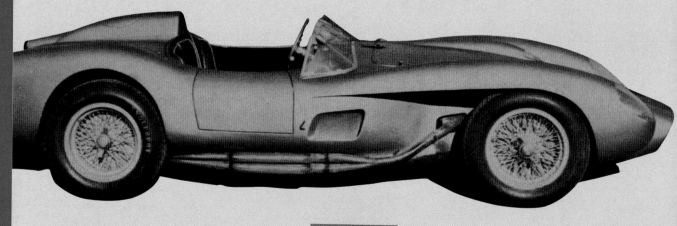

MODENA **Ferrari** ITALIA
automobili

250 testa rossa

motore   telaio

numero dei cilindri disposti a « V » con apertura di 60"   12

alesaggio e corsa   mm. 73 x 58,8

cilindrata totale   cmc. 2953,211

rapporto di compressione   9,8 : 1

potenza massima a 7200 giri-minuto con benzina 100 NO CV   300

monoblocco cilindri e basamento in silumin con canne riportate - albero
   motore su 7 supporti e bielle affiancate su cuscinetti a guscio sottile

valvole in testa disposte a « V » con camme e bilancieri a rullo, registro a vite

alberi distribuzione e pompa acqua azionati da catena silenziosa con tenditore

lubrificazione con pompa ad ingranaggi

accensione a batteria e due spinterogeni con anticipo automatico

alimentazione con pompa meccanica ed una pompa elettrica autoregolatrice

carburazione con 6 carburatori a doppio corpo

frizione a secco e mozzo elastico

raffreddamento con radiatore acqua a tubetti e lamelle - radiatore olio pure
   a tubetti e lamelle

cambio a 4 velocità sincronizzate e silenziose, comandate da leva centrale,
   presa diretta in 4ᵃ velocità

ponte posteriore del tipo rigido con puntoni laterali e triangolo di reazione

sospensione posteriore a molle elicoidali e grandi ammortizzatori oleodinamici

sospensione anteriore a ruote indipendenti con molle elicoidali e ammortizzatori oleodinamici

telaio monoblocco in tubi di acciaio

direzione ed articolazioni indipendenti, guida a sinistra

grandi freni sulle 4 ruote, con comando oleodinamico doppio sulle ganasce
   mediante pedale a doppia pompa e surpressore ; meccanico sulle ruote
   posteriori mediante comando a mano

		anteriore 1308
passo e carreggiata	mm. 2350	posteriore 1300
peso a vuoto della vettura carrozzata spyder		Kg. 800
capacità serbatoio carburante		lt. 140
consumo carburante ogni 100 km.		lt. 26 circa
		anteriori 5.50 x 16
ruote a raggi in lega leggera per pneumatici		posteriori 6.00 x 16

velocità raggiungibili a 7200 giri motore con pneumatici 6.00 x 16"

rapporto ponte	I vel.	II vel.	III vel.	IV vel.	in IV vel. x 100 giri
7 34	85 kmh.	125 kmh.	167 kmh.	198 kmh.	2,760 kmh.
7 32	90 kmh.	130 kmh.	176 kmh.	211 kmh.	2,930 kmh.
8 34	97 kmh.	143 kmh.	189 kmh.	226 kmh.	3,140 kmh.
8 32	103 kmh.	151 kmh.	200 kmh.	240 kmh.	3,350 kmh.
9 34	109 kmh.	160 kmh.	213 kmh.	255 kmh.	3,540 kmh.
9 32	123 kmh.	171 kmh.	226 kmh.	270 kmh.	3,760 kmh.

I dati del presente prospetto hanno valore unicamente informativo

16

CHAPTER 2
The Key Players

THE DOMINANT FORCE: Enzo Ferrari

Literally millions of words have been written over the years about this remarkable man, and still there is much about him we don't know. It is clear, however, that he is patriotic, single-minded, determined to be successful and desirous of making the name of Ferrari live forever.

Ferrari's *raison d'etre* is automobile racing, to which he has dedicated his entire life. With his talents he likely would have been just as successful in any other career, but fortunately for motor sport, he picked that arena to expend his energy. His personal racing record reveals a number of successes but his real capabilities are in organization, planning and strategy. His years during the twenties and thirties both with and operating in the name of Alfa Romeo, provided the proper training ground for starting his own firm. While those years brought success and honorary titles, such as Commendatore (commander) and Ingegnére (engineer), the glory always seemed to go primarily to the manufacturer. Ferrari determined to produce racing cars in his own name and took that step just before World War II erupted, setting up shop in Modena, a medium-sized, heavily industrialized Northern Italian city not far from Bologna. When hostilities ceased, he rapidly began implementing his plans, fielding his first competitive machines in 1947, using V-12 engine designs.

With the aid of some extremely dedicated workers, his dream turned to rapid fruition, initially based on sports car successes, and later with the Grand Prix program. Ferrari very astutely directed his company through a comprehensive growth plan, including new facilities in Maranello, a village near Modena, and by 1958 had captured several Grand Prix and sports car titles. In that short 10-year period the name Ferrari had achieved worldwide fame. Certainly Ferrari racing automobiles came to represent the Italian character to many foreigners, as his products were instantly identifiable. They had a look, sound and feel distinctly their own, implicitly reflecting Enzo's beliefs and ideals.

Ferrari, never actually a designer, nonetheless had an in-depth knowledge of racing car construction through years of intimate involvement with every aspect of the sport. While designs cannot be directly attributed to him, certain characteristics of his machines are clearly traceable to his beliefs. He insisted that any car bearing his name be built solidly and strongly, using only the best materials and the most highly skilled workers. Reliability, durability and driver safety were key goals. He felt that drivers could not possibly do well without absolute confidence in the construction of the car. Nothing was to collapse or fall off and they were overdesigned to withstand the stress of tremendous abuse. If the resulting cars weighed too much because of the strong construction, then the disadvantage must be overcome by more power.

To Ferrari, the racing cars bearing his Prancing Horse emblem were the critical element; they, not the drivers, were to receive the primary credit. Most drivers, if they wanted to stay on the factory team for very long, learned quickly to down play their role in bringing victory to the firm. The same dictum applied to privateers. Only "friends of Ferrari," i.e., those regarded by Enzo as truly recognizing the predominant role his namesake cars played in their successes could expect to purchase top-flight machinery. After all, Ferrari built cars, not drivers. He insisted on absolute loyalty from every worker in his employ; and any number of hours, no matter how long, were expected to be cheerfully expended by all hands to gain victory. Generally, Ferrari paid low wages, both to workers and drivers, with the money saved being plowed into the racing program. Ferrari felt that his workers should be as dedicated as he was in bringing glory to his name, and if low wages were a condition to be tolerated, so be it.

Ferrari's relationships with drivers were very complex. Basically, he tended to keep them at arm's length, so as not to be overly affected by their reactions to the stresses and strains of their chosen avocation. In addition, this inured Ferrari to a certain extent from the shock of a driver death in one of the firm's cars. This detachment was almost a necessity from his point of view, as he always remained confident that it was never the car at fault, but rather the driver.

Ferrari was a master publicist and worked tirelessly to promote his name and company. His annual yearbooks were of great graphic appeal, and the carefully staged press conferences made attendance a must for any serious motor racing journalist. His relationship with the popular Italian press was combative. On the one hand, the press extolled his glory to the heavens when victory was achieved, but tore him to pieces when a Ferrari driver was killed. Fortunately, the deaths were amazingly few, though when they did occur, all hell broke loose, such as the torrent of bombast resulting from the De Portago Mille Miglia tragedy.

Ferrari had suffered a grievous blow in 1956 when his only son, Dino, died unexpectedly following complications from a minor road accident. He had been groomed practically from birth to take over the firm, and his death ruined Enzo's plan to gradually retire and turn over to Dino the day-to-day operation of the business. In 1957, Ferrari was 59 years old, and instead of being able to relax and concentrate solely on his racing program, he had to continue carrying the full burden with no relief in sight. His son's death caused him great internal turmoil and sadness, into which he practically retired for several years. The result, after a long period of introspection, was to rededicate himself totally to racing and pursue his growth goals as long as he was able to, both physically and mentally.

Ferrari's relationship with his wife, Laura, has often been described as cold, and the death of their son undoubtedly affected them in different ways. When Enzo retreated to himself, Signora Ferrari felt more of a need to get out into the world. In the next few years she would attend various races, going as far afield as Nassau. In the course of these trips she sometimes became involved in the trials and tribulations that team personnel had to deal with on an everyday basis, as well as the methods of operation. She is reported to have served as a well-meaning but complicating intermediary on numerous occasions between team personnel and Ferrari. The positive effectiveness of her activity, if any, is difficult to ascertain, though the fact that it took place can be discerned in several incidents taking place during the Testa Rossa heyday.

THE CHIEF DESIGNER: Carlo Chiti

Throughout the early and mid-fifties, Ferrari design could be characterized as being composed of mediocre chassis and excellent engines, particularly the V-12. While chassis layout remained relatively insular within Ferrari, the firm's designers, led by Aurelio Lampredi, generally followed the flow of other concerns toward in-line racing engines in the 1952-1955 period. Jaguar, Aston Martin, Maserati and Mercedes-Benz all seemed to favor that form of design rather than a V-type. Ferrari went right along with the rest of the crowd, more or less de-emphasizing the V-12. The marque captured the 2.0-liter 1953 Grand Prix crown with an in-line 4-cylinder configuration and upgraded it to 2.5 liters for the 1954-1955 seasons. Neither year was very successful, leading Ferrari to conclude that fresh blood and new ideas were required.

In 1955, the Mercedes-Benz juggernaut flattened everyone, including Ferrari, and triggered a Maranello housecleaning. For Ferrari, a dismal 1955 suddenly brightened when his organization was gifted with the entire stock of Lancia V-8 engine Grand Prix team cars and spares. Lancias were top contenders, far superior to Ferrari, but in deep financial trouble. The gift immediately allowed the Maranello firm to once more become competitive. This stroke of luck also provided a breathing spell to put new designers into place and update or marry the Lancias into the Ferrari line and begin work on fresh designs. In 1956, with the now modified Lancia machinery on hand and Juan Manuel Fangio as number one driver, Ferrari once again garnered the Grand Prix championship. Of course it helped that Mercedes-Benz retired at the end of 1955 and that Maserati was bedeviled by over-expansion problems and general chaos. Lampredi had by then departed from Ferrari, his place being taken by Andrea Fraschetti, and he led the effort during 1956 to prepare new Grand Prix and sports racing designs for the 1957 season. These were primarily the Dino V-6 Grand Prix and 4-camshaft V-12 sports car lines. The Dino program was saddled with many difficulties and not as immediately successful as the sports cars. Unfortunately, Fraschetti didn't live long enough to see his ideas come to full term as he died in early 1957, the result of a Modena Autodrome crash.

Ferrari quickly replaced him by hiring Carlo Chiti from Alfa Romeo. Chiti was particularly desired by Ferrari as he possessed a fine theoretical engineering expertise, coupled within an innate skill at picking the right solution early in a design effort. Chiti's working mandate during 1957 included finishing the development of the Dino into a winner, updating the sports cars as required, and preparing new versions of the latter, as necessary, for 1958. The Dino program proved very frustrating to Chiti, as it had the power but not the handling required. Vanwall beat Ferrari in 1958 to gain the Grand Prix championship, and the rear-engined and much lighter Coopers claimed the title in both 1959-1960. It wasn't until 1961 that Chiti brought the Grand Prix

crown to Maranello with his own design, a rear-engine machine. The sports car effort was much more successful, as competitors were less challenging and hardware with winning potential already existed in one form or another.

In the U.S., emigration from other lands and a highly mobile society make regional identification inconsequential; not the case in many old world countries such as Italy. Modena lies in the province of Reggio Emilia and the bulk of Ferrari personnel comes from the immediate area. Chiti was a Tuscan from Florence, only 100 miles or so away. As strange as it may seem in these modern times, he was long considered an outsider by other Ferrari employees and had a great deal of difficulty in proving himself and getting his design ideas accepted.

Part of his problem at Ferrari was an inbred belief in tried and true methods; change was to be avoided. The small design staff tended to stick with obsolete concepts, and one of Chiti's primary tasks was to force the thinking level out of this rut and bring it up to date. It helped that he enjoyed Enzo's confidence in the early stages and that his decisions were to prove correct. He was a great experimenter, willing to try almost anything, and though there were plenty of failures, many useful and productive ideas flowed from his efforts. Certainly no one could fault his working habits, as he would not only put in the outlandish hours required, but willingly went to almost all the major races to supervise changes that the circumstances required.

Chiti is best described as a large and very bulgy man, with a rotund face set off by small, wire-framed eyeglasses that made him appear to resemble a great stuffed owl. His overweight condition likely resulted in equal measure from a decided distaste for exercise and a renowned reputation as a trencherman at the table. His capacity for food was simply prodigious and he could make vast plates of pasta disappear in a twinkling. It was a source of amusement to some people to see Chiti and Ferrari standing and talking to each other. They claimed the two had to wear eyeglasses simply because their stomachs prevented them from getting close enough to see each other without some visual help.

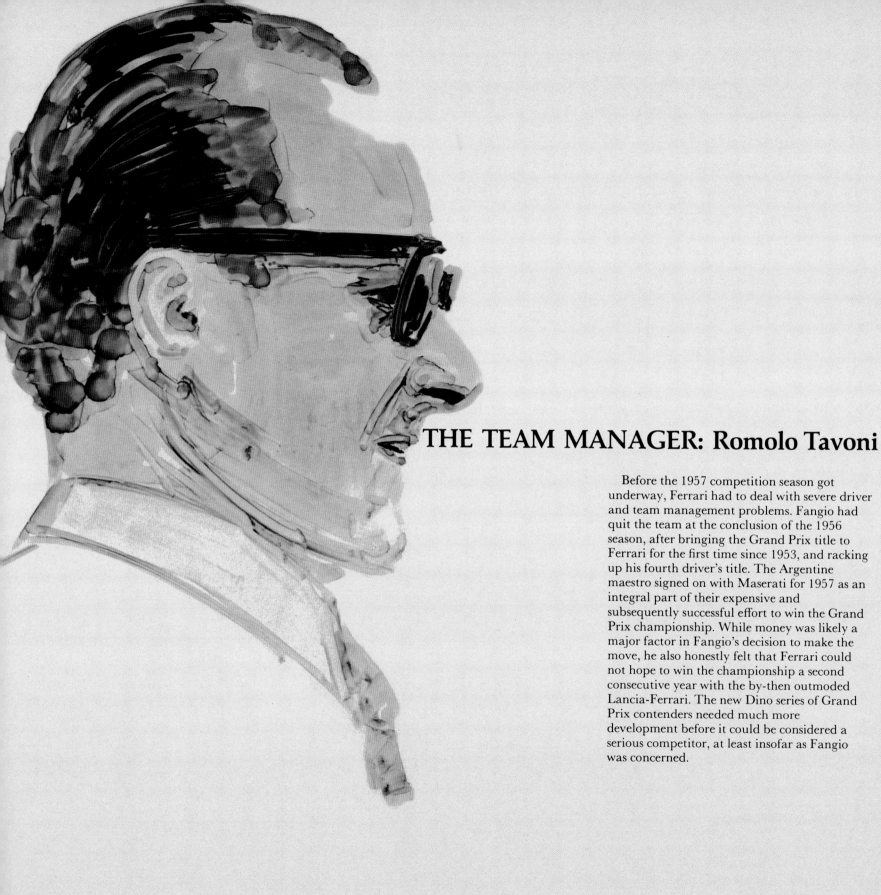

THE TEAM MANAGER: Romolo Tavoni

Before the 1957 competition season got underway, Ferrari had to deal with severe driver and team management problems. Fangio had quit the team at the conclusion of the 1956 season, after bringing the Grand Prix title to Ferrari for the first time since 1953, and racking up his fourth driver's title. The Argentine maestro signed on with Maserati for 1957 as an integral part of their expensive and subsequently successful effort to win the Grand Prix championship. While money was likely a major factor in Fangio's decision to make the move, he also honestly felt that Ferrari could not hope to win the championship a second consecutive year with the by-then outmoded Lancia-Ferrari. The new Dino series of Grand Prix contenders needed much more development before it could be considered a serious competitor, at least insofar as Fangio was concerned.

At about the same time and for similar reasons, the Ferrari team manager, Nello Ugolini, also defected to Maserati. The circumstances surrounding the departure, and the appointment of Romolo Tavoni to take his place, reveal much about the Ferrari organization's decision-making structure.

Tavoni, a tall, thinnish, dark-complexioned type, wore heavy spectacles and looked to be composed of equal parts scarecrow and studious scholar. He had come to the Ferrari firm as a young man after training as a secretary and worked in that capacity for some years, eventually becoming Enzo's personal assistant. During the mid-fifties his job took a different tack, that of on-site race data recorder.

The Commendatore had begun to stay away from the races more and more frequently, sending Tavoni along to function as his eyes and ears, with the mission of reporting everything that went on and putting it down on paper. Tavoni was initially at a loss as to how to do the job, having no prior experience as a designer, manager, driver or mechanic. He learned quickly to discern what was really taking place and impressed Ferrari by his astute comments and judgments about their racing effort. But many of the drivers and crew tended to regard Tavoni with disdain, considering him to be Ferrari's personal slave and something of a spy in their midst.

Ugolini particularly disliked Tavoni's presence, as he found that the secretary's reports to Ferrari often led to the countermanding of his decisions. A clever tactician in his own right, Ugolini insisted on running the show himself, without second guessing from the boss via inputs from Tavoni. The situation continued to deteriorate throughout 1956 to the point where Ugolini felt he could no longer function effectively as team manager. The inevitable clash with Ferrari occurred and he quit, being temporarily replaced by Eraldo Sculati. However, Ugolini's departure actually solved something of a problem for Ferrari. He had initially put Ugolini into the job so that he could physically remain in Modena, but found it impossible to restrain himself from managing the team, even on a remote basis. The arrangement with Tavoni, who quickly replaced Sculati as manager, was much more satisfactory from Ferrari's viewpoint. Tavoni would carry the title and operate by observing,

communicating with him in Modena and then implementing the commands. A perfect arrangement for Ferrari, as he could make objective decisions unaffected by race venue chaos or cross currents of team conflicts.

For poor Tavoni however, it was a doubly difficult task. Not only was he required to report accurately to Ferrari but, in addition, had to communicate and implement the decisions as well as run the actual race operation on his own volition, a definite tightrope job. By and large, Tavoni performed well in managing the team, though the total package of Grand Prix and sports car races must have been an exhaustive regimen. He was by nature a hard and meticulous worker, but there were times when the job got the better of him, and had an important bearing on the outcome of some races. He was also a compromiser and tried his best to keep everyone at least reasonably satisfied, but considering the personalities and egos involved, this was often an impossible task.

Tavoni also managed the pit stops, both scheduled and unscheduled. For the latter a set of standardized signals had been developed enabling the drivers to quickly and clearly communicate to the pits during the race. If a driver planned to come in for an unscheduled stop for example, he indicated so on the lap prior to coming in by pointing at the trouble spot and banging the top of his helmet with his hand. There were other, more specific signals too, such as holding up the right hand with a "V" for victory sign, which indicated the driver was coming in on the next lap for new brake linings.

Despite the attention to detail and easy-to-follow signals, pit stops were one area where Tavoni was frequently weak, not an uncommon Italian deficiency. Ferrari pit activity was always entertaining, and knowledgeable race

goers often camped out in close proximity to the team pits in hopes of being treated to a bout of zany madness. Invariably during any given race, at least one completely confused Marx Brothers occurrence would take place. For some strange and inexplicable set of reasons, the mere slowing down of a Ferrari as it entered the pits could cause the most peculiar things to happen. Knock-off hammers would suddenly grow wings and disappear, fuel hoses might shrink a foot too short to reach, electric plugs would fall out of the sockets, bolts miraculously reverse their threads, nuts mysteriously become the wrong size, tools get slippery with oil, and on and on.

Components that had worked perfectly from time immemorial would abruptly become obstinate, such as hood latches refusing to operate, light switches becoming recalcitrant, and starters binding up. All had to be repaired on the spot with tape and wire, accompanied by loud and inventive profanity, broken fingernails, bleeding knuckles and burned skin. The pit crews were obviously not well drilled in the art of staying calm and out of each other's way. When problems erupted, so did they. Great cries of anguish would rend the air, followed by everyone simultaneously descending *en masse* on the difficulty to try and beat it to death. The energy expended by the mechanics, each trying to perform his own chore plus five others, was truly prodigious. The result was a hysterical explosion of colliding bodies, loud voices, incomprehensible maneuvers, and often contradictory actions. Spectacular entertainment, no doubt about it.

THE AMERICAN INFLUENCE: Luigi Chinetti

Chinetti was the Ferrari distributor for the United States, and developed the U.S. into the Italian firm's most important market by tirelessly promoting racing car sales and encouraging development of streetable machinery. An Italian who came to the U.S. just as World War II began, he was, like Ferrari, shrewd, calculating, and in love with racing. His competition career was notable, highlighted by three victories at Le Mans, the last of these coming behind the wheel of a Ferrari in 1949, the first triumph for the make at the prestigious event. Chinetti was a tough man, as was evident from his performance at Le Mans that year, where he drove almost 23 of the 24 hours.

The success of Chinetti's import business was to a certain extent based on the tremendous growth of sports car racing in the U.S. during the fifties, as Ferraris seemed to be ideally suited to the then predominant airport courses. Of even greater significance was Chinetti's role in encouraging the factory to build and sell to him the kind of cars he felt would do best in his market. He kept in close contact with Modena, continually suggesting new ideas and contributing inputs from racing experiences to the design staff. He influenced the development of numerous models, particularly the customer version of the Testa Rossa.

Chinetti was very much like Ferrari in another way, as he, too, dreamed of forming a racing team and using that experience as a springboard to build cars of his own manufacture. His ambitions had long been frustrated by lack of financial resources, but events during the fifties were to provide him the opportunity to begin implementing his plan. The sport of racing in that period attracted numerous wealthy American patrons with money to spare and a desire to play in the big time. As Ferrari had used his relationship with Alfa Romeo many years before, so did Chinetti in establishing a team to campaign Ferraris. His creation was called the North American Racing Team (NART), with initial backing coming from George Arents. Though primarily intended at the outset to campaign Ferraris in the U.S., by 1958 the team began to compete at Le Mans with other European events soon to come.

The team began its glory days in 1958, when the Rodriguez family burst on the scene. Brothers Pedro and Ricardo, 18 and 16 years old respectively, had big ambitions and plenty of money from Papa Don Pedro to back up the attainment of their goals. Wild-eyed and fast, the hot-shot teenage pair also attracted plenty of press coverage. For Chinetti, who quickly allied himself with the Mexican group, it meant he could operate in a first-class manner with the best cars and equipment, as Rodriguez always insisted on buying the fastest available Ferraris. Throughout the Testa Rossa years, Chinetti's standard practice was to buy the Le Mans race-winning Ferrari for the Rodriguez clan in the name of NART. In 1959, the only year during the heyday of the Testa Rossa where one did not win at Le Mans, he bought the machine that led the race the longest. In numerous cases, the Rodriguez brothers would drive a particular Ferrari only once or twice before selling it to someone else, and between 1958 and 1962 likely used 10 to 12 different Testa Rossa examples.

Chinetti was highly regarded as an astute spotter and developer of driving talent. To him it didn't matter if a promising driver had money or not. If he did, he paid plenty to run a NART entry; if not, Chinetti would find someone else to foot the bill. When he found a super driver, such as Phil Hill, Dan Gurney, Richie Ginther, et al, Chinetti lobbied hard with Enzo to get them factory rides and acted as their sponsor and mentor until they were established. On the other hand, when drivers wouldn't follow his counsel, he was very quick to abandon them and many promising candidates never got very far in the Ferrari world for this reason.

Ferrari legend abounds with many tales related to the difficulties of dealing with Chinetti. If he didn't like someone, he wouldn't sell him a car, or a good car, or spares. However, if he liked a driver or car owner, and even if said person had little money, anything needed always got provided, sometimes at give-away prices if the situation demanded.

It is often said that Ferrari was both leery of and jealous of Chinetti, and it's certainly true that the two strong-willed Italians clashed on numerous occasions. Perhaps a measure of the relationship is that Ferrari never seemed to give any public credit to Chinetti, and perusal of Enzo's writings and official pronouncements during the fifties and early sixties shows scant mention of the American distributor's name. Not very fair in reality, as Chinetti was clearly one of the major forces that resulted in the outstanding Ferrari success story. He was not alone, however, as Ferrari never really gave anyone credit, keeping it all to himself. If you were associated with Ferrari, a seat in the back of the bus was a necessity of the relationship.

THE DRIVERS

The factory Testa Rossa driving corps was composed of a thoroughly fascinating melange of nationalities, temperaments and skills. Their only common denominator was that they all drove well.

Luigi Musso

Though Ferrari, after Fangio's departure, habitually did not designate any driver as number one, Musso came closest to occupying that position entering 1958. Certainly Enzo Ferrari regarded him as his favorite, and it's easy to understand why. Musso, Italy's sole Grade One Grand Prix star of the period, had all the necessary attributes to be a winner. He was a handsome, athletic looking Latin with smoldering eyes and patrician bearing. An aristocratic Roman of wealth, Musso was intensely patriotic and very conscious of his burden as Italy's only driving hope. Musso could always be counted on to extend himself to the utmost in the quest for victory, no doubt partly to retain his position as Ferrari's favorite. The Commendatore reciprocated by generally assigning the fastest car to him.

Musso was also something of a prima donna and barely concealed his contempt for most of the other drivers. He believed himself to be a cut above the others, because of his superior intelligence, education, sophistication, and breeding. These characteristics and good machinery probably counted for something, but realistically, his excellent showing primarily derived from fierce competitiveness that forced him continually to the limit. He had almost a religious mystic's faith in achievement of victory as a divine mission and that Providence watched to prevent injury. With this outlook on his racing life, and actions to match, Musso was an Italian idol. Inside the team it was a different matter, and though he was good company when not on the track, most of the other members disliked him intensely.

Mike Hawthorn

In actual fact, the number one driver coming into 1958 was probably Mike Hawthorn, the life-of-the-party Englishman, then at the peak of his abilities. He generally disliked sports car racing, preferring single-seat machinery. However, he was childlike when it came to automobiles in that he would happily race anywhere in anything. In fact, he raced all the time, both on the track and street. The circumstances hardly mattered to him. How long it took to get from point A to B for dinner or drinks was more than a sufficient excuse to justify tearing around at a fearsome rate.

Hawthorn, however, detested the long grinds such as Sebring or Le Mans, though he usually drove flat out all the time, no matter what the course. He was often accused of flogging a car in a long race simply to make it break so he wouldn't have to keep going for the entire duration. As a result, he normally earned the assignment as "rabbit" to break the opposition. Hawthorn always raced to win, even against his own teammates, a habit frequently leading to violent wrangles with the team manager. Conversely, he was probably one of the most tactically conscious drivers of the period, and thoroughly enjoyed psyching out his opponents. His stunts were constant, and a successful, sly maneuver meant almost as much to him as victory.

Hawthorn's one particular hatred was the Targa Florio. He couldn't be bothered to attempt learning the course, claiming it had too many corners, and hardly ever drove over it during pre-race practice. His normal modus operandi during Targa practice was to ride along with another team pilot in a Fiat rental hack. Once they were out of sight of the pits, he would clamber into the back seat and promptly go to sleep.

He was fun to watch while racing, mouth agape and wearing a pained expression as though he'd just swallowed a bumblebee. He also was death on clutches, not only because of ragged shifting manners, but from a habit of slipping the clutch to build peak engine revs when exiting corners. His driving style also included beating on the sides of the car ala Nuvolari, shouting what must have been completely unintelligible epithets at his competitors, and occasionally, attempting to spit on them.

Peter Collins

Peter Collins, who had taken the trouble to become quite proficient in Italian, was an immensely likeable Englishman and the mechanics' favorite by far. He, like Hawthorn and Musso, was part of Ferrari's regular Grand Prix driver crew but seemed to enjoy sports cars just as much. Collins was also superbly skilled at nursing along a crippled mount, and further, could be relied on to be gentle with the machinery from the very start of the race. His high standing with team mechanics stemmed largely from never complaining about deficiencies in the preparation of a car. He just got in and did his best. Collins derived a great deal of satisfaction from his position in life, thoroughly enjoying every aspect of it. He was always humorous, courteous, and ready for a good time. In addition, he was smart enough not to take sides in the always ongoing hassles between drivers, mechanics, the team manager and Ferrari, preferring to lend a willing ear and stay everyone's smiling friend. These days we'd characterize Collins as a "good guy."

Wolfgang Von Trips

Wolfgang Von Trips, the fourth member of the team, was a wealthy German count of courtly demeanor when not on the track. He knew almost no Italian, had absolutely not the slightest mechanical knowledge, and perhaps should be considered the most consistent driver on the team. Like Hawthorn, he always raced to win, and consequently was usually paired with him to help lessen the potential for inter-team battles. Von Trips was a photography enthusiast and usually carried a camera in the cockpit. In the event of a breakdown on a course, he would occupy himself the remainder of the race taking shots of the other drivers. He and Musso did not get along at all, constantly sniping at one another. Von Trips felt he was even better bred, wealthier, and more educated than Musso, and the two would continually clash over the most picayune matters. It galled the German that Musso got to drive the Grand Prix cars whereas he did not, feeling that he was the better driver. Von Trips kept up a steady campaign with Ferrari to be allowed to pilot the single seaters, but this activity was infrequent coming into 1958.

The German was quite fastidious, and during the long sports car grinds made a general practice of taking a quick bath, even if only of the cat variety, and changing to a fresh driving suit after each driving stint. The strain of driving often left him thoroughly dehydrated and he would sometimes gulp down several quarts of mineral water while waiting to go out again.

Von Trips' biggest failing was his lack of mechanical awareness. He would just keep on motoring, no matter what was taking place around him and often missed crucial pit signals or obvious signs that his car needed some help.

Phil Hill

Phil Hill, the first of the crop of outstanding west coast American drivers to make an impact on world class racing, had just finished his initial full year of Ferrari team driving. Everyone believed the Californian to be a top-notch driver, but his true greatness had not become completely obvious by the end of 1957, though his success in 1958 would see him become one of the best and his reputation soar. Hill was something of an enigma to the Italians as they weren't really quite sure how to regard him. He could be unbelievably emotional and argumentative. His facial expressions and arm waving in the heat of discourse put the Italians, usually foremost in that department, absolutely to shame. He was also totally frank and blunt on any subject and never kept his feelings to himself. Hill probably had the worst case of pre-race jitters ever seen in a race driver and frequently would rush behind the pits just before a start and heave up the contents of his stomach. Once the race started, he was fine. It was the pre-race speculation and uncertainties that bothered him, not the race itself. He was also something of a hypochondriac, carrying around a large assortment of pills and potions suitable for healing almost anything. Further, he was always most ready to help other team members diagnose their ailments and then supply the necessary medication from his stockpile. Hill's overriding ambition was to drive Grand Prix cars, and he was frustrated by Ferrari's unwillingness to try him in that role until late 1958.

Olivier Gendebien

The last of the regular drivers on the sports car team was Olivier Gendebien, mentioned so prominently in the prior chapter on Testa Rossa development. Gendebien was reckoned to have superquick reflexes and was particularly adept at motoring rapidly on unfamiliar courses. His learning curve on a new circuit was unbelievably fast. Just a few laps were required and he would know it well and be able to record top competitive times. This is all the more amazing when observing the impassive Belgian with the sleepy, sad eyes. Even when wide awake, he looked like he was ready to take a nap on the spot. He tended to move very slowly, except when in a race car, and carefully chose his words. Gendebien, like Von Trips and Musso, was wealthy, and raced for the sport and glory rather than any major financial benefit. He was more than a bit vain and, for openers, considered himself to be the top Gran Turismo driver in the world, a view which he was probably entitled to, based on his performances to date. Like Hill, he also was something of a frustrated Grand Prix candidate, though he had at least gotten several opportunities. Gendebien was considered to be an extremely consistent and level-headed driver, his placid demeanor totally masking an almost ferocious desire to win. As the 1958 season progressed, he would become more regularly paired with Hill as their driving styles were very similar, and, furthermore, they didn't seem to irritate each other, not true with some of the other driver combinations.

Wolfgang Seidel

As a backup team member if something happened to any of the primary crew, or if needed, to partner a fourth car, was Wolfgang Seidel, another German driver. He cannot be considered a particularly rapid chauffeur, but possessed many other virtues, such as dependability, always obeying team orders, and driving habits best described as very clean. Seidel never seemed particularly at home on the Ferrari team or with its cars, and exhibited a marked preference for smaller cars such as Porsche, with whom he later had a number of successes. If a 4-car team were to be run, then a promising Italian driver would be paired with Seidel, as Ferrari continually kept searching for up-and-coming world class candidates from his country.

THE FACTS OF LIFE

While appearances to the outside world were generally calm, the factory team was almost always in a continuous state of turmoil. Enzo Ferrari tended to encourage competitiveness between his drivers, playing off their rivalries between one another. He would alternately encourage individual drivers with displays of friendliness, followed by periods of coolness, to keep them worried, on their toes, and always anxious to do their best.

For any given event during this period, race assignments were tentative at best until the completion of practice, wherein everyone had a chance to try out all the cars so that comparison times could be gathered. Tavoni would then call or cable Enzo Ferrari directly, announce the results of practice, discuss the competition prospects, the health of the team's cars, and his recommendations as to driver pairings and race strategy. Ferrari would make the final decisions and the word would eventually be passed to the drivers, in some cases only a few hours before the race start. The uncertainties, at least so far as the drivers were concerned, must have been most agonizing, not knowing which car and partner you were going to get, or what was to be the race strategy until the last possible moment.

This does not mean the job was a nightmare instead of a dream. It more likely could be characterized as a volatile mix of equal parts exhilaration, terror, hard work, boredom, frustration, and socializing, all fermenting in the company of a group of high velocity, totally dedicated and competitive people.

During the racing season most of the drivers lived at the hotel Albergo Real in Modena, which became the social center for everyone involved in the sport. It was also naturally the place where every aspect of the Ferrari world was thoroughly dissected and where the choicest rumors emanated from. Many were guaranteed to result in hard feelings or discontent on someone's part, and no driver was totally immune to their effect, with the possible exception of Peter Collins, who would laugh off just about anything.

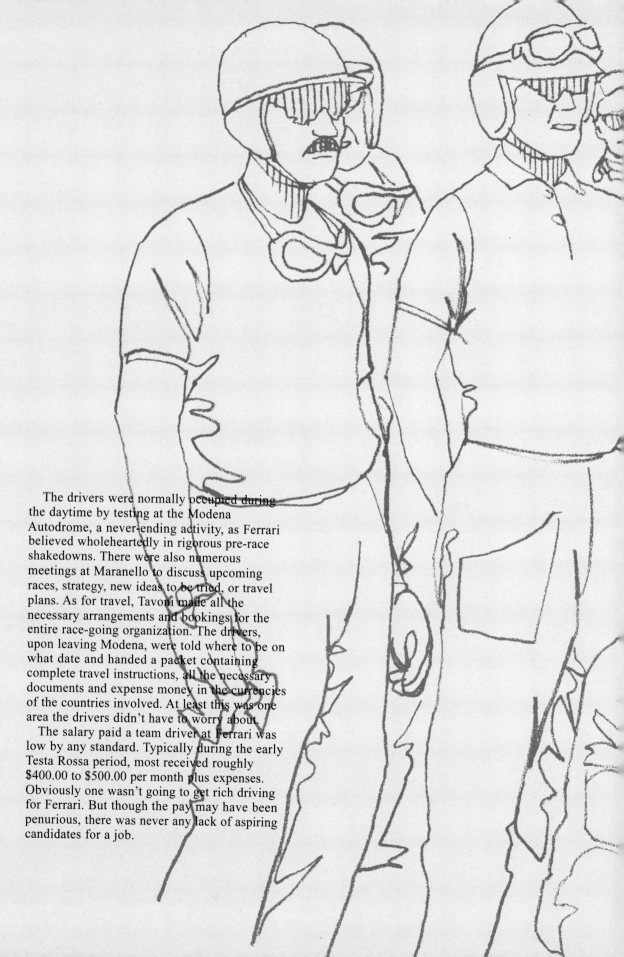

The drivers were normally occupied during the daytime by testing at the Modena Autodrome, a never-ending activity, as Ferrari believed wholeheartedly in rigorous pre-race shakedowns. There were also numerous meetings at Maranello to discuss upcoming races, strategy, new ideas to be tried, or travel plans. As for travel, Tavoni made all the necessary arrangements and bookings for the entire race-going organization. The drivers, upon leaving Modena, were told where to be on what date and handed a packet containing complete travel instructions, all the necessary documents and expense money in the currencies of the countries involved. At least this was one area the drivers didn't have to worry about.

The salary paid a team driver at Ferrari was low by any standard. Typically during the early Testa Rossa period, most received roughly $400.00 to $500.00 per month plus expenses. Obviously one wasn't going to get rich driving for Ferrari. But though the pay may have been penurious, there was never any lack of aspiring candidates for a job.

34

CHAPTER 3
1958: Triumph For The Testa Rossas

THE COMMENCEMENT OF THE 1958 season, with its new 3.0-liter limit, found Ferrari in a very strong position as a result of their thorough advance planning. They were practically assured of the championship, barring unforeseen circumstances. The Testa Rossas appeared to be fast enough to win, with the required reliability on hand, and the team drivers were all first-rate, experienced on the courses to be used and familiar with Ferraris.

The new formula had been promulgated to encourage more entrants, but circumstances prevented 1958 from being another outstanding competition year, with indications of the problem becoming apparent very early in the season. Maserati completely withdrew from factory sponsored racing due to grave financial difficulties and, in any event, their only 3.0-liter entry, the 300S, was not really competitive due to a lack of power. Jaguar did not feel inclined to produce a successor to the live-axle, heavy, but sleek D-type, leaving private competitors to carry on as best they could. The D could realistically be considered a potential threat only at Le Mans, and even there it would be a problematical proposition. Rumors indicated that the redesigned 3.0-liter version of the D engine was both under-powered in comparison to Ferrari and very fragile. The only other major contender for outright wins would be Aston Martin, known to be as fast as Ferrari and possibly even faster with Stirling Moss at the helm, but handicapped by a weak transmission. Astons appeared unlikely to field a full team for all the events which would probably make it extremely difficult for them to have a chance at the championship. Porsche continued to make great strides forward, but except for the Targa Florio, could not be expected to challenge for victories.

The 1958 championship races, all at least 1000 kilometers (620 miles) or longer, were scheduled for Buenos Aires, Sebring, Targa Florio, Nürburgring, Le Mans, and Goodwood, in that order. The Mille Miglia had been cancelled forever following the 1957 Portago tragedy. The races in Sweden and Venezuela had also been removed from the calendar, both primarily due to financial reasons. The Goodwood circuit in England had been entered on the list to replace the Dundrod, Ireland, course last used in 1955, and viewed by everyone as being unsuitable for racing anything faster than a turtle.

AN INAUGURAL SUCCESS IN ARGENTINA

The opening round of the 1958 World Sports Car Championship was, as customary, contested at Buenos Aires, Argentina, on January 26. The sports car race, known as the Mil Kilometros de la Ciudad de Buenos Aires or 1000 Kilometers of the City of Buenos Aires occupied the middle of a 3-week speed orgy called the Temporada. The Argentine Grand Prix had been run the week before, and a week later the Grand Prix of the City of Buenos Aires would be contested. As it was the height of the South American summer, the Europeans usually looked forward to the sunshine as a welcome break from the cold and dark northern clime at that time of the year. Unfortunately for all concerned, the Argentine organizers always took a financial bath on the 1000 Kilometer races as spectators could watch for nothing along the freeway section, rather than paying for seats in the Autodromo.

The sports car course, last used in 1956, was 5.88 miles long, requiring a minimum of 106 laps to cover the required 1000 Kilometers. Locally known as the "Circuit Routier," the course consisted of two very dissimilar sections. One part was a twisty portion of the Buenos Aires Autodromo race track, with the balance consisting of a section of the adjacent divided main freeway connecting the city and suburbs. The course was rather rough in spots, but relatively undemanding on the machinery nonetheless, as the bulk of the circuit really involved only two long straightaways. On the freeway section you blasted up one side, made a 180 degree turn around a water fountain in the center of a traffic circle, and then charged off in the opposite direction parallel to the way you had just come. The freeway portion had one very interesting virtue in that it was easy to track your relationship to competition. Just check the other side to see how they were faring.

The official Ferrari team entries for the race were composed of 0666 and 0704, shipped down to Buenos Aires from Caracas and augmented by a new left-hand drive, live-axle machine (0716) sent directly to the Argentine from Italy.

Backing up the factory entry were two privateers, both left-hand-drive live-axle customer cars. Piero Drogo from Venezuela entered his new Testa Rossa (0714) to be co-driven by a compatriot, Sergio Gonzalez. Drogo's car was somewhat distinctive as he had fitted small intake ducts down low on each side of the body just under the doors to funnel additional cool air to the rear brakes. The other private entrant was John Von Neumann, who had air freighted his press conference car (0710) from Los Angeles at great expense to participate in the event. The factory had asked for his support, possibly due to reliability worries, and he was only too glad to comply. His co-driver was a Ferrari team member, Wolfgang Seidel. This particular arrangement is likely the only occurrence during that period wherein a Ferrari team member competed in a championship race driving a privately-owned car.

John Von Neumann.

Avenida General Paz

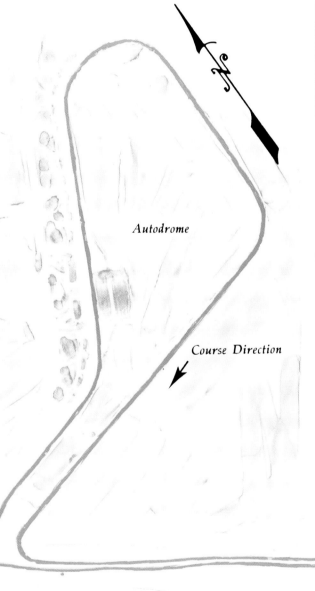

Von Trips straight-arms
0666 at Buenos Aires.
Musso and Gendebien also
helped bring the car home second.

Autodrome

Course Direction

Their opposition was mediocre indeed, as no Jaguars or Aston Martins appeared. Actually, the sole other factory entrant was Porsche with a 1600-cc RS spyder for Jean Behra, who gained Stirling Moss for a co-driver when the latter's privately-owned 300S Maserati broke its crankshaft during practice. The only other major opposition expected was from the Juan Manuel Fangio/Francesco Godia combination in Godia's new 300S Maserati.

All was not entirely sanguine in the Ferrari camp, however, as the Testa Rossas exhibited brake juddering characteristics in practice. The second prototype (0704) proved to be the fastest of the team cars but it had a unique concern all its own, fuel feed problems. The reason for the difficulty baffled the mechanics, resulting in a carburetor, fuel pump and gas line teardown that revealed nothing amiss. When screwed back together, everything worked just fine, and the problem never reappeared.

The earlier Testa Rossa (0666) exhibited some instability during practice, suspected to be caused by a bent or misaligned De Dion tube. Whatever the problem, it could not be resolved by the start of the race, at least to Musso's satisfaction, who had been assigned that mount.

Hawthorn Tries A Suntan

Hill set the fastest practice lap with a timing of 3 minutes 27.5 seconds (102.12 mph) in the second prototype, with Fangio, by dint of much trying, just behind in the Maserati at 3 minutes 28.2 seconds. Musso, originally slated for the other De Dion Testa Rossa, gave up on the car and switched to the live-axle version. In this machine he recorded the third fastest time of 3 minutes 28.5 seconds, followed by Seidel in Von Neumann's entry at 3 minutes 31.6 seconds. Collins managed a 3 minutes 32.0 seconds in Musso's vacated mount, as did Von Trips. Drogo and Moss both clocked 3 minutes 34.0 seconds as the next closest qualifiers. Hill's timing seemed to indicate that a Testa Rossa was within easy striking range of the existing circuit record set by Collins in 1956 with a 4.9-liter Ferrari at 3 minutes 26.7 seconds (102.55 mph). Hawthorn had hardly practiced at all due to suffering from a painful blistered sunburn on both legs acquired a few days earlier while relaxing in the Argentine summer sunshine after the Grand Prix, and further, his car did not fit him very well. He fervently hoped he wouldn't be required to drive at all in the sports car grind.

Top: *Peter Collins shared Buenos Aires win with Phil Hill.*
Bottom: *Musso's bent 0716 lies abandoned after first lap accident.*

The problem with Hawthorn resulted in some reshuffling of driver and car assigments, exacerbating an already touchy situation involving Musso. What resulted is perhaps typical of the kinds of problems that the Ferrari team was continually embroiled in.

Musso had originally been down to pilot the first prototype (0666), which was supposed to have been the fastest of the lot. Considering himself the number one driver, the Italian insisted on being switched to the fastest car, in this case, 0704. Further, because Hill and Collins protested the action (they were down to drive it), Musso got really upset and refused to have either one as a partner, notwithstanding that they were the only drivers to have run the car extensively during practice. In essence, Musso wanted to be assigned to the fastest car, which he had not even driven, and be partnered by Von Trips or Gendebien, who also hadn't been in it.

The problem was not settled until just before the start of the race. Hill and Collins kept their mount. Von Trips and Hawthorn took 0666. This made Hawthorn happy, as he figured that the car would break before his driving stint, relieving him of the necessity to suffer further. Of course, if it didn't break during Von Trip's tenure behind the wheel, then perhaps one of the others would, allowing its crew to take his place. Musso, having driven the live-axle machine a few practice laps, was assigned to that Testa Rossa with Gendebien as partner. The Italian was more than a bit unhappy with his lot and approached the race start in a black mood indeed. He made it more than abundantly clear he was going all out to win, no matter what, and that the others had better keep out of his way. The Ferrari team could hardly be characterized as one big, happy family.

At the Le Mans-style start, Collins jumped into an immediate lead with Von Trips close behind. Musso got off rather slowly and promptly got sandwiched in between some small fry. Coming into the first corner, Maurice Trintignant in a Ferrari GT attempted to dodge a spinning competitor and, in the course of the maneuver, shut the door on a charging Musso. Musso slammed into the side of the GT and careened straight off the road into a curb, breaking the Testa Rossa's left steering arm in the process, and then slewed into a concrete wall. Musso was only shaken up a bit. The car was out of the race for good, with Musso (very reluctantly, it must be noted) and Gendebien switching to co-drive with Von Trips. This relieved Hawthorn of the necessity to drive at all, no doubt to his delight.

The Von Neumann/Seidel machine only lasted nine laps before coasting into the pits sounding like a cement mixer gone berserk. The ring and pinion bearing had failed, and so ended their day. Fangio moved up to challenge the leaders, Collins and Von Trips, but on lap 22 he overdid things a bit and messed up the front of the 300S considerably, withdrawing for good several laps later.

The race settled down with Collins/Hill securely in 1st, Von Trips/Musso/Gendebien a lap back in 2nd, harried all the way by Moss/Behra who put on a brilliant driving exhibition in the little Porsche. Holding 4th were Gonzalez/Drogo, who had a trouble-free run all the way in their new car.

They finished the grind in this order, with the Collins/Hill duo winning at an average speed of 98.568 mph. Hill set the fastest lap of the race and also cracked the old mark on the 94th circuit with a clocking of 3:25.9 for an average of 102.957 mph. The pilots of the 2nd place Testa Rossa had their hands full, as the car seemed difficult to control throughout the race. One measure of the problem was given by the telltale tachometer needles at the conclusion of the race. The winning Collins/Hill car read 7700 rpm while the 2nd place Testa Rossa revealed 8400 rpm. Quite a difference.

The Argentine race could hardly be considered a stirring event by any standard. Still, Ferrari raked in the all-important eight points for winning, and perhaps more significantly, proved once again that reliability could be counted on from the Testa Rossas.

Basking in Florida sunshine are the cars of (L to R) Hawthorn/Von Trips, Hill/Collins, and Musso/Gendebien.

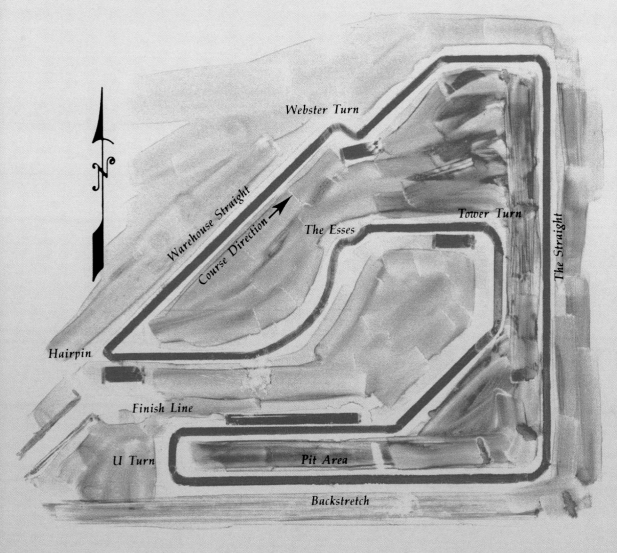

Webster Turn

Warehouse Straight

Course Direction

The Esses

Tower Turn

The Straight

N

Hairpin

Finish Line

U Turn

Pit Area

Backstretch

SEBRING AND ANOTHER HILL/ COLLINS VICTORY

The eighth running of the Sebring 12-hour Grand Prix of Endurance was scheduled to be contested on March 22, 1958, commencing at the customary 10 a.m. As darkness descended at about 6:30 p.m., the last 3½ hours were run in nighttime conditions. Sebring enjoyed that one distinction amongst the championship races, for it was the only event ending at night. Unfortunately it had precious few other distinctions and almost no favorable attributes. It was truly an unlikely race in an unlikely place. The course, laid out on the runways and feeder roads of an abandoned World War II air base near the Florida town of the same name, totalled 5.2 very flat miles per lap. The road surface was not only rough and bumpy, but abnormally abrasive, and therefore hard on both suspensions and tires. Brakes suffered the most, however, as the course layout featured a number of long straights ending in sharp corners, requiring the faster cars to slow down from 160 mph to 30 mph repeatedly per lap. No other championship event was in the same class as Sebring when it came to brake severity. The drivers considered the course to be very difficult, as it had very few distinguishing characteristics to guide them on turns, braking or shifting points.

Ferrari team driver/car assignments were predetermined after the brouhaha at Buenos Aires, with Collins and Hill keeping their Argentine victor (0704). The other Argentine team entries had been returned to the factory and replaced for Sebring by two entirely new cars, chassis numbers 0726 and 0728. Both were left-hand-drive, pontoon fender, De Dion versions assigned to Musso/Gendebien (0726) and Hawthorn/Von Trips (0728).

40

Supporting the team were three American-owned privateer Testa Rossas, all left-hand-drive, live-axle types. These included John Von Neumann/Richie Ginther (0710), E. D. Martin/Chet Flynn (0730) and Ed Hugus/John Fitch (0732), the first named in all cases being the owner.

The first real competition of 1958 to Ferrari was expected to come at Sebring as Aston Martin had entered a pair of DBR1s for Stirling Moss/Tony Brooks and Carroll Shelby/Roy Salvadori. Also, the newly revised 3.0-liter Jaguar engines were due to debut there, installed in a brace each of Cunningham-entered Listers and Ecurie Ecosse D-Type Jaguars. The 3.0-liter derivations were something of an unknown quantity, though pre-race press speculation intimated them to be fragile and only producing a relatively mediocre 250 bhp. Porsches were at Sebring in force, and though unlikely to be as fast as the 3.0-liter machinery, the little silver speedsters could be reckoned to make at least one less fuel stop over the 12-hour duration, potentially a significant factor in the final results.

Pre-race practice was thoroughly dominated by Moss, who set a new lap record of 3:22.8 (92.4 mph), breaking Behra's 1957 mark of 3:24.5 in a 4.5-liter Maserati, without seemingly extending himself or his mount at all. The Jaguar-engined entries were all well off the pace, with the Ferrari timings falling in the middle between the two extremes. The best Ferrari clocking, by virtue of much trying, was achieved by Collins at 3:23.4, with the other team drivers just behind and Von Neumann recording the fastest privateer time of 3:25 flat. The final Ferrari strategy for the race was to send forth Hawthorn/Von Trips as the rabbit in an attempt to wear out Moss, leaving the other team members to pick up the pieces. Actually, Hawthorn and Von Trips were not exactly displeased at their assignment as they figured the Testa Rossa's brakes would never last out the race anyway, so why not go fast for a while and get the chore over with early.

Brakes: Disc vs Drum

On the subject of brakes, none of the team drivers could be characterized as overly thrilled at the prospect of running at Sebring with the Ferrari drum-type stoppers. This feeling was based on two primary considerations. In order to make the linings last out the 12 hours, they utilized an extremely hard compound, and as Ferrari brakes were not servo assisted, very high pedal pressure was required. The drivers would have to practically stand on them at every corner to slow down. After a several hour driving stint, leg cramps were a certainty and by the conclusion of the 12 hours, most of the pilots would be barely able to walk. The team drivers, particularly Hawthorn, who had driven D-Type Jaguars with disc brakes on numerous occasions, had been complaining bitterly to Ferrari about the antiquated drum system used for several years.

The Commendatore, conservative as usual, continued to insist that drums were superior to discs and his position had at least some merit relative to the sports cars entering 1958. The situation had seemingly been long since resolved in the favor of discs for Grand Prix competition, but those contests were both shorter in distance than the sports car endurance grinds, and the single seaters weighed a good deal less than their

2-seat brethren. Discs had also proven to be advantageous at the easy-on-brakes Le Mans races, as the pads could be made to last for at least 12 hours before requiring fresh substitutes. The five or six minutes required to replace pads was considered an inconsequential time loss over the total 24 hour period of the race.

Much more inconclusive relative to the drum versus disc argument and pad longevity were the other sports car endurance grinds. They were all 12 hours or less, but uniformly much tougher on brakes. At Sebring, as an example, the disc technology in early 1958 was such that minimally one pad change was necessary during the contest, and possibly two, if competition persisted throughout the entire race. Over the Sebring race duration of 12 hours, approximately 200 laps could be covered, and one pad replacement would be equivalent to losing about 1.5 seconds a lap over the distance, possibly the difference between victory and 2nd place. Two stops might mean a very likely insurmountable disadvantage, as an average 3 seconds a lap would be lost. To Ferrari, the decision was easy to make: stay with the old reliable drum brakes which never gave any trouble whatsoever, except fade in the late stages of a race. Insofar as he was concerned, the fade could only be caused by improper and

injudicious use of the brakes by his drivers. Further, disc brakes were still not completely trouble free, though making great progress. New rotor and pad improvements in early 1958 would tip the scales irrevocably in favor of the discs, but for that year's sports car endurance races Ferrari would continue to rely on the old faithful drum brakes.

Moss Pours It On

The Sebring start at 10:00 a.m. proved Ferrari's worst fears as Moss jumped into an immediate lead, which he and Brooks continually increased as the laps rolled by. Hawthorn made a poor start, completely failing in his assignment as rabbit. The job of upholding Ferrari honor fell to Collins/Hill, who were in and out of 2nd in a bitter fight with the Shelby/Salvadori Aston Martin.

Early in the race Gendebien had an unusual collision with Archie Scott-Brown when the latter's Lister-Jaguar blew up suddenly while exiting a corner, causing the car to slow abruptly. The Ferrari rode right up the back of the Lister and stayed there, leaving tire marks on the Englishman's helmet. After both drivers had leapt out to inspect the damage, Gendebien fired up his engine, engaged reverse and backed off the crippled and unable-to-continue Lister. The

damage to Gendebien's left front sheetmetal was fixed at the pits and he resumed the race some 3 laps in arrears.

Moss continued to pour it on, setting new lap records in the process with the Collins/Hill, Hawthorn/Von Trips and Von Neumann/Ginther Testa Rossas panting along behind and steadily losing ground. The new 3.0-liter Jaguar engines proved to be failures as they all dropped out within the first four hours. Moss led until a long pit stop caused by a burst tire allowed the Collins/Hill team to gain 1st place. He rejoined the race in 2nd spot and proceeded to narrow the gap rapidly, with little prospect of failing to retake the lead as both the Collins/Hill and Hawthorn/Von Trips cars were practically without brakes, and clearly unable to hold out long at the pace being maintained.

By 3:00 p.m. the worry was over, as both Astons retired, the Moss/Brooks entry exiting with a cracked rear axle and the Shelby/Salvadori mount suffering a broken universal in the gear shift mechanism. Their exit left Ferrari in a commanding position, controlling the top four positions and no competition in sight. The Musso/Gendebien Testa Rossa had moved into 3rd, displacing the Von Neumann/Ginther team, who were having a fine run in their private entry.

The other privateers did not fare so well. Flynn, while running 6th, flipped his car in the Esses during the early afternoon, the consequence of a minor collision with a slower competitor. He broke a shoulder and seriously injured his left eye, though both subsequently mended well. The remaining private entry of Hugus/Fitch ran as high as 8th before dropping out in mid-afternoon with a broken valve spring and other assorted ills.

Privateer Flynn flipped after catapulting off a sand bank, but survived despite car's appearance. Going through Warehouse Chicane is the Hugus/Fitch 250TR.

Though the Ferraris only had to parade around without breaking to clinch the victory, as the afternoon wore on it became apparent that the two leading cars were engaging in a heated duel. The contest dragged on for several hours with the leaders running nose to tail in spite of continuous threats and pleadings from Tavoni, who was in an absolute rage over the ridiculous state of affairs. The duel finally ended in the ninth hour when the Hawthorn/Von Trips car retired with an unfixably burned-out generator drive unit in addition to being rather bereft of gears, with only top cog operative.

Taking a shortcut to the cockpit, an eager Hawthorn caves in a fender top and part of the tonneau cover as he goes, then gestures apologetically to the dismayed mechanic.

Shown in practice, Von Neumann (right) retired in the 11th hour while running third, but Gendebien/Musso held on to finish second. Gendebien (below) climbs back in after the last pit stop.

Musso/Gendebien and Von Neumann/Ginther moved up to 2nd and 3rd respectvely, with everyone now content to hold position and finish out the remaining hours of the race. Early in the 11th hour, Von Neumann had to retire once more, as he had in Argentina, with a broken rear pinion bearing.

The race ended in a 1-2 finish for Ferrari with the Collins/Hill victory setting a new distance record of 1040 miles for the 12 hours.

Collins picked up Hill on his way to the victory stand, shouting to everyone to keep out of the way as the car had no brakes whatsoever!

With Sebring completed, Ferraris had won both of the races run so far in 1958 and would take a commanding lead into the Targa Florio, the next scheduled event. Aston Martin appeared to be the competitor to fear, but the Ferrari lead made it difficult to imagine they could not win the war.

A HAPPY TARGA FLORIO FOR ITALY

The 42nd edition of the Targa Florio, the oldest surviving motor race in the world, was contested on the almost 45-mile (72-kilometer) Little Madonie Circuit on May 11, a change from the originally planned June 28 date. While the Targa Florio had been on the schedule since early in the year, it wasn't until about a month before the event was actually run that it

received official confirmation as a championship event. The problem stemmed from 1957 Mille Miglia repercussions, forcing that year's Targa Florio to be run as a rally. Vincenzo Florio labored mightily to gain permission to stage the event as a true racing contest once more in 1958, not fully succeeding until that April. And as the Sicilian heat could be unbearable in late June, the event was moved up to early May.

The circuit itself is a total test of man/ machine stamina against the treacherous Sicilian mountain roads. Narrow, twisty, indifferently paved, high-crowned, and rising almost 2000 vertical feet, they contained only one stretch of four miles along the coast that could be considered straight. The race consisted of 14 laps with some 702 corners, curves or turns in each, totalling just over 1000 kilometers. Even the most rapid machinery would require almost 11 hours to complete the grind.

Ferrari sent a 290 MM down to Sicily a week in advance so the drivers could get in practice laps on the circuit. There was not any official practice period where the entire circuit would be closed to normal traffic, so a driver never knew what might be lurking around the next bend. The 290 MM logged some 40 odd laps in practice, and though totally worn-out afterwards, gave absolutely no trouble mechanically whatsoever. On the other hand, the body was junk. The score sheet featured entries such as demolishing a Fiat delivery truck (Hill), a scooter (Gendebien), a chicken (Von Trips), a brick wall (Seidel), and so on. The mechanics simply hammered out the body after each incident and sent the car out once more. The mere fact that any car could survive 40 laps on the Little Madonie Circuit is amazing in itself and a testimonial to Ferrari's ability to build solid machinery.

Ferrari entered four team cars for the race, with the drivers pre-assigned. Three of the entries were Sebring veterans, with two of them essentially unchanged from that outing and assigned to the same driving pairs, Collins/Hill (0704) and Hawthorn/Von Trips (0728). Seidel with an Italian hopeful, Gino Munaron, were handed 0666. Hawthorn, who hated the Targa Florio, had hardly practiced at all and let Von Trips take the first stint in hopes that the German would stuff the car or blow it up before his trick came.

The Final Improvements

The third ex-Sebring team entry (0726) was entrusted to Musso/Gendebien, and represented the first outing for the final derivation of the 1958 Testa Rossa. To catch up a bit with design changes that had taken place over the winter, the always experimenting Ferrari organization had modified the second prototype (0704) by removing the up-front transmission and live-axle rear suspension and replacing it with a De Dion 4-speed transaxle suspended by coil springs. The primary motivation was to move more of the weight to the rear of the chassis to reduce the Testa Rossa's front-end heaviness. The success of the experiment led to the decision to construct three new cars employing this rear-end design and left-hand drive. Two of them, 0726 and 0728, were completed in March and saw service at Sebring, while the third, 0746, was finished in April. For the Targa Florio the new car (0726) was modified to an envelope body style similar to the earlier 1957 sports racing shape, to which form 0704 and 0728 were also later converted. Chiti had concluded that the pontoon fenders did not appreciably improve air flow to the front brakes and tended to produce undesirable high speed instability. Henceforth, only customers' cars would continue to be fitted with the pontoon-fender body style. The envelope body styling resulted in a slight change in model nomenclature, the derivation being known as the TR58.

For the Targa Florio, 0726 was additionally equipped with a 6-Solex carburetor setup that looked almost like a continuous 12-choke instrument and in this guise the engine was reckoned to pump out a solid 330 bhp, but with a rather limited peak power band. Musso was clearly the fastest Ferrari driver in practice with this new weapon, the power likely of more importance in the speed department than the body shape, which could not have been a factor on the slow Little Madonie circuit. Of course, his achievement must be viewed in the proper perspective, as Musso wouldn't allow anyone other than his planned partner, Gendebien, a chance to try out the car. The fine hand of Enzo Ferrari was in evidence here, as he had decided in advance to supply Musso, an Italian and Targa Florio master, with the fastest machine for the contest. After all, as Musso was the only Italian star on the team, he rightfully should be given the best chance to shine in front of his countrymen.

Of the competition, Aston Martin had sent a single DBR1 for Moss/Brooks, and though very fast in practice, it could not be considered seriously as a potential finisher because of unsolved gearbox gremlins. Actually, Aston originally intended to send a full team, but late official confirmation of the event's championshp status left them insufficient time to prepare more than one car. Porsche entered one of the latest RSKs for Behra and Giorgio Scarlatti, who were much more feared, as the car's handling qualities on the tight course, coupled with Behra's skill, could make them a potential overall winner.

First Lap Chaos

Race morning began as cloudless and hot, giving promise that the day would turn into a real broiler. Due to the heat and length of the race, starters began leaving at the crack of dawn in 40-sec intervals, with the smallest displacement contenders off first.

The first lap was rather chaotic as Moss clouted a marker stone while attempting to squeeze by a slower car on the narrow Sicilian mountain roads, damaging a wheel which he was forced to change himself. He limped slowly back to the pits and lost a great deal of additional time there while wheels were changed and a fractured crankshaft damper was

repaired. He went like blazes to catch up, setting a new lap record of 42:17.5 (63.33 mph) in the process, but was never in contention for top honors before withdrawing with gearbox maladies.

Von Trips also had a whole bunch of excitement on the first lap when he momentarily caught his foot under the brake pedal while entering a tight corner and slammed into a bridge parapet, extensively damaging the left front sheetmetal. After wrestling out the offending panels, he continued charging on, the Testa Rossa not affected mechanically, except for a wheel changed at the pits.

Meanwhile, the end of the first lap confirmed Ferrari's wisdom in selecting Musso to handle the fastest car when he recorded the quickest lap time of 43:56, a full 11 seconds faster than Collins, who followed in 2nd place. The leaders remained the same for the next few laps until Collins handed over to Hill at the beginning of the 4th lap. Hill promptly proceeded to make contact with a mountain side, damaging both right side wheels, not to mention the body work. He put the spare on the rear and limped all the way around to the pits with the right front tire flat. After the mechanics changed both wheels, Collins took over once again, leaving a highly agitated Hill some time to calm down.

Von Trips accelerates away at the start of Targa Florio, only to crash on the first lap.

Munaron climbs into 0666 at a pit stop.

By the mid-point of the race, the Musso/Gendebien Testa Rossa had an easy 7-minute lead over their 2nd-place teammates, Hawthorn/Von Trips. Moving up rapidly in 3rd was the Behra/Scarlatti duo in the works Porsche after a rather slow start while Munaron/Seidel held a secure 4th, with Collins scrambling to make up time after Hill's incident.

At the end of the 11th lap came some real excitement. Musso charged into the pits waving his arms wildly and shouting that he was "nienti freni" (brakeless). He proved this by over-shooting the pit by a good 50 yards with the Ferrari mechanics chasing like madmen after him, and pulling the Testa Rossa back. All his brake fluid had boiled out, an ill omen indeed. However, upon refilling the reservoir, the brakes, by some unexplainable miracle, once more seemed to respond as they should, so an apprehensive Gendebien was sent off to resume the battle, the team never losing the lead amongst all the chaos.

Behra Steals Second

Meanwhile, Behra had shown the potential of the little Porsche by moving into 2nd spot ahead of Hawthorn, before dropping back to 3rd when he handed over to Scarlatti. When he resumed the controls once more on the 12th lap, the Ferrari team began to get really worried, as both their leading cars were experiencing brake trouble and could motor no faster if Behra pressed the issue.

In addition, it's always difficult to know where you stand on a 45-mile circuit, especially when everyone starts at different times. By the time a team manager has calculated positions at the end of any lap and relayed them to a driver at the end of the next lap, or at some inter-mediate point, a whole lot of ground has been covered.

Hawthorn fell victim to the problem as Behra passed him into 2nd, timewise, on the next to last lap. During the interval before word got to him of the potential peril, the deed was done. It could not be undone, as Behra entered the last lap with a 35-sec advantage over Hawthorn that the Ferrari pilot could not do much about, though not from lack of trying. The Englishman tried every trick in the book to regain 2nd, but his brakes, which had practically gone away by then, made the task impossible.

Mechanics work on the Von Trips/Hawthorn car, battered from an early accident.

Of course, Musso/Gendebien were secure in first, which they held to the end, an extremely popular win with the race spectators. Behra came in 2nd, with the crinkled and brakeless Hawthorn/Von Trips mount 3rd. The Munaron/Seidel Testa Rossa held down a solid 4th spot well into the last lap, when Seidel entered a corner too fast, locked up the wheels and slid off the road into a rocky field. He backed out onto the pavement and charged off once again, not realizing the sump had been split open and all the oil was rapidly running out. Only 5 km from the finish, the engine seized solid. If he'd been aware of the problem, a stop to add more oil and then proceeding at a reduced speed would have likely gotten him to the finish still in 4th place. Altogether a real shame after their fine drive for so many hours. Upon their demise, the Collins/Hill Testa Rossa moved up to finish 4th. Once again the Testa Rossas had demonstrated outstanding ruggedness and reliability with a 1-3-4 finish.

Ferrari now occupied a commanding position in the series with a total of 24 points in hand by winning the first three races of the year. Porsche had 14 points, while luckless Aston Martin had been shut out. The next race at the Nürburgring would be critical, as Aston Martin, who had shown consistently superior speed to the Testa Rossas so far in 1958, would be on hand with a full team for the first time in the season.

Winner Musso races along a flat section of the Sicilian countryside.

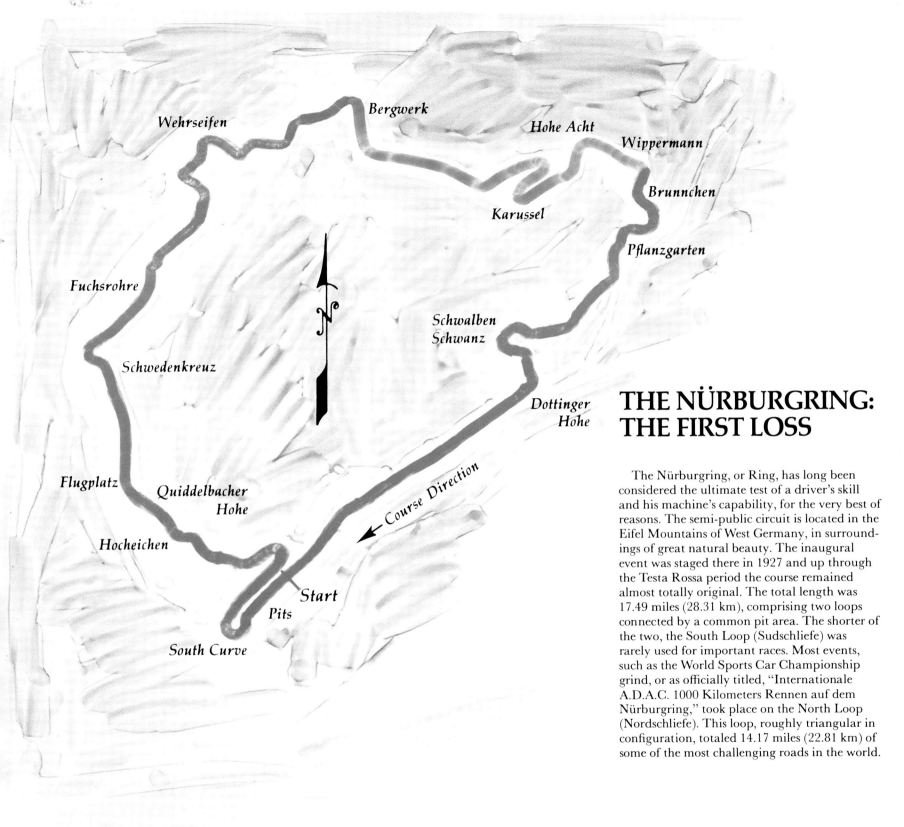

Wehrseifen

Bergwerk

Hohe Acht

Wippermann

Brunnchen

Karussel

Pflanzgarten

Fuchsrohre

N

Schwalben
Schwanz

Schwedenkreuz

Dottinger
Hohe

Flugplatz

Quiddelbacher
Hohe

Course Direction

Hocheichen

Start

Pits

South Curve

THE NÜRBURGRING: THE FIRST LOSS

The Nürburgring, or Ring, has long been considered the ultimate test of a driver's skill and his machine's capability, for the very best of reasons. The semi-public circuit is located in the Eifel Mountains of West Germany, in surroundings of great natural beauty. The inaugural event was staged there in 1927 and up through the Testa Rossa period the course remained almost totally original. The total length was 17.49 miles (28.31 km), comprising two loops connected by a common pit area. The shorter of the two, the South Loop (Sudschliefe) was rarely used for important races. Most events, such as the World Sports Car Championship grind, or as officially titled, "Internationale A.D.A.C. 1000 Kilometers Rennen auf dem Nürburgring," took place on the North Loop (Nordschliefe). This loop, roughly triangular in configuration, totaled 14.17 miles (22.81 km) of some of the most challenging roads in the world.

The private entry of Scuderia Ferrari Finlandia.

It ran down from the pit area start toward the village of Adenau and back up through the Hohe-Acht hills. The total vertical rise was just over 1000 feet (310 meters), but the course constantly went up and down with hardly a level stretch to be found. Covered in a clockwise direction, the circuit officially contained 85 right-hand bends and 91 left-handers, many almost unpronounceable to non-Germans and equally difficult to negotiate. These ranged from mere kinks to the famed 180 degree banked Karussel, with the humpbacked Flugplatz, narrow bridges, abrupt changes in camber, and assorted other surprises to challenge a driver.

A complicating factor at the Ring was the weather. It was, in a nutshell, totally unpredictable. It might be bright and sunny at the pits and raining three miles away. The circuit was intimidating in another way: there were very few guard rails, escape roads or spinoff areas. An off-course excursion was usually spectacular, as ditches, gullies, and steep dropoffs abounded to trap the luckless driver. Most pilots treated the course with the greatest respect, most certainly the reason behind the Ring's low fatality rate.

The Nürburgring circuit was owned by a semi-public corporation who maintained it and kept the course open year around. When actual races were not being staged, anyone, for a small fee, could have a go at the challenging track and play hero driver to his heart's content. The Ring encouraged spectator camping and drew simply tremendous hordes to the major Grand Prix and Sports Car events. Any quantity less than 300,000 paying spectators was considered a smallish crowd.

Up to 1957 it was firmly believed that no man had ever driven a full lap of the torturous Ring at his own and his machine's absolute limit. That year, during the German Grand Prix, by common accord, the unattainable was done. It took Juan Manuel Fangio, in one of the epic drives of all time to pull it off. Even today, spectators of the historic happening shake their heads in wonderment and awe at the feat. But then again, Fangio, the Maestro, was simply the best.

Ferrari Threatens To Withdraw

The 1958 edition of the 1000 kilometers took place on June 1, requiring 44 laps to be completed. Enzo Ferrari entered four Testa Rossas for the event and, with typical behavior for him, did not assign driver pairs to particular cars

until just before the race, letting everyone try them all out in practice.

Practice took place in conditions of frustration and anger, leading to a major confrontation between Ferrari and the race organizers. The reason was the organizers' insistence that all competitors use the same fuel, a brand made available by a competitor to Ferrari's supplier. The gasoline on hand was obviously inferior to what the Testa Rossas were normally fed, and required extensive retuning of carburetor jets, chokes and timing, a task continuing all through practice. Ferrari threatened to withdraw completely at one stage, but the organizers would not back down, and Tavoni finally got his orders to go ahead and compete in the race only a few hours before the start. Even with all the fiddling in practice, the Testa Rossas were not running up to par, possibly a key factor in the outcome of the race.

Part of the logic behind Ferrari's decision to run anyway was his fierce desire to win the race, achieved only once by the firm back in 1953. On that occasion, the first running of the 1000 kilometers, Alberto Ascari and Giuseppe Farina paired to drive a 375 MM 4.5-liter roadster to victory. Actually, it was something of a fluke win, as a pair of Lancias were leading by a veritable ton of miles, but couldn't restart on weak batteries after a pit stop. The regulations

allowed no exteral pushing or charging, so they were out, letting the Ferrari, crippled with rear suspension problems, stagger home to win. Ever since, Ferrari had been shut out and the Commendatore wanted to capture the event badly, at least to silence all the critics who called his Testa Rossas truck-like.

Due to the problems caused by the fuel situation, Tavoni allowed the team drivers to experiment in practice with all the cars, not fixing any assignments until after getting Ferrari's decision to run in the event. Ferrari, concerned about Moss, decided to pair the drivers and cars strictly according to their performance in practice, regardless of who wanted to pair up with whom. Hawthorn had recorded the quickest practice time of 9:43.4 with the right-hand-drive De Dion, pontoon-fender protytype (0704), and was assigned to it partnered by Collins, who had clocked the next closest time. Von Trips and Gendebien were given a left-hand-drive, transaxle, envelope-bodied Testa Rossa (0746) that had been run by Hawthorn at Silverstone May 4, equipped for that outing with a 3.0-liter V-6 Dino powerplant. For the Ring, the engine had been replaced by a normal V-12 Testa Rossa unit, believed to be number 0760, to which the entire car may have been temporarily renumbered. This example also had front brake assemblies and drums straight off a Grand Prix car, and further, was utilizing a rear carburetor air intake. Musso and Hill were down to pilot the same left-hand-drive machine (0726) utilized so effectively to win the Targa Florio, now equipped with Weber carburetors instead of Solexes. The last team car (0728), just modified to an envelope body, was the slowest of the lot by far in practice, and became assigned to Seidel/Munaron. Of the team cars, this particular one did not seem to respond at all to the mechanics' earnest efforts in reducing the negative influence of the poor fuel supplied.

In addition, three privateers were entered, all in left-hand-drive, live-axle customer cars. These included an Austrian, Gottfried Kochert, with a German co-driver, Erik Bauer, in their brand spanking new car (0748). Ecurie Belge supplied a mount (0736) for Willy Mairesse and Alain De Changy. The last entry, a Swedish/Finnish team composed of Curt Lincoln and Pentti Keinanen, were sponsored by Scuderia Ferrari Finlanda, sometimes referred to as Scuderia

Askolin after its primary backer, Carl-Johann Askolin. There didn't seem to be anything amiss with their Testa Rossa (0724) but the Finnish drivers proved to be embarrassingly slow in practice. Embarrassing is the proper term as they only managed to post the 23rd fastest time!

Aston Martin, the primary opposition, had a full team on hand for the first time in 1958, headed by Moss and Jack Brabham piloting the same car that had won the event in 1957. Practice was somewhat inconclusive as far as demonstrating the true potential of the Astons, for their drivers had been issued strict orders to motor with restraint and save the cars for the race. The Ferrari camp was more than a bit worried about the Astons, though none had finished a single race so far in the season. Still, there existed a nagging fear of Aston at the Ring, so Hawthorn/Collins were assigned to be the rabbit in hopes of hounding Moss to wear out his car.

Moss Gets The Last Laugh

The Le Mans-style start was rather unusual to say the least, as Hawthorn started running well before the gun sounded, hotly pursued by Moss shouting various unprintable epithets at his dastardly action. Hawthorn got to laughing so hard that he had trouble starting his car and Moss shot off in the lead, heading into the South Curve, and shortly reappeared going past the pits with better than a 100-yard lead over Hawthorn. When Moss once more appeared at the end of the first lap, he had a lead of 11 seconds over Hawthorn, who was obviously not able to keep up, much less play hound. Behind the leading pair came Brooks in another DBR1, just ahead of Von Trips, and farther back were Musso, Bauer, Seidel and Lincoln. The last mentioned was very far in arrears. One of the Astons dropped out two laps later, with Von Trips taking over a solid 3rd, but neither he nor Hawthorn could do anything about Moss, who steadily increased his lead.

A bare-armed Luigi Musso in 0726.

Moss built up a 40-sec-plus cushion before coming in on lap 10 and handing over to Brabham. The unfortunate Brabham, unfamiliar with the track due to Aston's practice conditions, was fair game for Hawthorn, who needed only two laps of tigering before he caught up, passed, and then proceeded to build up almost a minute's lead by lap 14. At that point, Brabham turned the car back to a fuming Moss, who took off in frantic pursuit.

The next lap found Hawthorn in trouble. He came limping into the pits with the left rear tire in shreds due to a blowout. The flailing remains had burned all the paint off the surrounding bodywork, but luckily hadn't severed the brake lines. The blown tire made the back of the car so low that the jack couldn't be fitted into place. Consequently, the mechanics had a real struggle in lifting up the rear high enough to ease the jack in position, an exercise accompanied by considerable loud shouting and equally loud profanity. Once in place, the old tire was removed and a new one installed while the drivers swapped, and Collins screamed off just as Moss tore by to take the lead once more. Von Trips also went past, now 2nd, so Collins actually rejoined the race in 3rd place.

On the 18th lap, Hill, occupying 4th spot at the time, also blew out a rear tire but, unlike Hawthorn, he was considerably further away from the pits. Hill stopped and installed the spare, a much smaller unit intended for the front, before limping back to the pits. His action led to a fine argument, accompanied by a considerable amount of profane verbiage in several languages and much arm-waving, as to whether he should have just continued into the pits on the rim, rather than change to a fresh tire. Musso took over, but not before the delay and arguing dropped the entry to 7th position.

Moss, in absolute top form, began pulling away from a frustrated Hawthorn, who gave it all he had, but seemingly to no avail. The Testa Rossa just couldn't run as fast as the Aston Martin. Hawthorn continued motoring to the very limit, until overdoing it on lap 34, when he hit a patch of wet tar in the Little Karussel and spun off the road into a shallow ditch nose first, from which the car refused to budge, though not damaged. Hawthorn leapt out of the Testa Rossa and levered it back onto the road with a handy fence post that he tore out of the ground, not doing Scaglietti's beautiful body work a great deal of good in the process. His performance elicited enthusiastic applause from the assembled spectators, which Hawthorn acknowledged by an elaborate bow before restarting. He took off after Moss without even losing 2nd place, though all hope of catching up was gone.

At this stage of the proceedings, Von Trips/Gendebien were 3rd, followed by Brooks in another Aston Martin. Musso/Hill had moved up to 5th, with Seidel/Munaron 6th. The race ground down with Moss triumphant and the Ferrari team occupying 2nd through 5th places, as Brooks crashed on the last lap while trying to pass a slower car.

Oliver Gendebien in 0746.

A Cool-Off Tragedy

Even two of the privateers managed to finish, Kochert/Bauer in 10th, and Lincoln/Keinanen 12th, though tragedy struck on the cool-off lap. The Nürburgring rules required that the leader in each class must complete the full 44 laps. When that occurred, all competitors in the given class would receive the checkered flag. Bauer, on his last lap, came by the start-finish line just behind Harry Schell's Porsche, and mistakenly believed the checkered flag to have been given to the Porsche and not to him. He continued to charge on, and in rashly attempting to pass on a curve, ran straight off the pavement and into a tree. The German driver sustained serious head and chest injuries to which he succumbed several days later.

The Ecurie Belge Testa Rossa had a rather unfortunate day. Mairesse was running 7th on the 2nd lap when one of Mr. Englebert's products blew out. After limping into the pits and effecting a tire change, a resolute though discouraged Mairesse re-entered the race in 51st or last position. He charged around the circuit to such effect that the Testa Rossa gained the 29th spot before handing over to De Changy. The rapid rise in standings continued until the 27th lap, when the team reached 13th place. Maybe it was an unlucky number for them as the Testa Rossa suddenly retired on that lap with a broken pinion bearing.

Though Ferrari was once again foiled in winning at the Ring, his team still put on a wonderful demonstration of reliability. Four factory starters and all of them finished, a marvelous achievement. The race did prove that the Aston Martins, at least when driven by Moss, were faster than any Testa Rossa driver combination Ferrari could muster. Still, the six points gained by the Hawthorn/Von Trips 2nd place ran Ferrari's point total to 30, an insurmountable lead for the championship. From a mathematical standpoint, Ferrari could do not worse than tie for first place, even if they failed to garner a single point from the remaining two events.

Erik Bauer, who died after crashing on the cool-off lap.

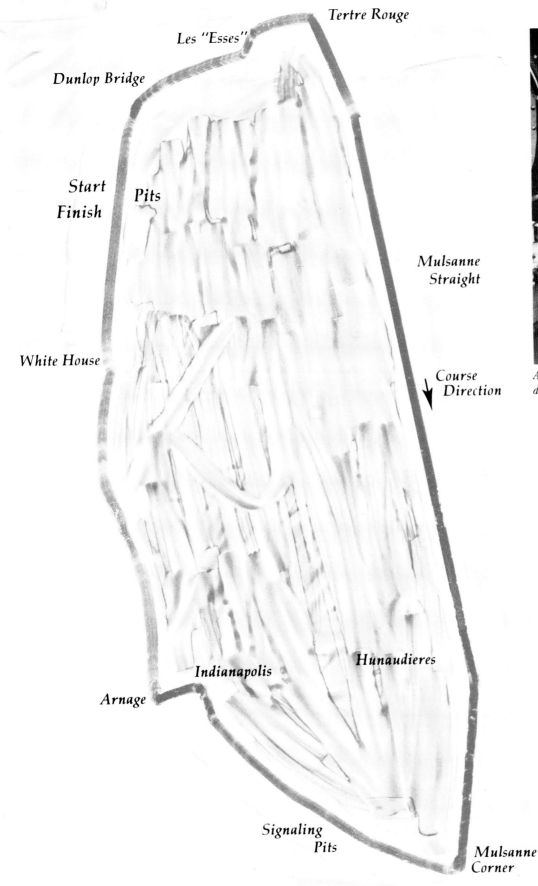

Tertre Rouge

Les "Esses"

Dunlop Bridge

Start
Finish

Pits

Mulsanne
Straight

White House

↓ Course
Direction

Hunaudieres

Indianapolis

Arnage

Signaling
Pits

Mulsanne
Corner

A Testa Rossa shows its top at Le Mans scrutineering day. Preposterous but part of the rules.

CHAMPIONSHIP AT LE MANS

The next event on the championship schedule was Le Mans on June 21/22, 1958. The grind, as usual, was easily the most prestigious prize on the racing calendar, and the one that most manufacturers tried the hardest to capture. Known officially as Les Vingt-Quatre Heures du Mans or the 24 Hours of Le Mans, the race was certainly the longest and perhaps the most dangerous of the world's championship events. The circuit, laid out in the gently rolling terrain of the Sarthe region northwest of Paris, comprises 8.366 miles of the smoothest road surface to be found anywhere. It is a very fast circuit, featuring several long, flat out sections, such as the famous Mulsanne Straight of 3.5 miles.

The Le Mans race qualifies as one of racing's great spectacles. Typically, crowds of 250,000 or more were on hand, some to watch the race, but most to take advantage of the carnival fair atmosphere surrounding the event. There was a big amusement park with all kinds of rides, hundreds of eating places and bars, dance halls, circus acts and every other manner of gimmickry to help the racegoers while away the long race and spend money.

Willy Mairesse sits in the privately entered 0718.

Le Mans is really a test of endurance for all concerned—drivers, cars, mechanics, spectators, timekeepers, and anyone else on hand. Twenty-four hours may be a short period in a human's life, but for a motor race it is a very long time. The result is total tiredness of men and machinery, contributing additional hazards to what is from the very beginning a dangerous sport. Even under the most ideal racing conditions, Le Mans is nerve jangling for drivers due to the wide disparity of speeds in the competing cars. Imagine a 120-mph machine fighting to pass a 100-mph tiddler when suddenly a 160-mph car blasts up from behind looking for a way to get by both of them. Drivers of slower cars, being occupied with their own duels, would frequently be caught unaware by faster machinery suddenly appearing on their tail. Next stir in the other elements such as 10 hours of nighttime racing, rain, the usual early morning fog and mist, oil on the track, and mechanical derangements, and you have a situation primed with danger and uncertainty. Finally add the fatigue factor, which radically increases the risk of errors by mechanics and drivers, and the total package becomes a grueling test of endurance.

Ferrari Plays It Safe

Enjoying a commanding lead in the championship stakes, Ferrari decided to play it safe, and made minimal changes for Le Mans. Like the Nürburgring, Ferrari had been shut out of the winners' circle at Le Mans for some time, as the last victory for a Maranello product had been 1954. Three team Testa Rossas were brought to the race, all TR58s constructed with envelope bodies and employing 4-speed trans-axle De Dion rear ends. Two were left-hand drive (0726 and 0728) while the third was the second prototype (0704), now sporting a new body, but still retaining the right-hand drive feature.

A 4-car effort, which included 0760, was originally planned to start the race, but Ferrari found himself with only six drivers in attendance when practice got underway, as both Musso and Munaron had been injured in prior accidents and were not up to snuff. Tavoni was concerned about the driver situation anyway, and his concern turned to horror when Collins walked up to him at the start of practice faking a broken arm complete with sling, and announced he would be unable to compete. The excitable Tavoni almost fainted dead away

from shock as all the other drivers burst into uproarious laughter over the success of their carefully arranged joke.

When practice concluded, final driver assignments were determined. Hill/Gendebien were installed in a left-hand-drive TR58 (0728) with a rear carburetor air intake. The other TR58 (0726), identical except for having a normally positioned air intake, went to Von Trips/Seidel. The third team entry (0704) would be driven by Hawthorn/Collins. On the surface the logic is clear, give Hawthorn/Collins, English natives who grew up on the right-hand drive, such a machine, with the other two cars going to left-hand-drive naturals. Very logical, but likely not a factor in Ferrari's assignments of drivers to cars.

Backing up the team were a truly international group of privateer Testa Rossas. Dan Gurney/Bruce Kessler were paired in a NART-owned right-hand-drive, De Dion, pontoon-fender ex-team car (0666) that had been purchased by Chinetti after the Targa Florio and rebuilt at the factory. This entry represented a last-minute switch of equipment on Chinetti's part, as he had originally entered and homologated a left-hand-drive customer's car (0756) for his American driving pair, but switched to the right-hand-drive machine when it became available. The balance of the private entrants, all in left-hand-drive, live-axle customers' versions of the Testa Rossa, were not expected to be as fast as the team cars or Chinetti's entry. This list included Alfonzo Gomez-Mena, a Cuban driver who entered 0722 with Piero Drogo as his partner, E. D. Martin over from

the U.S. in 0730, rebuilt at the factory after Chet Flynn's Sebring accident, with a Frenchman, Fernand Tavano, as co-driver, and the all-American entry of Ed Hugus/Ernie Erickson in 0732. Ecurie Belge brought two Testa Rossas to the event, 0736 to be managed by Alain De Changy and "Beurlys," a pseudonym for Jean Blaton, and 0718 for Lucien Bianchi and Willy Mairesse. Last was the French entry (0754) of Charles Pozzi to be driven by Francois Picard and Jaroslav Juhan, a Guatemalan who owned the car. Altogether, ten V-12 Testa Rossas were on hand, one of the most imposing assemblages of Ferraris ever to come to the fabled circuit.

The chief opponents included the Aston Martin team, with the dreaded Moss once more the team leader, backed up by the Whitehead brothers' semi-antique DB3S, the 2nd-place finisher in 1955. The D-type Jaguars, represented by a pair of Ecurie Ecosse cars, were on hand endeavoring to run their string of victories to four straight at the Sarthe battleground. Porsche had an entry for Behra and Edgar Barth, but it seemed unlikely they could do well at Le Mans, where brute power and a smooth track would negate any handling superiority.

Practice turned out to be the reverse of the Nürburgring as Aston Martins were out on the course constantly compared to Ferrari, who ventured forth but occasionally, and then slowly. Ferrari knew that the Astons would be the fastest, and saw no reason to run the Testa Rossas hard in practice and risk a crash or blowup before the race.

In the stampede at the start, the Hugus/Erickson TR is at far left, partly out of the picture. No. 17 is the Gomez-Mena/Drogo entry, while No. 21 is DeChangy/Beurlys.

A Le Mans Start

The most rousing spectacle at Le Mans has always been the start, a method established at that circuit and a standard fixture at almost all Championship Sports Car races for many years. A Le Mans start was composed of all the competing cars lined up on one side of the track and the drivers on the other. The cars were ordered in descending displacement capacity with the largest at the front of the line and working back to the tiddlers at the rear. They faced out, usually at about a 45-degree angle to the direction that the course took. The drivers stood opposite their steeds, and at the appropriate moment, signaled by a flag dropping, gunshot or cannon fire, they dashed across the track and leaped (or squeezed, as the case may be) into their mounts. Everyone would, depending on his engine starting, depart simultaneously and sideways. Hopefully, they missed everyone else. For sheer excitement, a Le Mans start is tough to beat, with the shattering noise of thousands of horsepower at full cry, peeling rubber and clouds of exhaust smoke.

The race began at the customary 4:00 p.m., with the champion starter of them all, Moss, making his usual lightning departure with the rest of the field howling after him. While the grind settled down after the first few laps, he continued to pour it on, pulling out an ever-increasing lead over Hawthorn, who had seriously wounded his clutch at the start, in 2nd, and Von Trips secure in 3rd. Gendebien cruised along in 7th, biding his time and quite content to let the front runners wear out their machinery. In fact, all the Ferrari team drivers had been given strict orders to drive to finish, and no inter-team clashes, please.

Racing under the Dunlop Bridge, Von Trips leads Hawthorne just before the deluge.

The team cars all wore spats on the fenders behind the rear wheels for Le Mans.

Fire In The Rain

By the time three hours had elapsed, the complexion of the affair changed completely as Moss blew up his engine, and shortly thereafter, the rapidly darkening sky unleashed a tremendous deluge, causing numerous accidents and totally confused pit stops. Drivers reported that it was literally like driving into a wall of water in the almost black, premature darkness. While everyone seemed to slow to a crawl, Hill, who had taken over from Gendebien in 3rd position just before the storm erupted, proceeded to put on an outstanding exhibition of fast motoring while charging into the lead.

The downpours continued intermittently throughout the night, making everyone thoroughly miserable and creating conditions almost beyond coping. The Hill/Gendebien mount clung tenaciously to first place all evening, continually hounded by the Ivor Bueb/ Duncan Hamilton D-Type, as Hawthorn/ Collins gradually dropped back with clutch maladies caused by the early chase of Moss.

There were many accidents during the night caused by the rain, most of which seemed to result in fires. Von Trips came upon such a scene near Mulsanne just after midnight, finding an Alfa Romeo coupe upside down in the ditch and burning, with its unconscious driver lying in the road. The German took to the grass verge to avoid running over him, stopped, ran back, and dragged the injured driver off the track surface, staying with him until the nearest marshals could get there. Eventually the marshals ran out of fire extinguishers and just had to let some of the conflagrations burn themselves out.

While running in 3rd spot just past midnight, Seidel spun off the road when he overshot Arnage during a particularly heavy downpour and got stuck in the mud. He couldn't restart, and wound up hoofing it back to the pits after struggling for over an hour in the darkness and rain to extricate it. In spite of his effort, he was roundly berated by Tavoni for leaving the car there. After all, he got it stuck and he should get it out. Of course, it's easy to say that when you are warm and dry in the pits. Not long afterwards, the Hawthorn/Collins Testa Rossa was forced to retire for good with no clutch and a damaged transaxle from clutch-less shifting, stranding Collins out on the circuit with a several-mile trudge back to the pits. This left the Ferrari team quite debilitated, with only Hill/ Gendebien in contention. They were passed by the Jaguar just before Seidel's incident, but regained the lead when the English car made its scheduled pit stop to change brake pads an hour later.

Headlamps blazing at 6:00 p.m., Hill heads into approaching storm darkness.

Hill And Gendebien Hang On

In fact, when Bueb reentered the fray, Gendebien, who had picked up a whole lap during the Jaguar pit stop, craftily tucked himself behind his adversary and followed him around in close formation for a number of laps. Eventually, the Jaguar pulled ahead out of sight, gradually gaining ground on the only remaining Ferrari team car. Hill and Gendebien hung on to their first place in spite of continuous hounding by Bueb/Hamilton all that long, miserable night and through the morning hours. They speeded up only enough to keep their lead, and nursed the car for the final battle, expected to come in the last few hours of the race.

The Martin/Tavano TR during a nighttime pit stop.

The rain began to abate in the morning hours, causing a general increase in speed of the two contenders, until around 11:00 a.m., when it started coming down in sheets once again. Gendebien backed off accordingly and the Jaguar began to catch up at an extremely rapid rate, causing great anxiety in the Ferrari pits. The chase came to a violent end when Hamilton had a tremendous crash at Arnage, which was like a skating rink, while trying to avoid a spinning competitor.

With almost 10 laps in hand over their nearest competitor, the Whitehead brothers' Aston Martin DB3S, the Hill/Gendebien team simply cruised around the course for the remaining four hours, as the weather gradually cleared, to clinch the race and the championship for Ferrari.

Phil Hill takes the checkered flag at Le Mans, the first American ever to win.

Three privateers: Picard/Juhan (left), DeChangy/Beurlys (center) a disheveled but sixth place finisher, and the Hugus/Erickson car (right) with Hugus up.

Only two of the private entries finished the grind, Beurlys/De Changy in 6th and Hugus/Erickson just behind in 7th place. The others did not fare very well. During the worst of the storm, the Gurney/Kessler car, with Kessler up, had a tremendous collision and fire about 10:00 p.m., with a D-Type Jaguar, whose Belgian driver was killed. Kessler's injuries put him in the hospital and the car had much of its body burned off. The Drogo/Gomez-Mena entry exited at about the same time with no clutch, and steering problems caused by an off-course excursion into a tree near the Mulsanne corner. The Picard/Juhan mount also went out violently when it spun and hit the remains of an abandoned Lotus, already clouted by several others before they got their chance. The Martin/Tavano Testa Rossa stopped soon after midnight, sans clutch, and a similar problem later halted the Bianchi/Mairesse mount.

The victory at Le Mans clinched the sports car championship for Ferrari, and he elected not to enter the last race of the season at Goodwood. Aston Martin scored a 1-2-3 sweep of that race, somewhat of a hollow victory in Ferrari's absence, but indicating clearly that reliability had been achieved at last.

The 1958 season, though perfectly satisfactory from the Ferrari viewpoint, showed that the firm could not expect to rest on its laurels in 1959, but must proceed to continue further developing the Testa Rossa. As Le Mans took place in June, this meant that Ferrari had almost the entire second half of the year to experiment, test and prove the changes in their cars for 1959.

Heaped with earth used to quell the fire, the ravaged Gurney/Kessler 0666 lies beside the track.

TURMOIL STALKS THE SECOND HALF

The last half of 1958 turned out to be a period of turmoil at Ferrari. The firm finished second to Vanwall in the Grand Prix championship, though Hawthorn pipped Moss by one point to capture the driver's title. A major contributing factor in the Ferrari failure to win the championship was the deaths of Musso and Collins, both killed in Grand Prix accidents that summer. Musso succumbed to injuries suffered at the French Grand Prix at Reims on July 6, while Collins was killed at the Nürburgring on August 3. In neither case were their Ferrari single seat mounts at fault; the causes were primarily attributable to driver error.

At the conclusion of the season, Hawthorn announced his retirement from racing, having secured his lifelong dream of becoming the world's champion driver. Further adding to the luster of his accomplishment was the fact that he was the first Englishman to win the title. Unfortunately, he got to enjoy the realization of his dream for only a few months before dying in a road crash on January 22, 1959.

If the loss of Musso, Collins and Hawthorn wasn't enough to cope with, more was yet to come when Von Trips, the sole remaining experienced Grand Prix regular, accompanied by Seidel, quit Ferrari late in 1958 to go to Porsche. This action left only Hill and Gendebien to form the nucleus of the driving team. Gendebien, who had driven Ferrari Grand Prix cars on several prior occasions, became a regular on that circuit now in addition to sports and GT involvement. Hill also saw his wish realized, becoming a Grand Prix regular, though his first single seater drive actually took place in a Temple Buell-owned Maserati 250F at Reims, on the same occasion when Musso was killed. The net of all this uproar in the driving team meant that Ferrari faced a monumental task in late 1958-early 1959 rebuilding his forces.

Testa Rossa Development Continues

While the driver drama continued to play itself out, development efforts continued on an updated successor to the 1958 Testa Rossa. Competition could be expected to make gains over the year, particularly by Aston Martin, whose DBR1 (with Moss) was much feared in the Ferrari organization. Even though the 1958 version of the Testa Rossa had rather handily captured the championship, improvements for 1959 were clearly necessary to retain the firm's position. Chiti, with Ferrari's backing, went through a very diverse program of experimentation in 1958, trying out many combinations in search of the best solution for 1959. While some were unproductive, it's still worth reviewing the key ventures.

As mentioned earlier in this chapter, a 3.0-liter V-6 Dino engine was installed in a left-hand-drive, envelope-bodied chassis (0746), and driven by Hawthorn into 3rd place at Silverstone on May 4, 1958. The engine was removed after that event for additional development work, but never to be seen again in competition as events turned out. The chassis, after Le Mans, remained at the works in an inoperative state for two years, before being resurrected in late 1960. It would make a spectacular reappearance in 1961.

A further significant effort came to light that same month on May 18, when another experimental Testa Rossa of sorts (0744), appeared at Spa in Belgium. Entered in the name of Equippe Belge with Gendebien as the driver, it competed in the unlimited capacity sports car race known as the Grand Prix of Spa. The car greatly intrigued observers and became the subject of much speculation as a possible 1959 prototype.

This machine, based on the 290 MM chassis with an envelope body and right-hand drive, appeared externally identical to a normal team car, but was radically different in every other way. The engine, the very same 312 LM unit experimented with in 1957, featured a four camshaft conversion for the standard Testa Rossa block assembly. Displacement was now 3.0-liters and the carburetion remained as before, but output was reckoned variously at 320 to 360 bhp at 9500 rpm, depending on who did the talking. It appeared to have no power at all below 6000 rpm, indicative of extremely radical timing. Moving off from a dead stop was considered a major task for the car until the revs built up and the power came on. There wasn't much doubt that the power claimed was for real once it got going, as it went like a rocket with a ferocious exhaust note.

The engine, unfortunately, weighed some 125 lbs. more than a standard Testa Rossa unit, creating undesirable front end heaviness if not corrected. To help solve the problem the car was equipped with a new 4-speed transaxle, likely a Colotti design as it exhibited a marked resemblance to his previous Maserati efforts and was quite unlike any known Ferrari unit. The transaxle featured the gearbox to the left of the final drive assembly, and the half shafts driven from high up on the compact unit. Mounted forward of the transaxle was a hydraulically operated clutch assembly, accompanied by a starter triggered by a push-down lever protruding out between the seats. A normal De Dion transverse leaf spring rear suspension configuration was incorporated in the design.

The front suspension was the usual Ferrari practice, but the frame differed from the customary ladder type employed in that it basically followed the space frame concept, with elaborate bracing for the transaxle.

Unfortunately, this major experimental effort came to naught, as Gendebien found it quite impossible to keep the engine revs within the maximum power band, though the car was retired during the race for another reason: a broken input shaft in the gearbox. After Spa, the car returned to Maranello for some further development work, and then was brought to Le Mans, but not run there. Ferrari had originally planned on entering a 4-car team at Le Mans, but injuries to Musso and Munaron reduced his driving crew to six. He elected to run his three proven cars, rather than taking a chance on the still questionable 4-camshaft version.

The engine was later removed and saved for further development at a future date, while the chassis became reworked to accommodate the ex-Portago driven, 1957 Mille Miglia 335 S 4.0-liter, 4-cam engine, and then was sold to John Von Neumann as a type 412 MI.

Disc Brakes At Last

Another development effort took place during the summer and fall of 1958 that also turned out to be partly an abortive move in the long run. An envelope bodied left-hand drive TR58 (believed to be 0726) became somewhat modified after Le Mans. The engine, while basically unchanged, featured coil valve springs in place of the hairpin arrangement previously used on all the Testa Rossas. The body shape also remained original with the exception of a modified headrest and the addition of a plexiglass cover fitted over the carburetor air trumpets, as employed on the Ferrari Grand Prix machines.

Though enhancing appearance, it did not seem to make any difference from a mechanical efficiency standpoint.

There was one area of major difference. The car was fitted with Dunlop disc brakes, the first competition sports Ferrari so equipped. This transpired after Collins had fitted a set of these brakes to his own personal 250 GT and demonstrated their capability to the Commendatore by convincing him to try out the car for himself. This led to an invitation to Dunlop to come down to Modena in the early summer and assist in the installation on the Testa Rossa and a single seater. After testing proved their superiority over the previously utilized drum brakes, Ferrari began installing them on all the competition cars as well as 1959 production for street use. A number of existing drum brake Testa Rossas were converted to discs during the 1959 period, posing interesting originality problems for today's restorers.

The Dunlop success in the disc brake area provided that firm with an entry to become Ferrari's racing tire supplier. For several years Ferrari had been using Belgian-made Engelbert tires almost exclusively, but during 1958 had grown increasingly disenchanted with their capabilities. There had been several instances of blowouts traced directly to faulty construction, and tread chunking and separation had occurred at almost every race.

Dunlop racing tires were extensively tested on the TR59 prototype (0726) all throughout the late summer and early fall of 1958, and compared with Engelbert's latest offering. The Dunlops proved to be the superior tire and Ferrari promptly switched to the make for 1959.

This particular car was exhibited at Ferrari's annual fall press conference on December 9, 1958, as the new team weapon for 1959. In fact, the true 1959 cars were still being developed, and were not even close to completion. When finally appearing for initial testing in January, 1959, it was clear that they were quite significantly different from the announced 1959 contender. In light of these developments, the press conference car must be considered more of a 1959 prototype than an actual 1959 car.

No More Customer Cars

Though never really formally announcing the decision, Ferrari stopped constructing new examples of the customers' model Testa Rossa in the summer of 1958, after a total of 19 had been built and sold, a figure including the ex-team cars of similar specification. Purportedly, his decision was based on the belief that they represented a sufficient quantity to provide more than adequate representation at the non-championship races. Of more meaningful influence on the situation was his feeling that the cars were seemingly not being used very much, and were unable, in fact, to carry off outright wins in the United States against the larger displacement Listers and Scarabs, and furthermore, the privateer owners were always pestering him for the newest, latest goodies. Dealing with these private owners became rather a nuisance, and Ferrari felt his concern gained only a modest benefit from their activities, and one not in any way commensurate with the demands placed by them on his organization.

This led to a dictum that in the future there would be no further sports racers built for sale to customers. There were some specific exceptions over the next few years, but in almost all these cases they were deemed a necessity to fulfill particular needs not otherwise covered adequately by the sale of used or surplus team cars. Examples of this activity were the two 335 S 4-camshaft engined specials (0744 and 0764) built for Von Neumann and Chinetti respectively to enable Ferrari to more effectively cope with the Scarabs and Listers in America. The Von Neumann example, delivered in the early fall of 1958, was constructed on chassis 0744, which ran at Spa the previous May and was known as the Type 412 MI. Unfortunately, it proved unable to handle the Scarabs in the two major West Coast fall 1958 races and didn't finish either event. The Chinetti machine utilized a similar chassis (0764) featuring pontoon fenders and a clear plexiglass carburetor cover, and was shipped to the U.S. in early 1959. Alan Connell of Fort Worth, Texas, purchased the car and campaigned it extensively around the country later that year. This car was often referred to at the time as a Super Testa Rossa, and from a distance the resemblance is very similar. However, neither it nor 0744 can be considered true Testa Rossas, and did not influence any further development direction of the model.

All of the 1958 team Testa Rossas were sold off to Ferrari distributors subsequent to Le Mans. The Gurney/Kessler Le Mans wreck (0666) already owned by Chinetti, required a new body and complete mechanical reconstruction. After completion, Chinetti disposed of it to Rod Carveth of San Francisco, California, with delivery taking place in February, 1959. Carveth entertained a dream of entering the car in the full program of 1959 championship races, and through Chinetti he secured a firm entry for Sebring with others dependent on his showing there.

The second prototype (0704) now truly a TR58, went to Von Neumann in September, 1958, at the same time as his purchase of 0744, with both intended for October Riverside action. Carlos Kaufman, Ferrari's South American distributor, bought 0726, the left-hand drive TR58 that became the TR59 prototype for delivery to a Brazilian customer, Escuderia Lagartixa. The last 1958 team car (0728), the Le Mans winner, went to Chinetti for the Rodriguez family under an arrangement where it would be campaigned as a NART entry.

The cessation in building customers' cars created something of a temporary seller's market for the existing examples. It seemed as though there were more buyers than sellers, particularly in the U.S., where little other competitive 3.0-liter machinery was available at that time. This is more than a bit amazing when considering how infrequently the Testa Rossas were to be seen at American races.

THE PRIVATEERS

In addition to the world sports car championship races there were many other venues where Testa Rossas competed in 1958. In all cases they would be private entrants, as factory involvement was apparently limited to the major races, or entry of experimental machines for events such as Spa, Belgium in May. Rather than detail every Testa Rossa race appearance around the globe in 1958, it is likely more significant to describe their usage and successes in the most important races and their general position in the racing scheme of things. There is a distinct problem in dealing with Testa Rossa participation in these races that must be noted. This involves the difficulty in tracking ownership of the cars during their active racing life, as they frequently changed hands with bewildering rapidity.

Somewhat surprisingly, most of the privately-owned Testa Rossas were run very sparingly in 1958. It's a surprise because by late 1958 some 19 customer versions were in circulation in addition to the two prototypes and two TR58s sold by the factory during the year. In total, then, 23 Testa Rossas were available for active use in one form or another, though they were widely scattered geographically, and in numerous cases did not appear in the minor races due to being at the factory for rebuilds and not delivered until late in 1958 or early 1959. The vast majority of the total 1957-58 production quantity of 23 machines did eventually come to the United States, some as new cars, and others arriving later in varying degrees of used and abused. During 1958, only two privateers consistently campaigned Testa Rossas throughout the American racing season, these being John Von Neumann (0710) in the West, and Jim Johnston (0720) of Cincinnati, Ohio, in the East and Midwest. During the summer and fall a few others began appearing occasionally, such as E. D. (Edwin Dennis, to be exact) Martin (0730) and Ed Hugus (0732), both Le Mans veterans, Dick Morgensen of Phoenix, Arizona (0756), in Southwestern races, and Dan Collins with 0752, owned by Charles Hughes of Denver. The six represent most of the Testa Rossas to appear in American races during 1958. To gain more insight into the circumstances surrounding their usage, a review of the racing activity of Von Neumann and Johnston is illustrative in showing the situation.

A plug change at Watkins Glen for the Hugus 250 TR just before the start.

The Von Neumann Car In 1958

Von Neumann's Testa Rossa, as mentioned earlier, was the first actual customer's car to be built. It differed from any other pontoon fendered car constructed by having a detachable nose section. The Von Neumann Testa Rossa also was fitted with angled cooling fins on the front brake drums, an item taken from the Grand Prix cars and believed unique to this example, except those on 0746 which were removed after the Nürburgring.

After the Ferrari press conference on November 22, 1957, the silver painted car was immediately airfreighted from Milan to New York and thence by truck to Miami, Florida, and put on a boat for Nassau, where it competed in the Nassau Speed Week held from December 2 to 9, 1957. Its arrival at Nassau marked the first actual competition appearance for the newly announced V-12 Testa Rossa series. Unfortunately, the car had only cursory testing before shipment from Italy, and initial practice at Nassau revealed severe front brake grabbing and juddering problems. Richie Ginther, then Von Neumann's chief mechanic and driver, temporarily resolved the brake difficulty by substituting front assemblies from another Ferrari. In addition to the brake problem, Ginther had to deal with carburetion difficulties that caused engine stumbling and hesitation, neither of which he could completely resolve at the time. These teething faults kept Von Neumann and Ginther from running the Testa Rossa extensively at Nassau, their best finish being a 3rd place in one of the minor races.

Richie Ginther in 0710 at Laguna Seca with damage from tangling with Daigh's Scarab. Ginther is shown again in 0710 at Riverside (center), while at right is Jim Johnston at Marlboro on April 20.

After Nassau, Von Neumann took the Testa Rossa back home to Los Angeles, fixed the brakes, resolved the carburetion problem and ran the car in the Argentine and Sebring championship races, failing in both due to disintegrating pinion bearings.

It continued to lead a very active competitive life throughout the remainder of 1958 in West Coast racing events. Von Neumann, Ginther and John's adopted daughter, Josie, all ran the Testa Rossa. There were few outright wins as the car had to compete against the Scarabs, Listers and other assorted American-built specials, such as Max Balchowsky in Old Yaller, or

American-engined foreign sports machinery, all of which could command much more power than the Testa Rossa. In 1958, the Lance Reventlow Scarabs ruled the roost in the West, and Von Neumann had to be content with class wins for the most part, though the Testa Rossa racked up more than a modest record by any standard of measurement.

As examples, Ginther took 3rd overalls at Santa Barbara on June 1, Reno on August 3, and Laguna Seca on November 9, plus a fine 2nd at Santa Barbara on August 31. Von Neumann seemed to drive the Testa Rossa only rarely, though he scored an excellent overall win

at Vaca Valley on July 6. The primary driver of 0710 was Josie Von Neumann, who competed regularly in the women's-only races where she was practically unbeatable, winning, among others, at Riverside on June 29, Reno on August 3, and Santa Barbara on the 31st of the same month. She was quite capable of dealing with the men as well, such as at Pomona on November 23, when she had a lock on 3rd overall until the pinion bearing broke. Josie would continue piloting the car in the 1959 season, becoming even more proficient as she gained additional experience.

ing the title, but with the lowest point total of any class winner that year. It wasn't his fault, but simply resulted from the paucity of entries in the D Modified class that usually relegated him to run in the next larger displacement group, C Modified (3000 to 5000 cc). In 1958, that class usually produced the outright race winners, and most commonly in the East and Midwest it was dominated by the Briggs Cunningham team of Walt Hansgen and Ed Crawford in 3.8-liter Lister-Jaguars. Generally, Johnston turned out to be the sole Testa Rossa entry in a given National event and he secured the class title by placings in the C Modified class without ever notching an outright win.

The most prestigious SCCA event of the season was the annual Elkhart Lake, Wisconsin, 500-mile enduro held on September 7, 1958, a length very close to the required minimum international championship distance. The race, the biggest amateur do of the year, always attracted a top-notch field of competitors. The track, one of a new breed of road courses springing up at the time to replace the horrid and almost universally disliked airport circuits, was one of the finest to be found anywhere. Set in rolling hills some 60 odd miles north of Milwaukee, the course measured four very challenging miles (6.437 km) to the lap. It was very pretty, excellent from the spectator standpoint, quite safe, and renowned for outstanding local cuisine.

Johnston entered his car for the event to be partnered by Ebby Lunken and Bud Seaverns, and the trio brought the Testa Rossa home to capture a most meritorious 2nd overall and 1st in class. Though never able to challenge for outright victory, the three drivers served notice that they should be considered as formidable competitors at Sebring in 1959. The winners were Gus Andrey and Lance Reventlow in a 1957 335 S Ferrari owned by Luigi Chinetti and leased for the occasion to Andrey's sponsor, Mike Garber. They had more than enough experience and power to handily deal with any competitor. Still, Johnston and company did a fine job in finishing 2nd, as in the process they beat many larger displacement machines. Johnston would continue on campaigning his Testa Rossa, which he nicknamed "Big Red," in 1959.

0752 & 0756

Two of the Testa Rossas noted earlier, 0752 and 0756, need to be mentioned further. They, in conjunction with 0750, 0754 and 0758 were the last batch of customers' cars to be produced. This group differed from earlier versions in that they were fitted with slightly larger

Jim Johnston

The only other regular American Testa Rossa competitor in 1958 was Jim Johnston, who purchased his car (0720) through Luigi Chinetti and took delivery in February, 1958. Johnston, a veteran of Sports Car Club of America (SCCA) competition in a 2.5-liter, 4-cylinder Testa Rossa, intended to use his new car initially at Sebring and follow that with an attack to garner the SCCA Class D Modified (2000 to 3000-cc displacement) championship. He had been originally promised a Sebring entry for 1958 by Chinetti, who controlled matters for Ferrari for the 12-hour race. Through an unfortunate mixup, his entry became relegated

to the reserve category and the problem could not be resolved until just a few weeks before the race was scheduled. At that point, Johnston decided not to run the Testa Rossa as he felt insufficient time was available to properly prepare it.

He proceeded ahead with his plan to capture the SCCA Class D championship by competing in a number of the National races, where points could be gained, and additionally, ran the car at numerous regional events, though these did not count insofar as the point standings were concerned. Unspectacular to watch, the steady and cautious driver secured his goal by clinch-

intake valves (same as TR58s) and longer intake manifolds for greater ram effect of the air-fuel mixture. The increased intake manifold length resulted in the carburetor velocity stack height being higher than before, requiring the bulge on the hood over the carburetors to be raised sufficiently to compensate. This resulted in a much more obtrusive and obvious hood outline. Chassis 0762 was the last pontoon fendered Testa Rossa to be built, as 0760, originally intended to be the final example, was cannibalized to provide parts to rebuild 0748, the wrecked Nürburgring mount of Bauer, and 0666, which had been crunched and burned in Kessler's Le Mans accident.

The Testa Rossa of Charles Hughes (0752) had been painted a dark blue to his special order, much to the disgust of Ferrari, though delivered with standard issue red seats that were the worst sort of color harmony imaginable. The car was airfreighted from Milan to Chicago during the last week of May, 1958, where it was prepared for entry in the Elkhart Lake Sprints, an SCCA National held on June 22. Dan Collins, also from Denver, did the driving at Elkhart but was very unlucky in having to start way back in the pack in 25th position. He did a marvelous job during the race, run partly in a heavy rainstorm, by carving his way through the field to take 3rd overall. Only Walt Hansgen and Ed Crawford in the Cunningham team's 3.8-liter Lister-Jaguars bested him. Also competing in this race was Jim Johnston, who finished 5th, some distance behind Collins. Hughes decided that Ferrari had not painted the car to the exact shade of blue he desired, so after Elkhart it was stripped and redone completely. Subsequent to the repainting, Collins ran the machine twice more in 1958, notching the victory on both occasions, the first outing at Midland, Texas, on August 1, and the second at Fort Sumner, New Mexico, on September 23.

Dick Morgensen took delivery of his Testa Rossa (0756) in mid-August and ran his initial race with the new machine on the 31st of that month at Santa Barbara. He finished 7th after a cautious run to learn the car's characteristics. In September, at Fort Sumner, he finished 2nd behind Collins and then took his car back to California on November second, this time at Palm Springs, where he gained another 2nd. Morgensen then finished off the season at Phoenix on November 30, where he took 3rd overall.

Pedro Rodriguez gets thumbs up from another driver before running in the Nassau Trophy Race, where he finished second behind the Daigh/Reventlow Scarab.

The Riverside Times Grand Prix

Perhaps the best way to illustrate the general uncompetitiveness of the Testa Rossa would be to describe an event such as the grandiosely titled U.S. Grand Prix for Sports Cars sponsored by the Los Angeles Times newspaper and held at the Riverside, California, track on October 12, 1958. Unlike SCCA amateur events, this race was for a big wad of real American dollars and attracted a star-studded competitive field, including Jean Behra in a factory-entered Porsche RSK. Phil Hill was on hand to drive the Von Neumann 412 MI while the boss himself would be piloting a 335 S Ferrari, and Richie Ginther running the lone Testa Rossa (0704). The fearsome competition was led by Lance Reventlow and Chuck Daigh in a brace of Scarabs, Bill Krause in a Chevy-engined D Jag, Max Balchowsky in Old Yaller, and the up-and-coming Dan Gurney in the Frank Arciero 4.9 Ferrari, all larger displacement machinery than the Testa Rossa. Truly, the field included the top guns of American road racing of the period, and they would race for a distance of just over 200 miles on the 3.275 mile high speed track, located some 60 miles east of Los Angeles near the San Bernardino mountains. The result was predictable, Daigh won, followed by Gurney, Krause, Behra, and Ginther, who also claimed a 1st in class. Neither Hill nor Von Neumann were around at the finish.

Nassau

The last of the trio of major Western Hemisphere 1958 races was held at Nassau in the Bahamas, the annual week-long speed orgy attracting another international field of strong entrants. The races were run on the 4.5 mile (7.24 km) Oakes Field airport course, one of the roughest circuits to be found anywhere. It featured scrub pine course markers, and an excursion off course into the sand dunes and pine thickets was to be avoided at all costs. The speed week, run by the flamboyant and highly arbitrary Captain Sherman "Red" Crise under the auspices of the Bahamas Tourist Bureau, was comprised of a whole series of races capped by the 252-mile Nassau Trophy on December 7, 1958. On hand were several Testa Rossas led by the NART entered 1958 Le Mans winner (0728) to be driven by Pedro Rodriguez. It now sported a front carburetor air intake and a fancy new paint scheme, but otherwise remained in basic Le Mans trim. Also on hand

was E. D. Martin (0730), who had so far in 1958 gained little success with his mount, not finishing at Sebring, Le Mans or Elkhart Lake, and taking a disappointing 10th overall at the SCCA Watkins Glen National on September 20. His sole success in 1958 appears to have occurred at a Dothan, Alabama, Regional race on October 26, when he scored an outright win. It should be noted that during 1958, Martin, a native of Columbus, Georgia, generally drove his 335 S Ferrari, using the Testa Rossa only infrequently.

A Scarab, piloted jointly by Reventlow and Daigh, easily won the Nassau Trophy race, though both Testa Rossas acquitted themselves very well. Rodriguez drove very smoothly to capture 2nd overall, with Martin behind in 3rd. Both were excellent accomplishments against the strong field.

E. D. Martin, shown at Elkhart Lake, campaigned his Testa Rossa sparingly.

Lucien Bianchi gets out of shape at Goodwood.

Around and About

Testa Rossas appeared at numerous other events in 1958, as a quick survey will show.

One of these was the Cuban Grand Prix held in Havana on February 24, 1958. The occasion is mostly remembered for the infamous kidnapping of Juan Manuel Fangio and for all the deaths from an early race accident that caused the ill-fated contest to be halted. Two customers' cars were on hand for the race, the first being Piero Drogo's (0714), shipped north from Argentina after the 1000 kilometer race, and the shiny new example (0722) owned by Alfonso Gomez-Mena of Havana. The unfortunate Cuban wrecked his car in practice and sent it back to Modena for a complete rebuild. Drogo started the race rather hesitantly and had really only begun moving rapidly when the race was stopped amidst monumental chaos on the sixth lap. He was credited with 13th position overall, though we will probably never know with any certainty what the finishing order really was.

Another race where Testa Rossas participated was at Goodwood, England, on April 7, 1958, in the Sussex Trophy contest. Ecurie Belge brought both of their cars, 0736 for Willy Mairesse and 0718 for Lucien Bianchi. The two pilots tried their best but achieved no signal success, with Bianchi finishing 5th and Mairesse dropping out sans clutch. Bianchi ran the same Testa Rossa a month later in England, this time a Silverstone race held May 4, 1958, and finished 6th.

Other 1958 Testa Rossa results in the rest of the world were very similar to those noted so far. Very, very few wins were recorded, the model seeming to be almost an also-ran in non-championship competition. Testa Rossas, or so it logically appeared, could win only the long grinds where reliability was of paramount importance, not the sprints when it counted for far less, and when larger displacement machines were on hand.

In conclusion, the 1958 non-championship racing season was very undistinguished from a Testa Rossa viewpoint, the highlights being the two 2nd place finishes of Johnston and crew at Elkhart Lake and Rodriguez at Nassau. Not a particularly inspiring record.

CHAPTER 4
1959: Not Quite Enough

T HE START OF THE international racing season began somewhat later than usual in 1959, as the Buenos Aires event had been cancelled. This meant the maiden race did not take place until Sebring on March 21, allowing Ferrari plenty of time to produce the finalized 1959 model. As mentioned before, initial testing of the actual 1959 type, denoted the TR59, began in January 1959, with the process continuing well into February.

Three new Testa Rossas were constructed for the 1959 season (0766, 0768, and 0770), all substantially different from the press conference car. The chassis, however, remained the new, full space-frame design, and continued the previous year's 92.5-inch (2350-mm) wheelbase. Right-hand drive was used, and from this point on became standard for all Testa Rossas.

The engine, seemingly unchanged in all essential details from the prototype, continued

to feature coil valve springs, again an item to be standard in the future. The conversion to the coil method of actuation had been long overdue, and was a great relief to the mechanics because of the difficulty in tightening down the cylinder heads. The 4-bolt stud pattern was almost impossible to work with, as the hairpin springs partially covered one nut. Besides solving that problem, the coil valve springs had another benefit in that engine limits could be safely increased into the 8,700-8,800 rpm range. This potential was left relatively unexplored, as peak power would be stated as 306 bhp at 7,400 rpm, a very modest increase and apparently achieved by minor revisions to camshaft timing. However, low end performance was considerably enhanced, and in general the engine featured a very wide, almost flat peak power range. Not readily apparent to the casual observer was that the engine had been lightened by changing

the sump, timing case and several other castings from aluminum to magnesium. Some 20 pounds were pared off in the process, which perhaps sounds minuscule, but every reduction in front end heaviness was desirable.

While the engine remained basically as before, its location in the chassis changed radically, now being mounted 4 inches to the left in order to line up with a newly designed 5-speed "barrel type" transmission. This design, another Colotti effort, had the primary shaft lined up with the engine, and the secondary shaft offset lower to the right, outputting power to the centrally aligned driveshaft back to the differential housing. The transmission case, made of magnesium, was something of a novelty for Ferrari, as most previous units had been constructed of aluminum. The engine offset also required modification of the exhaust manifold shapes to compensate for the unequal lengths dictated by the new location in the chassis.

Two views of the differential unit used in the TR59.

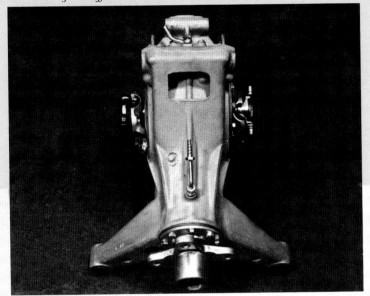

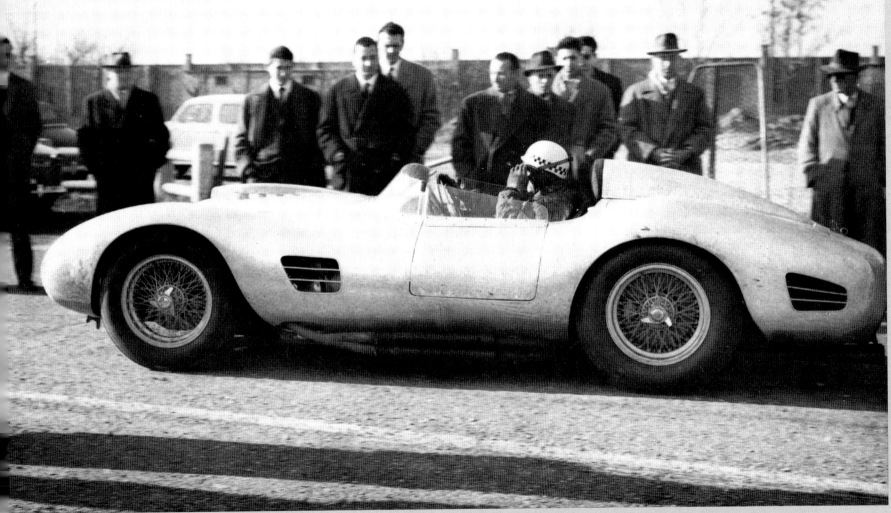

Jean Behra prepares to take the first TR59, 0766, for its initial test run at the Modena Autodrome in January 1959.

Various detail refinements such as access doors for the radiator and oil cooler can be seen on the unpainted but beautifully finished 0766 built by Fantuzzi.

The First Fantuzzi Bodies

Fantuzzi, who left Maserati when that concern quit building racing cars to found his own firm, took over the construction of Ferrari competition car bodies from Scaglietti. The rapidly rising rate of Ferrari production car sales left Scaglietti quite unable to cope with the demands of the racing department as well. The three team TR59s were Fantuzzi's first effort for Ferrari, based on a design by Pininfarina that greatly resembled the 1959 prototype, but incorporating numerous detail improvements.

The front brake vents in the nose of the body were now almost horizontal and slightly rounded, rather than vertical, and the rear brake cooling side vents disappeared altogether. A round trap door was fitted high on the nose over the radiator cap, with another placed on the left front of the hood, directly above the oil breather. The latter door allowed oil to be added without removing the hood. Also located on the hood, but in the right rear, was a rectangular flip-up opening meeting up with a conduit under the hood to funnel cool air into the driver's compartment. The need for more cool air had previously been a source of numerous driver complaints. The plastic cover over the carburetors was retained, and otherwise the body generally resembled the prototype.

Though not readily noticeable, the body was lower and more compact than either the prototype or the 1958 team cars. In addition, it was beautifully finished, a Fantuzzi trademark.

There was one very slight but readily noticeable difference between the first TR59 constructed (0766) and the others. The hood at the point of the carburetor air intake was a bit too low and fouled the fuel line, so a dimple was put in the sheet metal at that point. On the later cars, the profile of the hood was raised sufficiently to clear the fuel line. Not a significant difference, but one that certainly makes it easy to identify 0766.

The TR59, with all these changes, weighed some 170 pounds less than the 1958 team cars, a very gratifying and worthwhile achievement. The combination of lower weight, slightly more power, and wider usable power range enabled the new model to be considerably faster overall and presumably now able to deal more effectively with Aston Martin.

The TR59s appeared initially with dual exhaust manifolds on both sides of the engine, each covering three ports and leading to a separate full-length exhaust pipe for each manifold. This differed from 1958 practice, wherein only one 6-port exhaust section was fitted to each

side of the engine, collecting the group into one pipe before exiting the body. This single unit then became expanded to two exhaust pipes. Obviously, Ferrari was experimenting with scavenging and back pressure conditions to optimize engine output. Later in the 1959 season, one TR59 (0766) was converted back to the 1958 exhaust system style, evidently for comparison purposes. As 1958 was the year of front and reverse carburetor air intake experimentation, 1959 would be the dual versus single exhaust pipe trial.

The substitution of disc brakes for the drum system had several benefits, the most obvious being their resistance to fading, but in addition, they also saved about 50 pounds in total weight. Extensive testing took place to select the optimum disc and caliper sizes, brake master cylinder types and the brake pads themselves. Sebring would be the true test, as not only was it the first battleground of the season, but also the toughest course on brakes.

The Driver Situation

While the TR59s were being prepared and tested for the coming season, Ferrari remained continually occupied in rebuilding his shattered driver corps. He secured the services of Jean Behra, with Porsche in 1958, when Von Trips left for that concern. Behra, the only French Grade One Grand Prix driver of the period, brought a wealth of experience in both Grand Prix and Sports Cars to the team. Unfortunately, the tough, gritty little man also brought along a record of some dozen serious crashes over his career, as he seemingly knew no fear and always pressed on at or above his limits, regardless of the situation. Probably his worst crash occurred at the 1955 Tourist Trophy when his Maserati 300S plowed into a ditch, sliding along on its right side for many yards. In the process, his right ear was scraped off and Behra ever after wore a plastic ear which he would remove before a race start, carefully lodging it in his pocket. Actually, he had two plastic ears, one for the summer months and the other for the winter. Because Behra always drove flat-out to win, he was viewed as a particularly valuable replacement for Hawthorn, and would likely assume the unofficial team charger position. Behra possessed a mercurial temperament, alternating between sulks and rages, that could easily lead to hard feelings all around on a team,

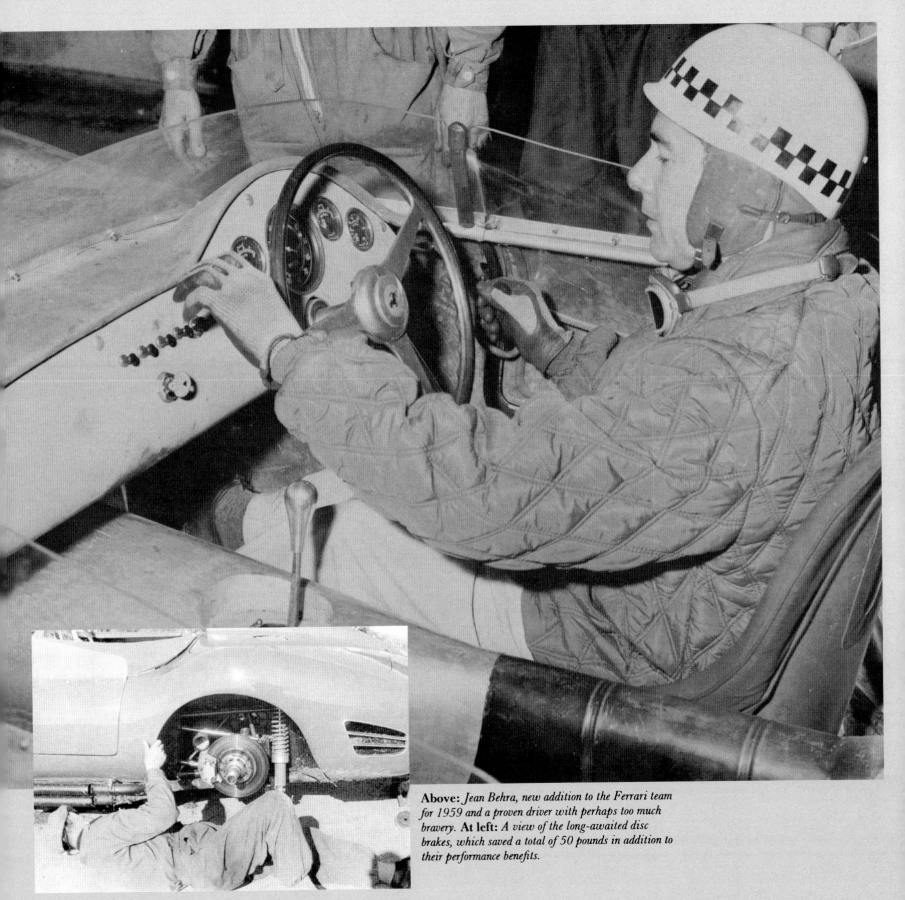

Above: *Jean Behra, new addition to the Ferrari team for 1959 and a proven driver with perhaps too much bravery.* **At left:** *A view of the long-awaited disc brakes, which saved a total of 50 pounds in addition to their performance benefits.*

Tony Brooks, smiling here, but a serious-minded Englishman who Ferrari found necessary to force into line.

as he could be absolutely caustic about a car's deficiencies, the mechanics' capabilities, other drivers' habits and the team manager's tactics. Nonetheless, his talents were very real, and the Ferrari organization would have to treat him gingerly if top notch performances were to be achieved.

A lucky break came Ferrari's way when Tony Vandervell quit the racing game completely after winning the 1958 Grand Prix Championship. This freed Tony Brooks, whom Ferrari quickly signed to a contract. Brooks, a very serious and almost completely humorless Englishman, first came to prominence in winning the 1957 Nürburgring 1000 kilometer race for Aston Martin, and became a key figure in Vandervell's 1958 effort to gain the championship. He had a reputation as an extremely cool driver and one who could be counted on to obey team orders. Like Behra, Brooks came to Ferrari with his share of faults and foibles, the main one being a dislike of sports car racing acquired in 1958. He felt it was unsafe to mix very fast and very slow cars in the same event, as incidents were bound to happen. As proof, he was only too ready to recount his last lap tangle with a tiddler at the Nürburgring in 1958, the contretemps costing him a sure 3rd-place finish. The Englishman intended to drive in Grand Prix events only, irrespective of what his contract said.

Ferrari didn't realize the depth of Brooks' feelings until he flatly refused to drive at Sebring. But Enzo Ferrari was never the type to allow drivers to flout his wishes, and put the screws to Brooks very quickly. He used two classic methods to bring Brooks around to his point of view. The first was to favor the rapid development of Hill's and Gendebien's Grand Prix capabilities, and the second was to give Brooks the worst car to drive. It didn't take Brooks long to catch on: if he wanted to win in single seaters, then good performance in the sports cars was a prerequisite. Brooks saw the light by the time the Targa Florio took place and thereafter remained a generally regular, though reluctant, sports car team member.

Another Englishman signed in the same period was Cliff Allison, of whom much was expected. His driving style emphasized caution, smoothness and consistency, all desirable attributes for long distance racing. A member of Ferrari's team for several years, he turned out to be

Cliff Allison, shown here before the Nürburgring. Note the jack and tool kit, standard Ferrari equipment on long circuits where a tire might need changing out on the course.

reliable in every way, though not compiling a particularly distinguished record during his tenure. He never seemingly wanted to adapt to the organization's method of operation, and generally remained aloof to inter-team rivalries, staying relatively unaffected by Enzo Ferrari's unsettling driver maneuvers.

The Unknown American

The real prize for Ferrari was the signing of Dan Gurney, whom Luigi Chinetti touted as the finest driver he'd ever seen. Gurney, almost totally unknown in Europe at that point, quickly made a name for himself with a series of sparkling drives during 1959. Coupled with a winning personality and cheerful disposition (though basically an introspective loner) he was clearly the find of the year.

With Gendebien and Hill, the four new team members formed a group that held promise to be as good as the 1958 team. To Ferrari's great disappointment, he was completely unable to find any Italian driver capable of qualifying for the team. There was no lack of applicants, but none performed well in track tests. It galled Ferrari that the great run of Italian pilots over the preceding years, such as Nuvolari, Varzi, Farina, Ascari, Castellotti, etc., seemed to come to an end with Musso's death.

With the cancellation of the Argentine event, only five races counted toward the 1959 Sports Car Championship. These were, in order, Sebring, Targa Florio, Nürburgring, Le Mans and the Tourist Trophy.

Competition in 1959 looked to be considerably more difficult than 1958, as Aston Martin announced it would be making a serious bid to win the championship. With proven cars and Moss leading the team, they would be tough to beat. Porsche, now with more powerful cars and additional driving talent, also announced its intention to compete across the board. No other major competitors appeared, as Jaguar seemed to lose interest completely, and the fire went out at Lister with Archie Scott-Brown's death. A considerable number of rumors about Maserati's new and radical sports racer, known to be extremely quick in initial tests, circulated amongst competitors, but it did not appear in championship racing in 1959.

Unlike Ferrari's 1958 breeze to the title, 1959 was shaping up early on as a real 3-way competitive struggle.

78

The Johnston/Lunken/Pabst 250 TR being refueled from five gallon buckets. Mechanic at right sops up overflow while "plombeur" at left waits to reseal gas tank

STORMY WEATHER AT SEBRING

The Sebring 12-hour race took place on March 21, 1959, marked by bad weather very reminiscent of the previous year's Le Mans situation.

Ferrari sent over his three team TR59s with the driver pairings preselected, something of a departure from normal practice. Hill/Gendebien (0770) and Behra/Allison (0768) were assigned to two of the cars, with Gurney and Chuck Daigh handling the third (0766), the last named driver getting his ride at the behest of Luigi Chinetti. Daigh, essentially filling in for the still obstinate Brooks, had made his mark in 1958 as not only the brains behind the Scarab operation, but also as a first class chauffeur.

The Privateers

Backing up the team were four privately owned Testa Rossas, two of which were ex-1958 factory versions. Pedro Rodriguez and Paul O'Shea were expected to do well in the 1958 Le Mans-winning car (0728), now converted to a front carburetor air intake. Rod Carveth of San Carlos, California had purchased the right-hand drive, De Dion, pontoon fender Testa Rossa prototype (0666) after a rebuild at the factory and entered it via NART with Gil Geitner as co-driver. The other entries were left-hand-drive customers' cars. E. D. Martin shared his entry (0730) with Lance Reventlow, augmented by Bill Kimberly, and Jim Johnston (0720) had Ebby Lunken and Augie Pabst as co-drivers.

Chuck Daigh (left) and Paul O'Shea have a few quiet words before the race.

*A NART reserve 250 TR
practices, but did not
race as all the primary
entries started.*

Lance Reventlow splashes along in the afternoon, his TR showing the effects of his early mishap while chasing Geitner.

On the reserve list and appearing for practice was a customer car belonging to Jim Hunt of Miami, Florida. His car, 0722, had been purchased from Chinetti by Lloyd "Lucky" Casner a month earlier. As none of the confirmed Sebring entries failed to make the start, the car was not run in the race. Casner and Hunt switched to drive a 2.0-liter 500TR Ferrari in the race for which they had previously secured a firm entry. This particular car, chassis 0600, was the first four cylinder Testa Rossa built. In 1958 it had been rebodied with pontoon fenders and run at Le Mans by the Rodriguez brothers before coming to the U.S. and being sold to Casner. With the pontoon fenders it was very easy to mistake the car as a shortened right-hand-drive V-12 Testa Rossa. Only by looking closely could the distinctive 500 TR style hood air ducts to the carburetors be noticed. Otherwise, for all one could tell the car appeared to be a V-12 Testa Rossa that had been left out in the rain and shrunk a bit.

There was another pontoon fender Testa Rossa that also ran only during the pre-race practice sessions. This was 0724, owned by John "Buck" Fulp of Anderson, South Carolina. Again, it was a reserve entry that did not make the actual race.

The primary opposition consisted of a lone Aston Martin DBR1 for Salvadori/Shelby and three Lister-Jaguars entered by Briggs Cunningham. Two of these were his very successfully campaigned 1958 models, and the third, with the latest 1959 Costin body style, must be considered a Lister factory entry for Moss/Bueb, though managed by the Cunningham organization. The ever hopeful Porsche team fielded two of the newest RSK models, one a 1600-cc version for Von Trips/Bonnier, and another of 1500 cc for John Fitch/Edgar Barth.

A Flap Over Fuel

Practice had not even begun when a major fuel ruckus erupted between Ferrari and the race organizers. Sebring regulations for 1959 required the use of Amoco fuel by all competitors, as that firm was the event's primary financial backer. Ferrari had Shell as an important sponsor in 1959 and had issued a policy statement in advance of the race stating that he would use his own brand of gasoline if he so desired, but backed off that position when Sebring refused to acquiesce. However, the Amoco gas supplied to all competitors turned out to be contaminated with water and rust chips, causing a wholesale teardown of carburetors, fuel lines and pumps by everyone. This led to a further major confrontation over the matter, with Ferrari at one point making plans to airfreight over from Europe a sufficient quantity of Shell gasoline to allow his team to run the race. The matter was resolved when a fresh supply of Amoco fuel became available that contained no contaminants. However, Ferrari stated categorically that his team would not run at Sebring again if not allowed to select their own fuel.

Practice took place amid some very strong rainstorms resulting in a great river in front of the pits and deep puddles all around the course. It managed to rain every day of practice, with the track never drying out completely at any point during that time. Taking full advantage of one of the relatively dry periods, Behra set the fastest lap time of 3:24 and won the job of rabbit.

Ferrari discovered a major problem with pinion bearings during the wet practice sessions. It seems that when the TR59s accelerated away from wet corners, considerable wheelspin would occur, causing engine revolutions to rocket up accordingly. When the rear wheels finally hit dry pavement and grabbed, the shock loadings on the pinion bearings were so severe they began to disintegrate. Both the Hill/Gendebien and Behra/Allison TR59 pinion bearings broke in the last days of practice, and there were frantic phone calls to Ferrari's bearing experts for new, stronger assemblies. The night before the race all three team cars were torn down and fitted with the new bearings, but the Ferrari camp was still greatly worried about a possible race day failure.

Preparations complete, a mechanic battens down the hood and Dan Gurney contemplates the cockpit.

*Under overcast and threatening skies, the drivers dash
for their cars in the U.S. version of the Le Mans start.*

They're off! Behra in No. 9 grabbed the lead on the second lap.

Top: *Record-breaker Behra brakes for the Esses, the tail showing hasty repair of practice damage.*
Center: *Hill in the race-winning TR59 puddle jumper.*
Bottom: *Pedro Rodriguez in the TR58. Fender was bent by marker barrel.*

Murky Sunshine At The Start

The race began at 10:00 a.m. in murky sunshine, with Salvadori taking the initial lead, but only for the 1st lap, as he began dropping back positions steadily, first with electric problems and later with engine oil blowing by a seal onto the clutch. The car retired for good in the early afternoon when the shift lever broke off in Shelby's hand. So much for the Aston Martin opposition.

Behra snatched the lead on the 2nd lap, followed by Rodriguez, Gurney, Bueb in the 1959 Lister and Von Trips with a Porsche. Gendebien managed a spin at Websters Corner on the 1st lap, dropping him back a bit, but not for long. By 11:00 a.m., Behra, setting a new lap record of 3:21.7 in the process, held a lap lead on Gurney, followed by a rapidly gaining Gendebien, who had forced his way past Bueb and Von Trips.

Behra's long lead evaporated when he brought in the car for the first scheduled pit stop at 12:30 and it refused to restart for Allison. It took almost six minutes to fix the problem, a balky starter switch, and send Allison on his way, now in 3rd place behind Gendebien and Daigh. The other driver changes went more normally, with everything proceeding smoothly for Ferrari until 2:30 p.m., when Hill pulled in the pits with the leading car giving out suitably grating rear-end noises. The pinion bearing had failed once more. Tavoni, fearful of the same malady striking the other cars, hung out the go-slow signal, a very reasonable act considering that a light rain had just commenced. Moss in the Lister took full advantage of the situation to pass both Ferraris and go into the lead by 3:00 p.m., when all the leaders came in for refueling and driver changes.

The Behra/Allison Testa Rossa made a very quick pit stop, re-entering the fray in 1st place with Von Trips 2nd. The Hill/Gendebien team was installed in the Gurney/Daigh machine, but a 5-minute pit stop to change excessively worn brake pads caused Hill to rejoin the contest in 3rd spot, although he quickly pushed by Von Trips into 2nd position. Moss continued his pursuit until 4:00 p.m., when he ran out of gas and got himself disqualified for accepting a scooter ride back to the pits. With Moss out of the way, the race was expected to settle down a bit, though this was not the case as events turned out.

Rain-soaked but determined, Rod Carveth pushed his partner's out-of-gas TR four miles back to the pits in order to continue the race.

The Rainmaster

A torrential rainstorm erupted at 4:30 p.m., causing everyone but Hill to slow down. Repeating his wet condition mastery of the previous year's Le Mans, Hill pressed on, gaining 1st place for good just after 5:00 p.m., when Behra handed over to Allison. Allison, very unhappy about the rain, took one lap and came in to complain that his steering had gone awry. After a cursory check he was told in no uncertain terms that the problem was all in his head and to get back out there and do his job. He did, though very reluctantly, going just fast enough for awhile to keep 2nd place ahead of Von Trips. Finally, Allison put his right foot down and reeled off some very quick laps, the fastest at 3:21.6 for a 92.857-mph average that gained him the honor of recording the best time of the whole race.

Shortly after sunset, the rain finally stopped and a glorious rainbow appeared as the Ferraris ground away the remaining time to take 1st and 2nd places. Victory lane was chaos, with the souvenir hunters doing more harm to the winning TR59 than occurred during the race. Stolen were the nameplate, oil filler hood door, oil filler cap, rear-view mirror, gear shift knob, fire extinguisher, spare wheel and tire, and literally anything else not requiring a welding torch to get free. Tavoni probably had an interesting time explaining the situation to Ferrari.

Ferrari had the eight championship points for winning the event, and learned that several TR59 components needed further development, namely, brake pads and pinion bearings, both certainly resolvable.

Of the private Testa Rossas, the Martin entry finished 6th, in spite of an off-course excursion by Reventlow, closely followed home by the Johnston machine in 7th, both cars having relatively trouble-free runs. Rodriguez, while dueling with Salvadori in the early stages of the race, spun out, collected some marker cones in the process, and jammed the right rear bodywork onto the tire. After a pit stop to rectify the damage, he re-entered the race only to blow up his engine a short time later due to overrevving in a futile effort to catch up the leaders.

The Geitner/Carveth entry ran consistently in the top 10 until late in the afternoon when it sputtered to a halt about a mile beyond the pits out of gas. Geitner, driving at the time, walked back to the pits and announced he was too tired to continue, leaving Carveth to perform the heroic task of single-handedly pushing the Testa Rossa the remaining four miles around the course back to the pits. An hour later, during the rain, Carveth attempted to squeeze by a slower competitor and collected a marker barrel full of water for his effort. The front end of the Testa Rossa was pretty well stove in, and though the sheet metal could be hammered out enough to clear the wheels, the unfixable broken headlights resulted in the steward's refusal to let the car continue racing.

TARGA FLORIO DISASTER

The 43rd running of the Targa Florio took place on May 24, 1959 over the previous year's course. Vincenzo Florio had died earlier that year, and the family tradition was kept alive when his grandson, Vincenzo Paladino, took over the responsibility to organize and manage the event.

Ferrari sent down their 3-car TR59 team, all now fitted with reinforced pinion bearing assemblies. Behra/Brooks were paired in a basically unmodified TR59 (0768), while the Hill/Gendebien mount (0766) had been changed to a single pipe exhaust manifold. The Gurney/Allison TR59 (0770) had been revised considerably in the engine department, having 42-mm Webers and modified valve timing intended to produce more power lower down in the rev range accompanied by a flatter curve up to the limit. Reports indicated these changes resulted in a peak output of 330 bhp at 7700 rpm.

No Aston Martins appeared, as that concern concentrated on preparing a full team for the Le Mans event, scheduled four weeks after the Targa Florio. Porsche came in force to Sicily with the latest 1600-cc RSK models for Umberto Maglioli/Hans Hermann and Bonnier/Von Trips, backed up by a 1500-cc RSK for Seidel/Barth.

Partly because of Ferrari's repeated requests, the race organizers made a strenuous effort to completely close the course during the last practice session, so everyone could run without the risk of tangling with the locals' cars, trucks, cows, chickens or whatever. Though the effort was valiant, the course was secure for only a short time, barely permitting an unobstructed lap or two for most drivers. Practice did reveal the Porsches to be almost a minute faster than the TR59s, though none of the Ferraris were being pushed very hard, as all the drivers were under the strictest orders to spare the machinery for the race. Ferrari drivers were universally critical of the TR59 5-speed transmission's shifting characteristics. They considered the circuit to be basically a 1st and 2nd gear course, and the off-set 1st gear slot arrangement made downshifts extremely cumbersome and time consuming. The team members all wished they had the 1958 style transmission where 1st and 2nd were opposite each other in the quadrant.

The practice times of Porsche were a considerable worry to Ferrari, and as if that weren't enough, the more thirsty TR59s would require at least one additional pit stop over their smaller competition.

The race started this year at 5:00 a.m., with the last car off at 5:41 on what promised to be a typical scorching hot Sicilian day. Gurney held the lead at the end of the 1st lap with 45:01.0 timing, followed by Behra some 8 seconds in arrears, closely shadowed timewise by the two 1600 cc RSKs.

Gendebien coasted into the pits at the completion of his first lap, accompanied by crunching noises in the differential. A quick examination showed the problem to be a broken crown wheel/pinion assembly, and the car was withdrawn. The Ferrari camp began to get extremely worried that the 1st and 2nd gear demands of the Targa Florio might strike all of their TR59s with the same affliction.

The completion of the second lap saw Bonnier take the lead with a 44:05.0 time closely followed by Gurney and Behra. The 3rd lap was even faster as Behra cranked out a 43:57.0, to pass Gurney into 2nd spot, though both continued to fall farther behind Bonnier, who had piled up a 20-second lead at that stage.

Behra roars away from the start while Brooks (at right) takes a snapshot. Gendebien in No. 152 would soon retire with a broken pinion.

Gurney whips past a group of spectators in the most powerful TR.

After reluctantly taking on partner Behra's rolled TR and doing considerably more damage of his own, Brooks asks for help at the Ferrari tire depot in the Madonie Mountains.

Behra Takes A Dive

Bonnier continued adding to his lead on the 4th lap, when Behra, giving it all he had on the downhill leg toward the sea near Campofelice, overdid things on a left hander, slid broadside off the road into a drainage ditch and flipped over, coming to rest upside down in a small pasture. Behra had dived under the dash when he realized what was going to happen and crawled out from under the wreckage completely unharmed.

Most other drivers would have called it a day at that point, but not the tough little Frenchman. He recruited a trio of awestruck locals to help him push the car back over onto its wheels. Considering what had happened, he found the damage to be remarkably light. The tops of the front fenders were flattened against the tires, the windshield broken, the plastic airscoop demolished, the headrest somewhat crushed and one exhaust pipe dragged on the ground. Both the left front and right rear sheet metal suffered extensively, but a few strong kicks cleared room for the tires. Furthermore, nothing leaked, and by one of those amazing peculiarities of life, the TR59 restarted immediately for Behra, so he proceeded to motor around to the pits, slowly at first and then much more rapidly as he realized that the handling had not been impaired by the accident.

If anything, this episode illustrates particularly well the toughness built into the racing Ferraris. They might be heavier than opponents, but pieces didn't fall off and the cars could take a tremendous amount of abuse and live to fight on.

Gendebien Takes Lunch

At about the same time as the news of Behra's incident reached the team, the overdue Gurney motored sedately into the pits, calmly announcing that his ring and pinion had broken. The Testa Rossa was about to be retired when an unusually frantic Gendebien pleaded with Tavoni for a chance to take the car out once again to see how badly it really was affected. Tavoni shrugged his shoulders and Gendebien charged off into the mountains, only to quickly realize that fast motoring was indeed out of the question. He took a leisurely three hours to complete a lap back to the pits, stopping along the way to observe the race, chat with spectators and stranded drivers, and have a leisurely lunch.

Behra's arrival at the pits shortly after Gurney had limped in created instant chaos, with Brooks initially refusing to take over the very dilapidated-appearing car. The mechanics set to work repairing the damage as best they could, replacing all the wheels and beating out or tearing off the bent sheet metal, while Behra tried to convince Brooks that the TR59 was still running just fine and the handling had not been adversely affected. Tavoni and Brooks got into an abusive shouting match, with the former strenuously complaining that the latter was a coward and, further, was being paid to race the car, not to play prima donna. After a hands-and-knees survey around the car, Brooks dubiously took the wheel and motored off, still tossing out epithets in several languages at Tavoni.

A rumpled Denis Jenkinson looks on as Brooks' battered TR is examined by mechanics. Brooks then climbed out to join Gendebien for more consultation.

The wounded sole survivor of team Ferrari began the 5th lap some 20 minutes behind the leading Porsche, and continued to lose ground. Partway into his next lap Brooks piled into a rocky bank after overshooting a corner and caved in the front end. He managed to restart and limped into Ferrari's mountain depot, where the mechanics hammered out the body enough to clear the tires. However, the steering had been damaged, and though he managed to make it back to the main pit, the ring and pinion began to emit what were now familiar noises. A hasty inspection showed that the differential casing had split under the strain and the car had to be withdrawn.

So ended Ferrari's Targa Florio bid with all three Testa Rossas now retired. Furthermore, as the team pits were located on the inside of the course, they were imprisoned there for the remainder of the event, unable to escape the persistent and very distinctive snarl of the Porsches as they drove unopposed toward victory.

Sitting for a group shot are (L to R) Phil Hill, Tony Brooks, Mrs. Brooks, Oliver Gendebien, and Cliff Allison.

Gendebien makes a very precise point to a quizzical mechanic.

Dunlop technician checks tires while fuel levels are read during practice pit stop.

Behra gestures emphatically while the mechanic grimaces as he struggles with hood fastener.

ANOTHER SECOND AT THE NÜRBURGRING

Barely two weeks after the Targa Florio, the 1000 kilometers of the Nürburgring were contested, the actual race taking place on June 7, 1959, with everyone on hand several days earlier for practice. The short interval left Ferrari with precious little time to repair the Targa Florio's ravages, but by working around the clock, the task was just barely completed. All three cars were also fitted with stronger ring and pinion assemblies to prevent a reoccurrence of that debacle.

Behra/Brooks (0768) were once again paired in their Targa Florio mount, which still exhibited traces of that event's damage. The engine had now been updated to be similar to the Gurney/Allison machine (0770), another Sicilian veteran and once more to be driven by them. Hill/Gendebien retained the single pipe exhaust manifold car (0766). The TR59s were supported by the private entry of Carveth/Geitner in the same prototype (0666) they drove at Sebring in March.

Leading the most serious competitors were Moss/Jack Fairman, sharing an Aston Martin DBR1, supported by the Whitehead brothers in their similar privately-owned machine. Aston Martin was trying to run their string of Nurburg wins to three in a row and, with Moss in

the saddle, obviously had an excellent chance to do just that. The Porsche team consisted of the same car and driver match-ups so successful in the Targa Florio.

Practice revealed the Ferraris to be considerably faster down the straights than any of the competition, but troubled by excessive rolling in the corners. This led to much experimentation with both front and rear coil springs and shock absorbers, all manner of combinations being tried. When practice ended, Behra had achieved the best time of any entrant at 9:37, so all the TR59s became fitted with the combination of shocks and springs installed on his car. The suspension problems probably were the likely cause of Hill losing control of his TR59 during the last practice session near the Flugplatz, where he bounced off the road into a bank. The resultant front end sheet metal damage cost the Ferrari mechanics another sleepless night making repairs.

Gurney and Brooks both got in practice laps of 9:40, as did the RSK of Von Trips, a feat surprising just about everyone. Moss only managed a best clocking of 9:43, but no one took the time very seriously, believing he must be saving the Aston Martin for the race.

A sprinter out of the starting block, Moss (third from right) heads for his Aston Martin. Gurney (dark helmet, second from right) is a step behind.

A Clean Getaway For Moss

At the 9:00 a.m. start, Moss made his usual immaculate getaway, followed at a distance by Gurney. By the end of lap one, Moss had a 14 second lead over Gurney, followed by Hill, Whitehead, two Porsches and finally Brooks, who had experienced some difficulty persuading his car to start. The race settled down with Moss continually increasing his lead as it became obvious that all the Ferraris were still handling poorly. Moss kept on at a fiery pace, breaking the lap record repeatedly, finally getting down to 9:32 on the 11th circuit, some 11 seconds faster than his old record.

Gurney came in for his scheduled pit stop on the same lap, complaining of clutch disengagement problems. While this was being

attended to and Allison installed in the car, about six minutes were lost. Hill came in on lap 14 to change drivers and almost at the same moment, Brooks showed up for the same reason. Instant confusion reigned in the Ferrari pits as both cars were refueled, new tires installed and Gendebien and Behra sent on their way. By lap 15 Moss enjoyed a huge lead of more than five minutes. This rapidly got much greater as it began to rain and the Ferrari's handling really went sour.

Moss changed over to Fairman on lap 18 and Gendebien and Behra gradually began to catch him. He made matters easier by spinning into a ditch on the 23rd lap. By the time the unlucky Fairman managed to extricate himself, Gendebien had snagged the lead with Behra

just a short distance behind and gradually gaining ground. Moss regained the controls more than a minute behind Behra and whittled the lead away at a 15-second-a-lap pace. Behra, driving at the very limits all the way, did his best to hold off Moss, even passing Gendebien into the lead in the process, but all to no avail. On the 29th lap, Moss had passed both the Ferrari pilots to take the lead once more, in Behra's case when he came in to the pits for the scheduled driver change.

Of the other top contenders, the Whiteheads had long since dropped out with a broken gearshift lever, and the Gurney/Allison TR59 had been slowed by recurring clutch problems though circulating steadily in 5th place.

The rain showers had stopped and the track began drying when Moss came in once more to hand over to Fairman. Fairman's stay on the track was very short, as Brooks got by him into 1st within a few laps, and then Moss once more took over. By lap 39, Moss had regained the lead, and easily kept it to the finish. Brooks began to slow quite noticeably in the last few laps with severe brake fade problems, allowing Hill to pass him into 2nd place. They finished in that order, with a Porsche taking 4th and Gurney/Allison holding onto 5th.

The Carveth/Geitner Testa Rossa stayed in the top 10 almost the entire race, moving up to 8th on the final lap before Geitner spun at Karussel, got stuck in a ditch and couldn't get out.

The points struggle became even more critical after the Nürburgring as Porsche still led Ferrari by one point, but Aston Martin also could win the championship, depending on Le Mans and Goodwood results.

Sales Pressure From America

The discontinuance of the customers' version of the Testa Rossa, and the failure of the one-off 4.0-liter specials (0744 and 0764) to deal with competition at the major American events led to pressure on Ferrari to sell examples of the TR59s. In the United States, 1959 saw the Testa Rossas gaining class wins but relatively few overall victories at the major events. The most important of these were considered to be Nassau, Elkhart Lake 500, Riverside Times Grand Prix and Laguna Seca Examiner Grand Prix, all contested in the fall of the year. Both American distributors, Chinetti and Von Neumann, desired an example of the latest 1959 team Testa Rossa in order to improve their likelihood of success.

Ferrari, who had constructed two more TR59s (0772 and 0774) in April, acceded to their requests, by agreeing to sell each one of the previous batch of TR59s built earlier in the year. Delivery would be dependent on how the season progressed, and might not take place until after the Tourist Trophy finale in early September.

Regarding the two new TR59s, 0772 became something of a rolling test bed for an experimental 3.0-liter V-8 engine and 4-speed trans-axle layout and was not campaigned in 1959. 0774 was readied for Le Mans, as Ferrari always preferred to keep at least one new machine in reserve for that race.

Above: *Behra undulates around one of the 'Ring's unending curves.* **Below:** *Hill in the Karussel in 0766.*

DNFS AT LE MANS

Two weeks after the Nürburgring came the 24 hours of Le Mans. This event, the 27th of the series, took place on June 20/21, 1959, with several new regulations taking effect. The most important called for a minimum 30-lap distance between taking on *any* fluids—water, gas or oil. Another change for 1959 was the addition of a test day in April, when all entrants could try out their machinery with plenty of time to make final adjustments.

Ferrari took advantage of the occasion to bring his TR59s to the track, where it became apparent that they were uniformly undergeared for the Mulsanne Straight and sprung much too stiffly for the super-smooth course. The drivers also complained of excessive brake fade and impossibly high pedal pressures. None of these problems prevented the TR59s from proving that they were extremely fast and easily more powerful than any other competitor. It was on this occasion that the larger choke carburetors were first tried on the car which was clearly the fastest of the lot and later to be run at the Targa Florio.

As Le Mans time rolled around, Brooks became obstinate once again, absolutely refusing to drive. He considered Le Mans not a true road course, and fraught with danger due to the tiddlers expected to run. In spite of every threat Ferrari could muster Brooks held to his position. Finally, Fernando (Nano) Da Silva Ramos, a fairly experienced Brazilian driver, was taken on in his place for this one event. The initial driver pairings became Allison/Behra, Gurney/Da Silva Ramos and Gendebien/Hill (0766). As Behra wanted Gurney instead of Allison as co-driver, Tavoni found himself being hounded continually by the argumentative little Frenchman, who insisted on his right, as the fastest team driver, to pick his running mate. Tavoni finally caved in at the end of practice, pairing Behra/Gurney in the new TR59 (0774) and putting Allison/Da Silva Ramos together in 0770.

In addition to the factory entries, a supporting contingent of three privateers was on hand: Rod Carveth/Gil Geitner in the prototype (0666) they had driven capably at the Nürburgring, Lucien Bianchi/Alain DeChangy in their Ecurie Belge mount (0736) and the Americans, E. D. Martin/Bill Kimberley (0730) with their Sebring 7th place finisher. Both of the latter entries were left-hand drive live-axle customer versions.

The competition primarily consisted of Aston Martin, entering a full 3-car team of DBR1s for the first time in the season with pairings of Moss/Fairman, Salvadori/Shelby and Trintignant/Frère. Backing them up were Peter and Graham Whitehead. Porsche had a full complement of cars entered, but could not be considered as serious contenders for a high finishing position.

The 24 Hours of Over-Revving

The opening practice sessions revealed that Ferrari apparently had learned little from the April test day, as the TR59s were still seriously undergeared, though the other problems had been licked. The undergearing situation did not prevent them from proving they were still easily the fastest cars on the track and surely capable of seeing off the Astons. Tavoni had decreed a rev limit of 7500 rpm, to which none of the drivers paid the slightest attention, all continually coming in after practice periods with telltale needles reading well into the 8000s, causing Tavoni to fly into fits of rage. The payoff came when Behra pulled in after establishing the fastest practice lap of 4:03.0 with the telltale pegged at 8900 rpm. Tavoni literally exploded at Behra, causing the other drivers to join in to defend Behra's and their positions, all simultaneously carrying on in English, French and Italian, not to mention energetic arm waving. Tavoni finally realized there was no way he could win and stalked off to sulk alone in a corner of the pits, after warning everyone that the engines would not possibly last 24 hours of over-revving.

98

At the height of his powers, Jean Behra drove with total abandon to go from 16th position in the second lap to first place on the 18th, setting a new record for 3.0-liter cars in the process.

The start of the race at 4:00 p.m. took place in good weather, and though it clouded over later in the evening and even drizzled for a few moments before clearing for good, the conditions were far better than 1958. Moss made his customary rapid getaway, closely followed by Gendebien and Da Silva Ramos. Behra stalled his car twice at the start, the delay putting him back into 16th place of the end of the 1st lap, though not for long. Incensed at the poor start, he turned into an absolute tiger, obsessed with gaining the lead. He began rocketing around the circuit with total abandon, broadsliding the corners and screaming down the straights, literally pushing slower cars out of the way as he moved rapidly higher in the standings. Tavoni realized immediately that Behra had gone wild, and hung out the go-slow signal for several laps. All he got in return was Behra's raised fist as he tore past.

Hill leaps from his TR, instructs one of the mechanics, and follows up with even more emphatic instructions. Gendebien looks on, as calm as Hill is excitable.

No one could possibly hold off Behra's attack, and he continued to circulate ever faster, getting down to 4:00.9 on the 17th lap, setting a new 3.0-liter record in the process. He capped the epic breathtaking drive on the same lap by blowing off Moss on the Mulsanne Straight, and then slowed only slightly after taking over 1st place. Over the next several hours, Behra moved out to more than a lap advantage over Moss, who clung to 2nd spot, just ahead of the two other team Ferraris.

Behra came in for his first pit stop on the 30th lap, followed in quick succession by Da Silva Ramos and Gendebien. Why all three cars came in at practically the same time has never been explained, but a poorer example of team management cannot be imagined. The confusion was total, a true Italian comedy. Tavoni took one fearful look at Behra's telltale needle, saw it read 9300 rpm, and just walked away, leaving the mechanics and drivers on their own to figure out how to manage the refueling, tire-changing mess.

The Bianchi/DeChangy customer's car (0736) follows the Allison/DaSilva Ramos TR59.

Too Much Water

Behra was not the only one to over-rev. The other cars had been subjected to similar, though somewhat less brutal treatment, and it became clear that the engines were suffering when all three required a half-gallon or more of water to top up the radiators. The high revolutions had probably caused the blocks to expand, allowing water to leak past the gaskets. How long the engines would stand the abuse could make the difference as to whether they might last out the many remaining hours, for succeeding pit stops required adding ever greater quantities of water.

After the first spate of pit stops, the leading group remained the same, though the order did not continue that way very long. Allison somehow forgot to use the clutch pedal properly on one occasion when shifting up from 4th to 5th and damaged the synchro rings. This caused the TR59 to jump out of 5th gear more and more frequently as the problem became worse, with attendant high revs. The engine finally dropped a valve after numerous such occurrences and the car had to be retired. Meanwhile, Hill had slowed drastically after the pit stop with what, at the time, was suspected to be carburetor flooding. In fact, it was simply water leaking past the head gaskets into the combustion chambers. As the water level in the car's cooling system went down, the condition began to clear up, allowing him to go faster. This pattern was repeated through successive pit stops with both remaining TR59s. The Moss Aston Martin also dropped back in the same period, and exited for good shortly afterward with a broken valve.

All these retirements and problems led to a considerable reshuffling in the leading order, though the Behra/Gurney combine stayed in the lead. By 9:00 p.m. 2nd place was held by Shelby/Salvadori, and 3rd by Hill/Gendebien, nursing their sick car along as best they could.

Gurney Studies Italian

Just after darkness fell, one of Behra's headlights disintegrated, causing the marshals to black flag the car. Two pit stops were required to permanently effect a fix, and though they were short, the time lost resulted in the car rejoining the fray in 3rd place behind the Aston Martin and Hill/Gendebien. A short while later one of the headlights failed again with Gurney at the controls. Tavoni wanted to warn Gurney that a light had gone out, and instructed the Ferrari signaling pit halfway around the course near Mulsanne Corner to hang out an appropriate signal. The mechanics obligingly displayed a signal board reading "little," apparently the nearest they could come to "light" in English. The thoroughly mystified Gurney knew the Testa Rossa was wounded and only had one headlight, but upon seeing the signal, assumed he was being warned about a serious new malady not apparent to him in the cockpit. He immediately slowed and cautiously cruised around for the next several laps, waiting for disaster to strike. Meanwhile Tavoni was becoming frantic, as he couldn't imagine why Gurney had slowed so abruptly. Fuming in frustration, he ordered the "come in" signal. Gurney obediently pitted, expecting to be told what the trouble was, but instead caught a blast from the agitated Tavoni wanting to know why he had slowed down. The conversation quickly deteriorated from that point, and suffice to say the American took to the course once more in a rather bad mood.

Things went from bad to worse just after midnight, when Gurney broke off the gearshift lever, necessitating another pit stop while the mechanics jammed a piece of pipe onto the stub. By that stage, the car was seriously overheating and just barely making the minimum 30 laps before water could be added. After the

next pit stop, the car could be observed emitting steam from the left-hand exhaust pipes, a clear indication that the prolonged bouts of overheating had caused a cylinder liner to shift. Realizing the hopelessness of continuing, the car was withdrawn. This left only the Hill/Gendebien entry, now in 2nd place sandwiched between the Aston Martins of Salvadori/Shelby and Trintignant/Frère, to uphold Maranello's honor.

The Babysitters

But uphold it they did, taking the lead just after 2 a.m., when the leading Aston Martin made a long pit stop. Hill and Gendebien babied the car along, maintaining first place through the remainder of the night and during the morning hours, even though the TR59's condition gradually and inexorably deteriorated. By that stage, all of the supporting Testa Rossas had dropped out. Martin/Kimberley had exited with gearbox problems, the Ecurie Belge mount suffered initially from a faulty fuel pump, causing combustion chamber starvation that led to a holed piston, and the Carveth entry blew up on the Mulsanne Straight.

By 11:00 a.m. the situation became hopeless. Gendebien came in to the pits with a two-lap lead, but he had yet to cover the required 30 circuits before adding water and the engine was in imminent danger of seizing from overheating. No more water could be added, so the mechanics tried everything they could think of in an effort to make the engine run cooler. To add to the grief there was no oil pressure. As the engine overheated, water got into the sump and the combination of watery oil and extremely hot engine burned out the bearings. Nothing could really be done to solve these problems, so Gendebien went out once again with no hope of finishing. After a few very slow laps he coasted into the pits for the last time with a thoroughly seized engine.

Aston Martin went on to finish 1-2 in the event, capturing the all-important eight points and suddenly becoming contenders for the Championship. Though all the Testa Rossas had broken, Ferrari most fortuitously picked up four valuable points by virtue of the privately run "Beurlys"/Elde 250 GT 3rd place finish, the fastest of a group of Ferrari GT cars capturing a string of four consecutive places. All the Porsches broke, leaving the point standings with

Hill at speed.

Ferrari, 18, Aston Martin, 16, and Porsche, 15.

Ferrari really lost Le Mans because of the undergearing problem, completely inexcusable in view of the April testing results. Behra's fantastic performance at Le Mans remains one of the epic efforts in the history of the event, and a fitting remembrance of the little Frenchman's fighting ability.

Hill's car takes on gas and water during an early morning pit stop. By 11:00 a.m. however the situation was hopeless.

The dry-sumped 3000-cc TR59 engine with 38DCN Weber carburetors.

INTERIM DEVELOPMENTS

The 1959 season's European races had been run through Le Mans, at 2-week intervals. By the time the team cars got back to Maranello, only a few days were available to fix the obvious problems before the transporter had to leave once more for the next race venue. Fortunately Goodwood did not take place until early September, so after Le Mans the harassed organization finally had sufficient time to really go through the Testa Rossas properly for the championship-deciding season finale.

The torn-down Le Mans engines all exhibited bearing failure from the over-revving, over-heating problem. This led Chiti to decide the only proper resolution of the situation was to dry sump the TR59 engine. New sumps were designed and installed, with 10.0-liter capacity oil tanks placed in the left front fenders, partially blocking the engine room air escape vents. The camshafts and timing were also changed to allow a safe 8500 rpm limit, and carburetion reverted back to the earlier 38 DCN types.

At the team drivers' urgings, considerable experimentation took place during the summer at Modena and Monza to resolve the handling problems. Eventually, over a degree of negative camber was cranked into the rear wheels in an attempt to stabilize the back end, though potentially serious tire wear was to be expected. The front end got its share of attention too, all oriented toward reducing the severe understeer so apparent at the Nürburgring. Various front anti-roll bar sizes were tried to get some oversteering characteristics, but they only resulted in a modest improvement, due to the TR59s being basically front end heavy.

Behra Goes Down For The Count

The inevitable and long overdue eruption with Behra came at the French Grand Prix on July 5. Behra, convinced as usual that he had been given an inferior mount by Tavoni, seemed to almost deliberately blow up the car during the race in pure frustration. Afterwards he and Tavoni had a wild argument in the pits, to the great fascination of the onlooking horde of spectators. The disagreement, depending on the witness, culminated in one of three ways: Behra punched Tavoni, Tavoni punched Behra, or they both swung at each other. The conclusion of the argument was much clearer. Tavoni fired Behra, and Enzo Ferrari backed the action.

After Behra cooled off, he approached Ferrari to regain his spot on the team. The Commendatore refused to see him, accept his apology or reinstate him, and further even declined to sell him a car to campaign as a privateer.

Behra had for several years sponsored the building of Porsche-based specials which he would run in races where his involvement as a factory driver was not required. He competed at one of these events, held at the Avus track in Berlin on August 1, just two weeks after his dismissal from the Ferrari team. Behra's Porsche got out of control while running flat out on the high banking and flew off the top. The resulting crash was instantly fatal. For the unlucky Frenchman, it was the 13th major accident of his career. At his funeral there were no flowers from Ferrari, or factory official representation, or message of condolence. It was just as though Ferrari had never heard of him.

Still, Behra's death posed some serious problems for Ferrari. He had unquestionably been the fastest driver on Ferrari's sports car team in 1959 and had been counted on to spearhead the firm's attack at Goodwood. His departure materially lessened the team's chances of winning the championship, and probably was a key factor in the final results.

Ferrari, after a rather cursory search, signed Giulio Cabianca for Goodwood. An Italian pilot best known for some stirring Mille Miglia and Targa Florio drives with OSCA, he had driven a semi-official factory 2.0-liter Dino at all the major European races in 1959, giving a good account of himself. Though not yet of the caliber required for 3.0-liter competition, Cabianca was viewed as having more potential, and might eventually become a regular team member.

The Hill/Gendebien
0774, which dropped a
valve at the start and was
parked after one lap.

Hill and Gurney listen
attentively as Brooks
motors on at full throttle.

TOURIST TROPHY FINALE

The 1959 version of the Tourist Trophy, the 24th edition in the series, took place on September 5 at the Goodwood Circuit in Sussex, England. The race length was six hours, over a 2-mile airport-type course consisting of mostly fast bends and no real straights, hardly suitable for a championship event and considered by many drivers as strictly a Mickey Mouse course. Though much less of a meaningful road course than even Le Mans, Brooks was on hand for the event, primarily because he could hardly refuse to run on his native soil with the championship at stake.

For the first time in the history of the championship series, three competitors had the opportunity to win the title going into the last race of the season. Ferrari had to finish at least 2nd to tie for the championship, though if this occurred and Aston Martin captured the Tour-

ist Trophy the Feltham firm would garner the title due to scoring more victories during the season. The mathematics of the situation were very interesting and all manner of combinations could be imagined. The three competitors came to Goodwood fully prepared to do battle, and all believed they could win.

Ferrari's 3 team cars were preassigned to Brooks/Gurney (0770), Hill/Gendebien (0774) and Allison/Cabianca (0766), all updated to the latest specifications and identical, excepting the single pipe exhaust manifold on 0766. The Aston Martin and Porsche teams were at top strength for the vital contest, and both had a definite advantage over Ferrari by virtue of having competed in the 1958 edition of the race. Aston also sprang a new wrinkle on everyone, installing air jacks in their DBR1s for more rapid tire changing.

Handling Remains A Problem

When practice began, the Ferrari team quickly realized that the suspension testing and modifications had been for naught, as all the Testa Rossas had severe understeer which changed abruptly to excessive oversteer whenever power was applied. Consequently, the team mechanics spent the first two practice days altering rear spring stiffness, eliminating front anti-roll bars and generally fiddling with different combinations of front shock absorber settings and spring rates to effect a cure. The problem was never completely sorted out, though improving considerably over the practice periods. As testing took place using only small amounts of fuel in the tank, no one knew what to expect of handling once the race started with a full load on board, though rapid tire wear was feared.

At the start, Gurney in No. 9 is barely underway with G. Hill in a Lotus 15 (No. 29) about to cut in front of him. Moss is already out of sight, having jumped the start.

Standing by the cars along the pit wall before the start, Chiti talks to Gurney.

Practice degenerated into a fierce duel between the contending teams, with Moss, Brooks and Gurney all breaking the 1958 record of 1:32.6 held by Moss. Moss retained the distinction of being fastest at 1:31.2, with the two Ferrari drivers less than a second behind, and the quickest Porsche within a second of Maranello's best. The stage was now set for a dingdong battle.

The start at noon was most peculiar. Moss began running as the starter raised his flag, followed in ragged fashion by everyone else. As so many drivers had jumped the start, the officials wisely decided to just let the race take place. Moss left while most of the others were still running and all the Ferrari drivers made poor starts. Hill, in his great anxiety to get going, over-revved and dropped a valve, forlornly

0766 in for a pit stop, getting four new tires, gas and oil.

Above: *Allison in 0766 is waved past by D-Jag in early stages. The TR59 went on to finish third, taken over by Hill and Gendebien.* **Right:** *Brooks in ill-handling 0770.*

coasting back into the pits after one lap and retiring. Not a good omen for Ferrari that day. Gurney took off far in arrears and really began burning up the track during the first hour, gradually moving up into 3rd and pressing Shelby's Aston Martin for 2nd. Gurney's achievement is all the more remarkable as his car seemed to be handling particularly badly, and not improving as the fuel load lightened. Allison was similarly unhappy with his TR59's handling, but his mount appeared to be behaving considerably better than Gurney's. Allison played it cautiously, gradually moving up to 6th by the end of the first hour.

At the first spate of driver changes about an hour into the race, Brooks took over from Gurney, and quickly called back at the pits to complain about the car's steering. He was sent back out and promptly spun at Lavant corner, coming in to the pits once more, where both front wheels were changed. All this pit activity caused Brooks to rejoin the chase back in 6th place, and he began to really motor in an effort to catch up, breaking the race lap record several times before leaving it at 1:31.8. Meanwhile, when Allison came in for his pit stop and changeover, Hill and Gendebien took over his mount, and Cabianca never got to drive at all.

Just after 2:30 p.m., Salvadori, partnering the leading Aston Martin with Moss, came in for a pit stop and his car caught fire during the refueling activity, causing a spectacular blaze that ruined the car and pit. The 2nd place Shelby/Fairman Aston was called in and Moss took over, now as the leading car with the Von Trips/Bonnier Porsche in 2nd, and Hill/Gendebien 3rd.

Deliberately stopping a few feet from the finish line with the crippled TR, Gurney lifts himself out, getting ready to push it over at the appropriate time for a fifth place finish.

Moss Shuts The Door

As the race approached the final hour, lap times showed conclusively that the Hill/Gendebien-driven Testa Rossa would never be able to overtake the Porsche at the pace being maintained by both. This led to Tavoni bringing in the car and handing it to Brooks, clearly the fastest Ferrari driver that day. While this action took place, the 2nd-place Porsche came in for its final pit stop, a long one due to the time it took to replace its bolt-on wheels. When Brooks re-entered the fray, he assumed that the Porsche's time-consuming pit stop had enabled him to move up into 2nd place. This caused him to completely misread Tavoni's frantic pit signals

that he was actually in 3rd, some 12 seconds in arrears, though gradually gaining. Brooks finally realized his error during the last few laps when he spotted the Porsche in front of him, rather than behind, where he had expected it to be. He pushed the TR59 to the limit in an effort to catch up, but Moss, circulating between the two cars and knowing that Brooks must be kept out of 2nd place, successfully balked him for several laps. By the time Brooks managed to fight his way past Moss and take off after the Porsche, the race was in its closing laps, with the Ferrari crossing the finish line only 2 seconds behind the Porsche.

Gurney had moved up to 4th place in the sixth hour, performing commendably well in the obviously mishandling car, only to blow out a tire on the next to last lap. He coasted to a stop at the finish line and pushed his car over at the appropriate time to take 5th place.

Brooks, who should, by that stage of the season, have known how to read Ferrari pit signals, likely cost the team a tie in the championship. Ferrari lost the title by two points in an exciting finish to a competitive and hard fought season of racing.

1959 NON-CHAMPIONSHIP RACING

The 1959 season witnessed far more Testa Rossa activity than the prior year, though almost all the action occurred at American events. The Testa Rossas were but rarely seen in Europe, a state of affairs caused to a certain extent by the remarkable progress of the English constructors such as Cooper and Lotus, who were practically unbeatable in sprint racing. Their handling prowess more than compensated for any displacement or power deficiency against the Testa Rossa, though their usage was generally restricted to sprint events as durability continued to be elusive. The English were leading the revolution and it would only be a matter of time before their products began coming to the United States in force to irreversibly change the existing order of things.

In early 1959, the English invasion could only be discerned by the most astute American racing patrons and pilots, and the Testa Rossa still appeared to be the best bet to win the SCCA Class D Modified crown, though predicted to have only a mediocre chance to capture races outright, as they would normally be running against the larger displacement machinery. At that point there was literally nothing else competitive to the Testa Rossa in Class D. The old Monzas, 300S Maseratis and DB3S Astons were obsolete, and the DBR1s seemed to stay exclusively at home. A number of additional Testa Rossa examples arrived in the U.S. over the winter of 1958-1959, bolstering the ranks of steady campaigners and, as in 1958, most were run sparingly, though two competitors did compete extensively and their activities deserve to be described.

Alan Connell

One of the stars of American amateur racing in 1959 had to be Alan Connell from Fort Worth, Texas. A big, burly and well-to-do rancher, he took a sudden liking to racing, beginning abruptly in July, 1958 with a Maserati 250S. The Texan displayed an almost immediate skill far beyond what his limited experience would have normally indicated, though some of his initial outings were marked by an exuberant wildness. He seemed to learn very quickly how to drive well, was naturally aggressive, and further possessed the ambition to be a winner and the financial resources to buy the best equipment. At the conclusion of the 1958 racing season Connell had served notice that he would be a force to reckon with in 1959.

Desiring the latest, fastest, and finest machinery, Connell paid a call on Luigi Chinetti in October 1958 and purchased the freshly rebuilt ex-Piero Drogo pontoon fender customer car (0714) for a fling at the 1959 SCCA Class D Modified Championship. Some months later he also ordered for late Spring delivery the 4-camshaft 335 S pontoon fender special (0764) to campaign for outright wins in the major races. Here was a man who clearly could operate in the big time.

Connell hit the 1959 SCCA Nationals trail with a vengeance and consistently scored points, never finishing further back than 2nd in class at the nine races he contested, though not winning any event outright. He managed to snatch three firsts in class, these coming at Bridgehampton on May 31, the Elkhart Lake Sprints on June 21 and at Montgomery, New York on August 9. Montgomery turned out to be the last National event that Connell competed in with the Testa Rossa, as the point total gained by that stage safely secured for him the Class D Modified title. In addition to the Nationals, the Texan often drove the Testa Rossa at Regional events, his best performance probably coming at Mansfield, Louisiana on March 18, 1959, when he won 1st overall.

After Montgomery, Connell seems to have concentrated almost exclusively in running the 4-camshaft car in pursuit of outright wins at the remaining 1959 Nationals and other important races. There his competition was much more severe, as he had to contend with the likes of George Constantine in the Elisha Walker Aston Martin DBR2 and the Cunningham team Lister-Jaguars, as well as the American-built or engined specials. Connell would never again pilot a Testa Rossa, though his six months in campaigning one had been very fruitful for him and Ferrari.

Dick Morgensen

The other consistent Testa Rossa competitor in 1959 was 0756, owned and driven by Dick Morgensen of Phoenix, Arizona, who nicknamed his mount the "Ole Red Sled!" As noted in the prior chapter, he had actually run the car several times in 1958, gaining the experience that would see him become a formidable threat in 1959. Morgensen was a forceful driver and a tough competitor who enjoyed the cut and thrust of close combat. He was not above fender bashing to push slower cars out of the way, and consequently most fellow competitors gave him a wide berth in the corners. The Arizonan could not be considered a wild driver by any standard, but his cornering techniques certainly provided good value for the paying spectators' money.

Morgensen tended to restrict his activities to the Southwest, though he certainly had a busy year in 1959. His record was capped by victories at El Paso, Texas on March 1, and a string of California wins coming at Santa Barbara on May 31, Del Mar on September 20, Riverside (amateur) on October 10 and San Diego on November 15; his last win came at Tucson, Arizona on November 22. His California placings included a 1st in class at Pomona on February 1, 2nd overall at San Diego on June 21, 2nd overall and 1st in class at the Riverside National on July 18, following that up on the next day by a 3rd in class at the hotly contested Kiwanis GP, a 2nd at Santa Barbara on September 6, and a 3rd at Riverside on December 6. Morgensen also finished a worthy 4th overall at the most important American sports car race of the year, the 1959 version of the Times Grand Prix held at Riverside on October 11. All in all, Morgensen had an extremely busy and productive racing season and his efforts were rewarded by gaining enough points to capture the Pacific Coast Driver's Championship.

Some Of The Others

There were many other Testa Rossas around and about, but most seem to have been rarely used, for one reason or another, as a quick survey of their activity will indicate.

As in 1958, Testa Rossa participation in the SCCA National circuit was very spotty and well below what should have transpired. Even Jim Johnston (0720) ran infrequently, apparently surfeited with his 7th place finish at Sebring in 1959. Possibly Johnston's best National showing was a 1st in class at the tight Cumberland, Maryland track on May 17 where he bested Alan Connell for D Modified laurels. Later in 1959 he sold the Testa Rossa to David Biggs of Clarksville, Missouri, and gradually retired from active competition.

Amongst the rarely used Testa Rossas was the example owned by Charles Hughes of Denver, Colorado and driven by Dan Collins, who piloted it to a Regional race win at La Junta, Colorado on May 31, and followed that with a 2nd overall and 1st in class at the National held at Buckley Field, Colorado on July 12. Later in 1959, Hughes advertised the Testa Rossa for sale and eventually disposed of it to Alex Budurin of Tucson, Arizona, though it does not appear to have seen a race track again until 1960.

In 1959, Ed Hugus sold his example (0732) to Russell Cowles of Phoenix, Arizona. The new owner ran it only a few times in 1959 Southwestern events before blowing a head gasket at El Paso, Texas on November 1. Cowles had the car completely rebuilt at that stage and while at it, repainted the previous white-with-blue-stripes color scheme all blue.

Josie Von Neumann continued to campaign 0710 in West Coast races during the first half of 1959, now almost in every instance head-to-head with the men. She certainly acquitted herself well, as the results show a 2nd in class behind Morgensen at Pomona on February 1, 4th overall at Avandaro, Mexico on April 26, 3rd the following week in Mexico City and a 4th at San Diego on June 21. By that stage 0710 was definitely one very tired machine in desperate need of a rebuild and consequently became more or less retired to pasture. Not that Josie lacked for rides, as her father had imported a number of other Testa Rossas, one of which was always available for her use.

These included 0718, for sale by Von Neumann on behalf of its' Mexican owner, Julio Mariscal. The car was driven at Riverside on July 19, 1959 by Pedro Rodriguez and sold shortly thereafter to Gordon Glyer of Sacramento, California who scored a 3rd overall in his first outing with the car at Vacaville on September 27. Von Neumann still owned 0704, run at Riverside on July 19 by Josie, and 0754 which was eventually to become the property of George Keck of Vancouver, British Columbia, Canada.

Another sparingly used Testa Rossa was the example (0748) purchased by Gary Laughlin of Fort Worth, Texas from Chinetti in April 1959, though delivery did not take place until July. This was the 1958 Nürburgring mount of Gottfried Kochert and Erik Bauer which had been rebuilt at the factory after the latter's fatal crash. Laughlin ran the car rarely and his best performance in 1959 was probably a 2nd overall at Midland, Texas on October 11, the winner being none other than Connell in the 4-camshaft Ferrari.

E. D. Martin does not seem to have run his Testa Rossa at any 1959 American events, using it solely for Sebring and Le Mans that year and then had the car mechanically rebuilt before shipping it home to Columbus, Georgia. Martin discerned by racing at Sebring and Le Mans that the TR59s were far faster than his 250 TR and he had been rebuffed in his efforts to buy one for himself. At about this time the Maserati Birdcage was announced, and as it appeared to be far superior to the customer style Testa Rossa, he ordered one immediately. Martin then sold the Testa Rossa to Pete Harrison of Atlanta who ran it only a few times in 1959 after taking delivery in early September. His record included a 2nd overall at Tuskeegee, Alabama on September 6, behind Martin's 335. Harrison later dnf'd at Courtland, Alabama on October 11 when the differential casing cracked apart. Martin meanwhile took delivery of his Birdcage and in his second race with the new car at Daytona on November 15, he crashed mightily and suffered extensive injuries. He retired permanently after recovering from that accident.

Pedro Rodriguez drove the 1958 Le Mans winner (0728) on only a few occasions other than Sebring in 1959, mostly in Mexico. At Leon, Mexico on January 18, he finished 2nd behind his brother in a Porsche RS, and at the Avandaro race on April 26, he dropped a valve seat causing serious internal engine damage. The Testa Rossa was brought back to Chinetti in New York, rebuilt and then disposed of in October to George Reed of Midlothian, Illinois.

Jim Hunt sold his customer car in the summer of 1959 to Dr. David Lane of Miami, Florida with Lucky Casner acting as the broker, but the new owner failed to finish his maiden outing at Daytona on September 6, 1959 when the split race pinion bearing broke. Lane had the rear end repaired and took the Testa Rossa to Daytona once again to contest the last SCCA National of the year on November 15 where he took a first in class and then went on to Nassau.

The Big Three

As in 1958, the most important American racing events were the Elkhart Lake 500, Riverside Times Grand Prix and Nassau Trophy, the latter two being professional events with a prize money payoff.

The Elkhart Lake 500 event held on September 13, 1959 attracted the usual top-notch field of amateurs, but unlike previous years, the heavy hitters sat it out, the West Coast crowd preparing for Riverside, and many of the East Coast contingent waiting for Nassau. In the case of Von Neumann and Chinetti neither had yet taken delivery of their promised TR59s, though both were expected to arrive in time to compete at Riverside.

Two customer Testa Rossas did show up at Elkhart Lake, but were not an important factor in the outcome of the race. The best finish was an uninspiring 10th overall and 3rd in class by George Keck and Frank Beck in 0754, while Dave Biggs partnered by Martin Baoine brought 0720 home in 17th position.

With the side of the car crinkled from encountering a guardrail during practice, Phil Hill awaits the start of the L.A. Times Grand Prix at Riverside. He won easily.

At Riverside on October 11, 1959, Phil Hill easily won the 200-mile Times Grand Prix and the big bag of gold that went with the honor, in the Von Neumann TR59 (0768). All was not entirely serene for Hill as he did have a contretemps with a guardrail during practice that messed up the right side of the body considerably. Though looking decidedly secondhand, the TR59 ran perfectly as Hill stroked his way to victory, lapping, at least once, every other competitor in the race. Morgensen (0756) as recounted earlier took 4th place, and Glyer (0718) finished 8th. In retrospect, Hill's victory at Riverside would mark the only occasion where a Testa Rossa would win any major American race, amateur or professional, during this period.

All the heavyweights from the East and West Coasts along with a sizable contingent of European drivers descended on Nassau for the annual speed week festival held in early December 1959. Von Neumann sent the TR59 for Hill to once again pilot, but the competition was far more formidable than seen at Riverside. Heading the list were George Constantine in the Aston Martin DBR2, Alan Connell in the 4-camshaft Ferrari, Pedro Rodriguez in the NART TR59 (0766), and three of the new Maserati Birdcages to be piloted by Dan Gurney (about to leave Ferrari permanently) Loyal Katskee and Gus Andrey. Numerous other Fer-

A refueling stop for Pedro Rodriguez in the Nassau Trophy Race.

raris, Scarabs, Listers and Maseratis were there in force, and just about any one of them was capable of winning the 252-mile Nassau Trophy feature attraction on December 6.

Nassau ran its usual, almost bewildering plethora of races, one of which was a Ferrari-only bash won by Hill with Rodriguez 2nd. Prospects for a Ferrari success in the Nassau Trophy were a bit discouraging, at least on the basis of practice timing results, though race incidents were probably much more significant in keeping a Prancing Horse machine out of the winner's circle. Hill collided with an OSCA pilot who misinterpreted on which side he intended to pass, knocking him out into the pine scrub boonies. Altogether, he lost at least 50 seconds in getting back on the course and making a quick pit stop to check his tires to be certain they were undamaged.

Pedro Rodriguez was even more unfortunate as he tangled with Gus Andrey's Birdcage, the contretemps costing the Mexican almost 10 minutes to repair the damage. He re-entered the race with no chance for a high finishing position, and wound up 12th overall after a very dispirited drive. Poor David Lane was once again a non-finisher in the ex-Hunt Testa Rossa (0722) when the repaired pinion bearing failed, leaving him disgusted and discouraged with his mount. All things considered, Nassau was none too kind to the Ferrari marque in 1959.

Subsequent to Nassau, John Von Neumann sold the TR59 and all his other racing Ferraris to Jack Nethercutt of Los Angeles, the group including 0704, 0710 and the 412 MI. Nethercutt actually desired to purchase only the TR59, but to do so, had to buy all the rest as one package. Von Neumann, in addition to his Ferrari interests, also was the Volkswagen distributor for the West Coast, then in the midst of explosive growth. He had less and less time to devote to racing and had actually turned over the management of the Ferrari operation to his wife, Eleanor, who was not only a very capable businesswoman, but a racing enthusiast of long standing. John pretty much retired from racing at that point as Eleanor continued forward, though on a somewhat reduced scale. Nethercutt kept only the TR59, disposing of 0704 to Dick Hahn of Seattle, Washington, and the worn-out 0710 which went to a succession of owners over the next few years, none of whom did anything worth noting with it.

CHAPTER 5
1960: The Title Regained

THE LATE FIFTIES and early sixties were times of great technical upheaval in the motor racing world, as the many eras of front-engine domination came to an end and the rear-engine machinery gained ascendancy. The transition period was intense, and in retrospect, remarkably brief. Porsche and Cooper led the way, proving during the late fifties that the rear-engine layout permitted lower overall weight and better handling. Cooper won the 1959 Grand Prix Championship, and Porsche almost did the same in the sports car division. Enzo Ferrari had clearly recognized the coming trend, and by late 1959 had assigned essentially the entire design staff to develop rear-engine competitors. However, he continued to refine the front engine GP and sports cars for 1960, convinced they could still capture both championships. Stubborn? Perhaps. But mostly just a realistic assessment of the time it takes to develop winning new machines, and a sense of the winds of change then blowing through the CSI.

The winter of 1959-1960 found the CSI embroiled in controversy as to the future form of motor racing. The 2.5-liter Grand Prix formula, in effect since 1954, was due to end after the 1960 season. The proposed 1961 formula called for a 1.5-liter maximum engine capacity. This occasioned a great deal of jousting as the various forces competed to get their aims and biases accepted. From Ferrari's standpoint, it made no sense to build a new 2.5-liter car for the 1960 season, so he instead concentrated his Grand Prix efforts toward the new 1961 formula.

A GP Car With Fenders

Sports cars were the subject of even more eventful discussion by the CSI, particularly as a preponderance of members felt these machines had irretrievably strayed from the original guideline of being production, street-driveable cars with modifications as necessary to withstand the rigors of long distance competition. It was argued that "automobiles" such as the Testa Rossa could quite logically be considered as nothing less than Grand Prix machines with fenders and lights added. They were virtually impossible to drive in the street, custom built, not even remotely fitted-out like passenger cars, and prodigiously expensive to construct and maintain. It was further argued that this lack of reality to anything customers could purchase and use on an everyday basis probably inhibited many manufacturers from taking a role as active competitors. All in all, an undesirable situation that demanded relief, and quickly.

Responding to the pressures of many manufacturers, the CSI had been promoting a Gran Turismo class oriented toward streetable coupes with complete and fully operational road equipment. The class had grown by leaps and bounds during the past several years, supported both by a wide range of constructors and evident spectator enthusiasm for cars more closely resembling what they could drive themselves. The surge of Gran Turismo popularity provided an impetus to continue upgrading the importance of that series while gradually deemphasizing the special purpose sports racers. Making it yet easier to phase out the sports cars was the increasing difficulty of even being able to organize the required minimum of five 1000-kilometer events each year.

Compromise For 1960

The problems led to a proposal that the championship should be staged for Gran Turismo cars, with the sports cars still allowed to compete—but not for points. The discussions dragged on over the winter before a compromise was worked out along lines proposed by the Le Mans organizers. This called for the championship to be decided along 1959 rules, but with several new regulations aimed at making the sports cars more like their streetable Gran Turismo brothers. The principal changes included a full-width windshield with at least a 10 inch (34 cm) vertical rise from the cowl, operating windshield wipers, and space for a suitcase measuring a minimum 26 inches (65 cm) long,

16 inches (40 cm) wide and 8 inches (20 cm) deep somewhere in the body cavity, but not encroaching on the passenger compartment. Though not officially incorporated in the overall rules, the Le Mans organizers also had several special constraints of their own which were generally followed by the other 1960 major events. These included a maximum turning diameter of 45 feet (14 meters), minimum ground clearance of 4.75 inches (12 cm), and maximum fuel capacity for 3.0-liter machines such as the Testa Rossa of 31.7 gallons (120 liters).

In spite of these actions, the handwriting was on the wall. The out-and-out sports racer would not have much longer to live unless more competition materialized quickly, something that appeared quite remote.

The 1960 race schedule, as originally planned, called for seven events, starting with Argentina and followed by Sebring, Targa Florio, Nürburgring, Le Mans, Goodwood and a potential season finale in Venezuela. The Venezuelan event remained financially shaky for some period of time before being dropped from the schedule in May. The Goodwood organizers also vacillated because of their uneasiness about running a championship event when no English manufacturer might be in contention for the title. They felt that a Gran Turismo event would be far more popular with the fans, and in April, after several months of backing and filling, they announced that the championship race would be abandoned in favor of a GT event.

With the defection of Goodwood and the financial incapacity of Venezuela, only five events would decide the 1960 championship. Actually it would be four and three-quarters, because even though all the events were supposed to be for a minimum distance of 1000 kilometers, the Targa Florio organizers had already decreed that their 1960 edition would be over a distance of 10 laps, or 720 kilometers, and would not budge from that position. Technically speaking, the championship should not have taken place as the required minimum of five 1000-kilometer events was not staged, but the CSI, recognizing the difficulties involved, permitted an exception to the rules, supposedly only for that year. Not a good situation from anyone's standpoint, but the problems were indicative of the sorry state of long distance sports car racing at the time.

In the midst of these negotiations, Aston Martin dropped a bombshell by announcing their retirement from sports car racing. Having reached their goal of capturing the championship in 1959, they decided to now take aim at the Gran Turismo and Grand Prix championships. With Aston out of the running, only Porsche would remain to field a factory team against Ferrari. This state of affairs was significant confirmation to the CSI that Gran Turismo racing had to be the direction actively pursued. However, in consideration of the large expenditures already committed by Porsche and Ferrari, and the compromise worked out using the Le Mans rules, the CSI proceeded with the Sports Car Championship for 1960, though no one considered it a desirable state of affairs.

One new competitor appeared on the scene for 1960, the American-run and financed Camoradi U.S.A. team, entering Maserati Type 61s in the major championship races. No one really knew what to expect of this semi-factory operation, as the team and the car were essentially new and untried.

Driver Dissatisfaction

Over the winter of 1959, the Ferrari team underwent another disruptive upheaval, with half the driving force quitting for one reason or another. Generally, the drivers felt the organization had no chance of capturing the 1960 Grand Prix championship with the apparently obsolete front-engine single seater. Similarly, they did not see any substantial development activity taking place with the Testa Rossas that would result in significant benefits being achieved.

Dan Gurney, who had raced in 1959 for a purported pittance while proving his abilities, refused to sign a contract for 1960 when it did not contain the substantial raise he felt he had rightfully earned. Ferrari refused to budge, so Gurney left to accept more lucrative offers from BRM to drive their Grand Prix cars, and from Camoradi to handle Maseratis in the sports car events.

Olivier Gendebien felt that Ferrari's chances were poor to win either championship in 1960, stating his belief that the only potential victory might be at Le Mans. He moved to Porsche, where he signed on to drive their sports cars at every event other than Le Mans. Gendebien sat out the first few events of the 1960 Grand Prix season before hooking on with the Yeoman Credit team campaigning Coopers.

Tony Brooks, disillusioned with Ferrari's potential in 1960, tired of endless arguments over driving the sports cars, very negative on the potential of the Ferrari Grand Prix effort and getting bored with the whole game, quit completely late in 1959. He returned to England to stay out of racing until becoming involved with Vanwall and Cooper efforts later in 1960.

These defections and retirements left only Phil Hill and Cliff Allison to form the nucleus of the 1960 team. The shrewd Commendatore decided to lure Von Trips back to the Prancing Horse camp from Porsche. The bait was promise of the team leader's spot, and the blandishment worked, as the German came back to Ferrari's employ. Naturally, Hill was none too pleased at this apparent snub, fully believing he had rightfully earned the accolade as number one driver. The action created an instant rivalry between Hill and Von Trips to prove who was the better driver, a struggle continuing all through the year. Of course, that is exactly what Ferrari aimed to achieve by rehiring Von Trips.

Enter Richie Ginther

Another new driver joined the team in 1960, and the circumstances surrounding the situation offer an interesting view of Enzo Ferrari's calculating mental processes. The new man was Paul "Richie" Ginther, the third of the Californians to make the big time in that period. Ginther had compiled a very successful record in the U.S., generally piloting Ferraris owned by John Von Neumann. As the 1960 Sebring event loomed closer, Ferrari and the race organizer, Alec Ulmann, once again deadlocked over the mandatory gasoline requirement. Ferrari decided he would not officially enter factory cars, and further, would not allow team drivers to participate.

Richie Ginther, tireless tester, excellent mechanic and fine driver, whose affable personality belied his tremendous capacity for work.

However, the Commendatore wanted a chance to garner the all-important championship points. This led to the preparation and loan, for Sebring entry, of the latest type TR59/60 (0774) to Luigi Chinetti, who signed Ginther and Chuck Daigh as drivers. Ginther was sent to Modena late in the fall of 1959 to check out the car, and while there was pressed into service to test the new 1960 Formula 1 cars, as neither Hill nor Allison was available. Ginther turned in lap times very close to the Autodromo outright record, and highly impressed Chiti and Ferrari with his driving and testing skills. The upshot of the episode was that Ferrari offered Ginther a one-time drive in a Testa Rossa at Argentina, and then following Sebring he would be signed to a contract. In this manner, Ferrari not only obtained a new driver, but kept his position relative to Sebring inviolate.

The affable and technically competent little man became a regular in both classes of racing in 1960, being rewarded not only for his excellent performance, but also because he quickly and willingly took over the universally detested test driving chores. Ginther's mechanical aptitude and ability to communicate problems and potential solutions to the design staff, coupled with an inexhaustible capacity for putting up with both the physical rigors and mental boredom of testing, rapidly gained him Ferrari's favor. As most of the other drivers heartily disliked test driving, they were only too happy to let him do the job.

These four drivers formed the official factory team for 1960, as Ferrari normally entered only two Testa Rossas for the Sports Car events, with the exception of Le Mans. If other drivers were needed, they were hired on an event-to-event basis. It appears that those drivers handling Dino-series cars in support of the Testa Rossas in 1960 were also generally employed on a one-at-a-time scheme.

Evolution For The TR59

The Ferrari development organization was a beehive of activity during this period, with an astounding variety of projects underway. These included Grand Prix and Formula 2 front and rear engine design trials, the new baby Ferrari, changes to the 250 GT Short Wheel Base Berlinetta series just replacing the Tour de France model as the firm's Gran Turismo mainstay, and innumerable Dino V-6 experiments. The Testa Rossa received its share of attention, though the changes for 1960 were more evolutionary than revolutionary. In Ferrari's opinion, the 1959 championship loss had been partly a fluke, though he recognized that smaller cars had a distinct advantage over the Testa Rossas on the twisty courses. Therefore, a plan evolved to support the Testa Rossas with the Dino V-6, primarily at the Targa Florio and Nürburgring, where they might have a better chance of winning. Only Porsche would be a factory entrant in 1960, and Ferrari felt the Testa Rossas to be clearly superior at Le Mans and other long courses, so with the Dinos as backup for the twisty circuits, he believed the firm would have a more than reasonable chance of winning the championship.

An obvious inhibiting factor against a massive improvement program for the Testa Rossa was the likelihood that the Sports Car Championship might be aborted at the end of 1960. This made it financially unwise to expend any sums above those necessary to comply with the new regulations. Still, the 1960 model of the Testa Rossa was a bit more than a warmed over TR59, featuring several significant changes, though not readily apparent to a casual observer. The last TR59s to be built (0772 and 0774), were modified during the 1959 season and over the winter of 1959-60 in a number of ways. These included cutting the frames just behind the front wheels to shorten the chassis from 92.5 to 89.75 inches. This action, in conjunction with a minor front end re-working, resulted in the turning radius being reduced from a ponderous 55 feet to a more reasonable 45 feet, a figure necessary to meet the 1960 Le Mans regulations. The V-12 engines remained basically as in 1959, though now mounted about an inch lower and slightly further back in the chassis. The 5-speed front-mounted transmission, the subject of much driver criticism in 1959, was initially replaced with a 4-speed rear-mounted unit, aimed both at shifting weight rearward to improve the Testa Rossa's handling characteristics, and at providing an easier shifting arrangement for 1st and 2nd gear courses such as the Targa Florio. This unit was the subject of considerable experimentation throughout 1960, with a 5-speed version being tested as well, but at most events the two cars ran with the 1959-style front-mounted transmission. The De Dion rear suspension remained as before, no matter which transmission form was employed.

The bodies, once again built by Fantuzzi, were almost completely identical to the old 1959 style, though several inches shorter and very slightly lower. To meet the 1960 rules, they were equipped with the required high, full-width windshield and wipers, the added weight of this gadgetry negating any benefits from the lighter frame and body construction. The new cars weighed in dry at 1655 pounds, almost 20 more than the previous year's model.

The 1960 version of the Testa Rossa, as displayed at the annual Ferrari press conference held on December 29, 1959, was simply the modified TR59. The two cars involved (0772 and 0774) were variously referred to at the time as TR59/60, or TR60. For our purposes, we will define them as TR59/60s. As mentioned previously, two of the TR59s (0766 and 0768) had been sold, with the remaining 1959 team car (0770) being retained and updated to 1960 mechanical and bodily specifications. It continued to see service throughout the 1960 racing season as a factory entry. All three cars now had the gas filler cap located in the headrest without a sheet metal lid, a change from the TR59's middle of the back deck positioning.

Test sessions at the Modena Autodromo just prior to the first event of the new season showed the revised 1960 model to be less than a second faster than the TR59. While handling had been improved, the high windshield's negative aerodynamics cancelled out any meaningful performance increase. Also involved in testing at that time, and the subject of considerably experimentation all season long, were vented disc brake assemblies in various sizes, though invariably larger than the 1959 type.

A SCARE IN ARGENTINA

As in 1958, the Buenos Aires, Argentina, 1000-kilometer race, contested January 31, 1960, was held partly on the permanent Grand Prix track, combined with a section of the Buenos Aires freeway. The course again totaled 5.88 miles and 106 laps would be required to make the necessary distance.

Ferrari shipped two Testa Rossas to the Argentine for the pairings of Hill/Allison (0774) and Von Trips/Ginther (0770), accompanied by a 2.5-liter Dino 246 entrusted to Lodovico Scarfiotti and local hero, Froilan Gonzalez. Gonzalez, the aging veteran of some heroic battles in years past, was well past his prime as a driver, but the "Bull of the Pampas" still remained an Argentinian idol. In a slight change since initial testing, both Testa Rossas had vents cut in the front of the rear fenders, and the TR59/60 driven in the race by Von Trips and Ginther featured an air intake fitted in the valley between the right front fender and hood for additional cooling. Hill proved to be fastest in practice of all the Ferrari team drivers after unusually extensive practicing by all hands. He set a new record of 3:23.1 after much trying, handily beating his 1958 mark of 3:25.9.

Camoradi had entered a lone Tipo 61 Birdcage Maserati of 2.9-liter displacement for Gurney/Gregory, altogether an unknown quantity, as the only major previous racing appearance

for the model had been at Nassau, where all three present had broken or been involved in accidents. In practice, the Birdcage went very well, Gurney cutting a best time just a second slower than Hill, though there was some suspicion that the Maserati could go considerably faster yet. It was one of those situations where the Ferrari team couldn't figure out if they should be worried or not.

Tavoni Loses His Voice

Porsche appeared with a 3-car team of 1600-cc RSKs for Bonnier/G. Hill, Trintignant/Herrmann and Gendebien/Barth, none wearing the new high windshields prescribed by the 1960 regulations. As the lower windshields might reduce their lap speeds by a solid 3-4 seconds, Tavoni lodged an immediate and loud protest. Porsche's excuse revolved around their unanswered appeal to the FIA that the 10-inch-high windshield unfairly gave their cars an additional disadvantage because they were much lower than the Ferraris and as such, lost proportionally more aerodynamic effect. In addition, they had secured in writing a waiver of the regulation from the Argentine organizers for the event, while the matter continued in negotiation. Tavoni remained absolutely adamant that Porsche follow the rules, particularly as the 1960 fuel limits favored the smaller cars anyway. The

Testa Rossas could only carry 32 gallons (120 liters) while the 1600-cc RSKs were allowed 26 gallons (100 liters). There was no question in Tavoni's mind that the Porsches could go much further per tank of fuel than the Testa Rossas might. If the windscreen rules were not adhered to, then the RSKs, as compared to the Testa Rossas, would likely cover the 1000 kilometers with at least one less pit stop, saving possibly 4 to 5 minutes, plus being 3 to 4 seconds per lap faster than with the high configuration. In total, Porsche would pick up 8 to 9 minutes, and potentially be unbeatable.

Finally, on the last day of practice, Porsche gave in, but only after Tavoni, during all the strenuous arguments, had lost his voice completely. Just as he calculated, the RSKs suddenly slowed 3 to 4 seconds a lap, no longer remaining within a few seconds of Testa Rossa times. If practice results held up in the race, and Porsche managed to get away with one less pit stop, he calculated that the Testa Rossas could win, but by a very small margin.

Allison reported feeling unwell the morning of the race, so Gonzalez was quickly nominated as a reserve driver for him and allowed to briefly try out the car an hour before the start. As it turned out, Allison evidently made a swift recovery, negating the need for the Argentinian's services in the Testa Rossa.

The Sandbag Drops

The start of the race proved Gurney had been sandbagging in practice, as he tore off to an immediate lead and steadily increased it over Hill and Ginther, who were really trying to keep up. For almost two hours Gurney ground on, eventually gaining a lead of 1:45 over Hill and setting a new lap record of 3:22.4 in the process.

Shortly before the first round of pit stops were to occur, Gurney gradually slowed as the Birdcage began to handle more and more erratically. When the driver changes were completed, Allison, given the GO signal by Tavoni, didn't take long to overtake Gregory in the Maserati, charging past into the lead on the 40th lap. Gregory was quickly called in and Gurney took over once again, and though the car mishandled badly, started to close in on Allison. The Ferrari camp was convinced that whatever was bothering the Maserati had to eventually get worse, and refused to speed up their leading car. Though Allison knew that Gurney was rapidly catching up, he heeded Tavoni's pit signals and kept his cool. Finally, Gurney overdid it, spun, and clouted some hay bales. A few laps later the transaxle gave out, ending the Maserati challenge.

So ended the race for all intents, as Hill/Allison and Von Trips/Ginther cruised around serenely the remaining distance to capture 1st and 2nd place. The winners took six hours 17:12.1 to cover the distance at an average of 159.58 km/h.

The Dino 246 ran as high as 3rd before dropping out with a broken magneto wire, allowing the Bonnier/G. Hill Porsche into that position, where it stayed throughout the rest of the race.

Ferrari picked up the all important eight points for winning, with Porsche garnering four, in another demonstration of almost faultless Testa Rossa reliability.

Hill and Allison wear their victory wreaths. The issue was never in doubt after Gurney's Birdcage broke.

Ginther at the controls of 0774, loaned by the factory to NART. Car held second for many hours, but was a DNF with a seized engine.

Privateer Pete Lovely saved the day for Ferrari, coming all the way from 12th place to finish third. Hump over rear deck covers outsized fuel tank.

FERRARI BOYCOTT AT SEBRING

For the 1960 edition of the Sebring 12-hour grind on March 26, the organizers stood firm on their previous year's resolve that all competitors must use only the race sponsor's fuel. Ferrari refused to acquiesce to the demand and boycotted the event, and additionally would not allow any of his three team drivers to compete, even in privately owned machines. Ferrari's official withdrawal robbed Sebring of much of its importance as a championship event, but conversely put additional pressure on the firm to do well in the other events.

Ferraris were represented at Sebring exclusively by private entries. Jack Nethercutt entered his TR59 (0768) to be co-driven by Pete Lovely, and Luigi Chinetti's North American Racing Team (NART) fielded a factory prepared and loaned TR59/60 for Daigh/Ginther (0774), fresh from its Argentine victory, accompanied by a 2.0-liter Dino 196 for the Rodriguez brothers.

Porsche also objected to the mandatory fuel rule, but the desire to garner championship points outweighed their principles in the matter. While Porsche officially boycotted Sebring, all the factory drivers were on hand driving team RS60s "sold" to Bonnier the week before the event. Other serious competition was expected to come from a pair of Camoradi-entered Maserati Tipo 61 2.9-liter Birdcages, one for Moss/Gurney and the other entrusted to Shelby/Gregory. The Cunningham team entered Walt Hansgen/Ed Crawford in a Birdcage, with Dave Causey also on hand with his privately owned Tipo 61 to be shared with Luke Stear. Maserati hopes were high, particularly as Moss had scored a strong victory at Havana, Cuba, on February 28, with a Camoradi machine.

Pre-race practice was somewhat inconclusive as none of the top contenders seemed to be overly exerting themselves. It almost seemed as though the sunny, temperate Florida weather made everyone a bit more placid than usual.

Lovely Springs A Leak

At the 10:00 a.m. race start, Lovely got away very quickly into the lead, followed by Daigh and Hansgen. By lap three, Moss, after making an uncharacteristically slow start, charged by everyone to the front. Meanwhile, Daigh had to make a quick pit stop to replace a flat tire, temporarily dropping him far behind the front runners, but not for long.

At the end of the first hour, Moss enjoyed a comfortable lead over Hansgen, who had moved up rapidly in the field, followed by Daigh at a distance, trying to make up the time lost in the early pit stop. By noon Daigh had reached 2nd place, pushing Hansgen back one notch, and the Rodriguez brothers held 4th, though hounded continuously by Bonnier in the fastest Porsche. Lovely had been in and out of the pits several times with fuel leaking problems, dropping him well back in the standings.

The front runners held their same positions until the mid-afternoon, when the Daigh/Ginther Testa Rossa began to emit a thin wisp of smoke, gradually growing in size, an ominous portent that all was not well in the engine's innards. At about 3:30 the car clouted a slower mover in a corner and called in at the pits to get four new tires, repair a smashed headlight, straighten a caved-in fender, replace the front brake pads and take on a copious quantity of water. No question there, obviously a ruptured head gasket, but as nothing could be done about it, the car was sent out again.

The fuel leaking problems caused the Nethercutt/Lovely TR59 to come in for a half-hour pit stop so a permanent repair could be effected, dropping them back to 12th place. The Rodriguez brothers also had a pit stop of similar duration to replace a broken universal joint, and shortly afterward dropped out for good with a defective clutch.

The afternoon period was generally very unkind to the front-runners as Crawford got stuck on top of a sand bank, and though eventually freeing the Birdcage, it retired shortly thereafter with sand in the gearshift selector mechanism. Meanwhile, the fastest Porsche, driven by Bonnier and G. Hill, fell out with a rod through the side.

A Lovely Move

Shortly after 5:00 p.m. the badly smoking 2nd place Daigh/Ginther TR59/60 began to pop, bang, and throw sparks out the exhaust pipe. They had put on a tremendous performance with the very sick car in chasing Moss for some seven hours, but the run couldn't last much longer at the rate it was deteriorating.

Only a few minutes later the Testa Rossa slowly coasted into the pits with the engine seized solid, leaving only the Nethercutt/Lovely machine, far back in 9th place, to salvage some honor for the Prancing Horse.

Moss and Gurney, at this stage, had a 6-lap lead on their closest pursuers, a pair of Porsches, prompting them to slow down considerably. Maybe the slowing down did it, as just past 6:00 p.m. the Birdcage suddenly broke its ring and pinion. So much for the last of the big displacement front-runners and very reminiscent of Sebring in 1954 when the same circumstances prevailed.

Lovely regained the controls of the now properly fixed TR59 at the approach of dusk and began to really motor, picking off cars one by one in a masterful exhibition of nighttime driving. By 9:00 p.m. he had blasted his way up to 3rd overall with a good chance of snatching 2nd place from the Holbert/Schechter/Fowler Porsche, if he could only maintain the pace. By 9:30 p.m., with a half-hour to go, Lovely had caught up to within 20 seconds of the Porsche, but couldn't seem to narrow the gap any further.

At 9:45 p.m. Nethercutt, figuring Lovely couldn't possibly make up the time on the Porsche, called him into the pits and took over the TR59 for the few remaining laps. Even with the driver change they finished only 1:04 out of 2nd place. Conceivably, Lovely could have pulled it off, but Nethercutt owned the car and the decision as to who drove when was his alone.

By virtue of the Nethercutt/Lovely 3rd-place finish, four valuable championship points were gained, putting Ferrari and Porsche in a tie for the series lead at 12 points each. Like 1959, privateers' points kept Ferrari in contention for the title.

In April, the Goodwood organizers dropped their planned championship race, leaving only three firm events on the calendar: the Targa Florio, expected to be won by Porsche, Le Mans, at which Ferrari was favored, and the Nürburgring, a tossup between the two.

The TRI60 Appears

At the Le Mans test day held on April 9, 1960, Ferrari brought along a new variant of the TR60 (0780), shepherded by an anxious Carlo Chiti. It featured a revised chassis design on an 88.6-inch wheelbase and a fully independent rear suspension, composed of a dual wishbone layout almost identical to Ferrari's Formula 1 cars. It also had a remodeled 5-speed gearbox, heavily vented disc brakes, and weighed in at 1510 pounds, some 160 pounds lighter than the normal TR60. The new model, of which two were built (0780 and 0782), became known as the TRI60 to denote its independent suspension characteristics.

The TRI60 as it appeared in Monza on April 27, 1960.

Unusual shot underneath transporter shows air scoops to rear brakes and part of IRS wishbones.

The engine room of the TRI60.

A side view of the TRI60, also taken at Monza.

Le Mans Test Day and the TR160 gets some front suspension adjustments. Later Hill stands in the cockpit as ignition receives attention.

Hill, Allison and Ginther tried out the new car during the trials, and all were enthusiastic about its handling, though unhappy that Briggs Cunningham's new experimental D-Type Jaguar successor could easily pass them on the Mulsanne Straight. Of course this must be kept in perspective, as Hill turned the fastest lap time of the day, a sparkling 4:01.4, very close to the all-

time practice record set by Fangio in 1957 at 3:58.1. This compares to the best Jaguar time of 4:08, bettered by both the other Ferrari drivers. Unlike 1959, the TRI60 was overgeared, only reaching 7100 rpm maximum on the Mulsanne stretch, so the solution seemed to be simply a case of fitting a slightly lower fifth gear ratio to allow higher engine revs.

A more normal TR59/60 was also on hand, and though having greater top speed than the IRS derivative, would not lap faster than 4:04. On the basis of the trial, the IRS car certainly looked to be superior to the De Dion type.

THE TARGA FLORIO LOST AGAIN

The 44th edition of the Targa Florio on May 8 consisted of 10 laps on the delightfully named "Piccolo Circuito della Madonie," totalling 720 kilometers, instead of the normal 14 lap, 1000-kilometer grind. The shortened distance, supposed to be worth fewer championship points, was decreed necessary to permit spectators to clear out of the mountain roads before darkness fell. However, some suspicion lingered that it was really done to enhance Ferrari's chance of winning by reducing their fuel consumption disadvantage compared to Porsche. Over the full 14-lap event the Ferraris would need an additional pit stop, but at 10 laps, both makes would require the same number.

Ferrari came in force to the Targa Florio, sending down a team of five cars, all different from each other. Heading the list were the TRI60 (0780) as seen at the Le Mans trials, and a standard TR59/60 (0772) both utilizing 4-speed transmissions with first and second gears opposite each other in the quadrant. Supporting them were live-axle and IRS 2.5-liter Dinos, and a 2.0-liter Dino for the Rodriguez brothers under the auspices of Chinetti's NART. In addition, an ancient Monza 750 came along on the transporter to serve as a practice hack. The driver crew included the regulars of Hill, Von Trips, Allison, and Ginther, the latter newly signed to a contract, plus Giulio Cabianca, Lodovico Scarfiotti and Willy Mairesse. Also on hand to drive was Paul Frere, the Belgian driver/journalist, in his first factory-entered ride.

Opposing the Ferraris were a trio of RS60 Porsches to be managed by Barth/G. Hill and Gendebien/Herrmann/Bonnier. Because of a lack of drivers, the last named crew would handle two of the cars. In view of Porsche's 1959 Targa Florio performance and their showing to date in 1960, they were heavy favorites to win.

Phil Hill prepares to take out the TRI60 for a practice session.

The only other competition of note was the
Camoradi Birdcage entry for Umberto Maglioli, a 2-time Targa winner, with co-driver Nino
Vaccarella, a Sicilian lawyer reputed to
intimately know all 702 curves making up the
circuit. Camoradi had been very disappointed
by the failure of their Birdcages to last to the
finish in previous events, and only entered the
car after Maserati assurances that the weak ring
and pinion problem had been corrected.

Most of practice took place in the normal
Targa Florio conditions of local traffic hazards,
but the situation in 1960 was even worse than
usual. The severe winter of 1959-1960 had been
hard on the mountain roads, and now numerous work crews were out with repaving equipment, rollers, shovels and brooms attempting to
restore the surface to some semblance of
smoothness. This meant that even in the mountains, caution had to be exercised, as wandering
work crews might be encountered in the most
unlikely places.

The Monza "muletta," though looking thoroughly disreputable and suffering from a broken rear spring hastily wrapped in wire, went
like a rocket, seemingly perfectly suited for the
course. Even though the roads were cluttered
with normal Sicilian traffic, Hill managed a
highly respectable 48:20 lap in the old pig.
However, Ginther, ill at ease on the circuit,
finally did in the Monza when he piled into a
house on the last day of open road practice.

Scratch One TRI60

As in 1959, organizers completely closed the
entire course to normal traffic so that competitors could go flat out, at least for a few laps.
During this session Allison had a spectacular
accident with the TRI60 (0780) at the end of the
only straight section of the circuit. The straight
terminated in a gentle left-right-left "S" curve
normally negotiated in the 125- to 130-mph
range. As he entered the beginning of the curve,
the left front tire suddenly blew out, and unable
to make the right-hand turn following, he went
straight on into a deep drainage ditch, burying
the nose in mud. Allison escaped unhurt, but
the Testa Rossa was literally destroyed. Among
other items, the front suspension and frame were
caved in, the engine torn off its mounts and the
differential casing broken.

*Ginther (202) leads Von Trips in the IRS Dino 246,
but crashed only moments later, eliminating the only TR
to start.*

The TRI60 had been the fastest Ferrari in practice, with both it and the IRS 246 Dino performing particularly well in handling bumps, pot holes and bumpy turns. That form of suspension was clearly not yet completely worked out as turns with humps or ridges were more difficult for them than the normal De Dion TR59/60. Despite its smaller displacement, the IRS Dino beat the best times posted by the TR59/60. As this had not been expected, and the TRI60 was unrepairable, confusion ensued in the Ferrari camp as to who would drive which car. The situation remained up in the air until late that last night before the event, when final assignments were made. Hill and Von Trips got their wish and took the IRS Dino 246, leaving the TR59/60 to Allison and Ginther. The Rodriguez brothers kept their Dino 196, while Cabianca, Scarfiotti and Mairesse were assigned to the live-axle 2.5-liter Dino. This left a disappointed Frere without a ride, so he simply switched back to his original profession of motor-racing journalist.

The Ferrari crews' outlook could not have been encouraged by their prospects on the morrow, as both Porsche and Maserati were easily faster in practice than any of Maranello's best. For the first time since the Mercedes-Benz days, Ferrari would come to the starting line as a distinct underdog.

The Demolition Derby

Contributing to the general uneasiness on race day was a new problem confronting all the competitors, most of whom had never experienced such a situation in Sicily. It was drizzle and mist all through the normally bone-dry mountains, making the roads exceedingly muddy and treacherous.

By the end of the first lap, Ferrari fears were confirmed as Bonnier forged a 23-second lead over Maglioli, followed by Gendebien in another Porsche, then Allison, Mairesse and Von Trips in order behind them. Von Trips had come to grief on the initial lap when locking brakes caused him to smack a wall, requiring some frantic work to pull out a tire-fouling fender, though nothing could be done about the slightly bent front suspension.

The order remained this way over the next few laps as the bad mountain weather began to clear and lap times decreased. Bonnier pitted the leading Porsche on the 4th lap, allowing

Maglioli to assume the lead by virtue of staying out for an additional lap. Allison came in and handed over the best-placed Ferrari, the TR59/60 running in fourth, to Ginther. Only a kilometer beyond the pits he rashly tried to pass a slower car on the outside of a curve, lost control, got on the marbles and rammed a tree head-on. So much for the only Testa Rossa competing.

The race ground on, with Von Trips and Hill moving up to 3rd by the 8th lap, some six minutes behind the Bonnier/Herrmann Porsche, which in turn was more than four minutes in arrears of Vaccarella, who was really burning up the course in the Birdcage. His effort came to naught on that lap when the fuel tank, evidently punctured by a flying rock, ran dry at a most critical moment, entering a high speed corner. Bereft of power, Vaccarella crashed heavily, ending a fine demonstration of skillful driving.

The race ended on a predictable note after this incident, as the Bonnier/Herrmann Porsche took the victory with the Hill/Von Trips Dino 2nd, followed by another Porsche, and the Cabianca/Scarfiotti/Mairesse Dino in 4th place. The Rodriguez brothers finished 7th, an amazingly high position only when viewed in light of their heroic efforts not to finish at all. The Dino looked like the last survivor of a demolition derby, crunched in four separate accidents during the race. The most serious occurred when Pedro did a double roll, landing upright on the wheels and leaving portions of the bodywork scattered about the landscape in the process. In spite of it all, the poor, battered Dino kept on running to the end.

With Porsche's victory in the Targa Florio, they took a 2-point lead over Ferrari, 20 to 18, in the championship stakes. Though the TR60 in one form or another was Ferrari's primary entry in the title quest, on tight circuits it seemed to be slower than the rapidly improving Porsches and barely faster than the 2.5-liter Dinos. The glory days for the big front-engine sports racers were clearly running out.

Just after the Targa Florio, the Venezuelan race organizers admitted their inability to raise the necessary funding, and formally abandoned the shaky event, leaving only Nürburgring and Le Mans to finish out the season.

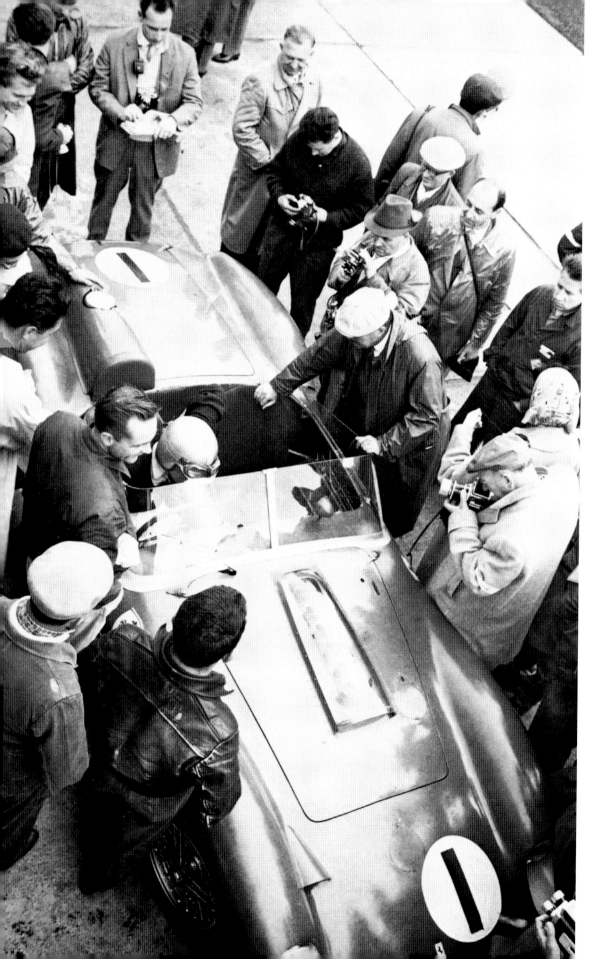

Von Trips gets ready to go out for practice, with Hill standing alongside, among the crowd.

NÜRBURGRING

Both Ferrari and Porsche badly wanted to win at the Nürburgring 1000 kilometers on May 22. Neither firm had rung up a victory since the event resumed championship status in 1956. Naturally Porsche wanted to succeed in front of the home folks, but more important, they were fully aware the 'Ring represented the last venue in the championship series where they had an excellent chance of winning. To Ferrari, the Nürburgring had proved to be total frustration: four consecutive 2nd place finishes, and the only championship event not captured by a Testa Rossa in the past two years.

Ferrari entered two Testa Rossas, both having the Targa Florio 4-speed transmissions replaced with 5-speed units. One had the standard De Dion rear suspension (0770) while the other was one of the new TRI60 (0782) independent rear suspension cars with stronger springs, plus modified brake caliper assemblies to reduce grabbing and locking problems encountered at the Targa Florio. Supporting them were two factory 246 Dinos, and a 196 Dino specifically entered by NART for the Rodriguez brothers. Driver pairings were intended to be Hill/Von Trips and Allison/Ginther in the TR60s, with Mairesse/Scarfiotti, Scarlatti/Seidel in the 246 Dinos.

Opposing the Ferrari team were 1700-cc RS60 Porsches for Bonnier/Gendebien and Herrmann/Trintignant, and a pair of Camoradi Maserati Tipo 61s for Moss/Gurney and Gregory/Munaron. This team, managed for the occasion by Piero Taruffi, could only be regarded as a dark horse, in view of Birdcage failures to finish any championship race to date. The only other opponents of note were a team of three Aston Martin DBR1s, now privately owned and not expected to be a serious threat.

Leaping About In The Rain

Practice took place during intermittent rain, drizzle and fog, for some years a rare occurrence at the 'Ring. Practice times were well off the 1959 record of 9:37 set by Behra, though Bonnier managed a 9:43 during one of the brief dry periods. The best Ferrari time of 9:59, bettered by four other competitors, was chalked up by Hill in the TRI60. Most of the other team drivers did much worse, Ginther in particular looking very unsteady while trying to learn the course under adverse conditions.

Ferrari always seemed to be tangled in some routine problem which turned into quicksand, and in this case it revolved around unsuitable rain tires and experiments with both 15-inch and 16-inch wheel sizes. All the team cars were very unstable wearing rain tires, leaping about under braking and appearing particularly treacherous on wrong camber turns. Most of the cars were switched back to dry tires, mounted on 16-inch wheels, and with these Hill managed his best practice clocking, though not representative of the Testa Rossa's potential if proper rain treads had been available. After practice, all the Ferraris were switched to dry tires, as the drivers opted for stability, even if it meant they would be slower than their opponents.

The final driver and car pairings were established at the conclusion of practice with Hill/Von Trips taking the TRI60(0782). Ginther was removed from partnering the other Testa Rossa (0770) with Allison, and replaced by Mairesse, who had considerably more experience at the 'Ring. Scarfiotti drew Ginther as co-driver in one 246 Dino, the other going to Scarlatti and Seidel.

The name of Willy Mairesse has been mentioned several times earlier in the Testa Rossa story, but his assignment to a team mount at the Nürburgring marked his first official factory ride in one. Like Gendebien, he was Belgian, and initially made his mark in Gran Turismo races, but otherwise the two drivers were totally dissimilar. Mairesse, of plebeian background, seemed to have no sophistication whatsoever. He was taciturn in the extreme and possessed what has often been described as a glowering countenance. His eyes were deep set and very penetrating, and it is said he could reduce people to incoherency by pinning them with an unyielding, ferocious stare. His reflexes were reputed to be incredibly fast and, in conjunction with extraordinary vision, he scored some outstanding GT successes in races over unfamiliar roads.

Mairesse had a driving style all his own and one quite lurid to behold. He had his own particular way of attacking corners, a method which appeared certain to end in disaster. More than once he exited a corner backwards, only to put himself right again with just a flick of the wrist. He lived only to race and seemed to have no interest in anything else. Like Hawthorn, just

Pit stop at the 'Ring for the TR59/60 of Allison/Mairesse/Hill.

getting into a car, any car, for any reason, race or not, was sufficient excuse to go just as fast as possible. With these characteristics, he naturally had some horrendous crashes, and most contemporary observers were sure he'd never live long enough to die a natural death.

Fog Sets The Pace

The day of the race dawned with the pit area coated by a fine drizzle and wrapped in fog. This pattern of fog and drizzle was repeated over various parts of the course, making the first time since 1936 that a Nürburgring event would be run in such conditions. On that last occasion, Bernd Rosemeyer had won the German Grand Prix for Auto-Union, earning the title of *Nebelmeister* or fog-master. While conditions

early on the morning of May 22 were similar to the event of so many years ago, no one could predict that the weather would turn far worse.

At the 9:00 a.m. start Moss got off quickly, and then the Maserati seemed to hesitate slightly, allowing Jim Clark in an Aston Martin to snatch first. However, Moss rapidly got by him to take the lead. Clark began to drop back and neither he nor any of the other DBR1s would further be a factor in the outcome of the race. Both Hill and Allison got off rather slowly but made up the lost ground very quickly, moving into 4th and 5th positions by the end of the first lap, though both Testa Rossas seemed to be handling rather erratically on their dry compound tires.

By the 7th lap, Hill began to close strongly on Bonnier's Porsche, then clinging to 2nd. Large areas of the track began to dry, allowing him to push the Testa Rossa harder. On the 10th lap he successfully made it by a very stubborn Bonnier to snatch 2nd, Allison also moving up to 4th on the same lap. That lap was not kind to Ferrari in another respect, as Ginther's 246 Dino retired with a blown head gasket.

Though Hill got by Bonnier, he could do nothing about closing the gap on Moss, who continued to steadily increase his lead over the next few laps. Tavoni was not greatly worried, figuring that in spite of the Moss/Gurney mastery of the 'Ring, the Birdcage would eventually break as the model had in every previous championship race that season.

The TR59/60 waits to leave as a Porsche slides by in the pit lane.

The leaders began pitting for the first scheduled stops and driver changes on lap fourteen. After their completion the order remained the same, though Gurney began pulling out an ever longer lead over Von Trips as the fog closed in and reduced visibility in many sections to 50 yards or less, hardly conducive to charging along flat out.

Firecrackers In The Pits

Ferrari suffered another grievous blow on lap 15 when Scarlatti brought in the sole remaining 246 Dino for refueling. The team was using a pressurized fuel feed system and the mechanic accidentally started pumping gas before the gas cap had been fully opened. The fuel hit the hot exhaust pipes and burst into a raging inferno, from which Scarlatti was extremely fortunate to escape practically unhurt. Compounding the severity of the fire was the mechanic's unfortunate act of dropping the fuel hose with the valve open, causing untold gallons of gasoline to continue pouring out. A tremendous conflagration ensued, reducing the Dino to cinders and destroying much of the Ferrari pits in the process, as tires exploded like firecrackers. When the fire was finally brought under control, Ferrari's pressurized system had also been destroyed, meaning that future pit stops would be long and laborious as the cars would have to be refueled from churns.

In recompense, though, Ferrari's hopes suddenly looked much brighter when Gurney dived into his pit with both himself and the Birdcage soaked in oil from a broken line. The cool day and extremely high oil pressure used in the Maserati engine had caused a line to burst and the over 5-minute pit stop to fix it allowed Von Trips to snatch the lead, with a several minute advantage over Gendebien in the Porsche, while Mairesse moved up to 3rd in the TR59/60.

On lap 22, the halfway mark, dense fog descended on almost the entire course. Windshields began to mist up inside and out as the wiper mechanisms were unable to cope. Drivers found it impossible to see, and the fallacy of the FIA windshield regulations was never more apparent. Many drivers attempted to improve visibility by cleaning the windshields with rags, practically lifting themselves out of their seats to do so, hardly safe at racing speeds. More amazing is that no serious accidents occurred.

The rear brake vents atop fenders were closed off to keep the brakes from getting too cool on the cold, wet race day.

Phil Hill surges through a downhill bend in 0782, chasing second place.

A New Company

Enzo Ferrari's heart and soul have always been in racing. While the rapid growth of Ferrari passenger car production had been extremely satisfying (and profitable), the time necessary to manage that side of the business tended to distract his attention from the competition effort. He had begun to begrudge more and more the necessity of expending ever greater energy on satisfying the demands of street machinery. Ferrari recognized that the profits supported his racing activity, but further growth was contingent on increasing his plant facilities and work force, as the organization was bursting at the seams. More production meant more headaches. He was now 62 years old and desired to concentrate strictly on the competition side of the business.

On May 22, 1960, an announcement was made in culmination of his dreams. Ferrari Automobili, founded in 1939, would be dissolved and replaced by Società per azione Escercizio Fabbriche Automobile e Corse (SEFAC). This organization would henceforth be responsible for designing and constructing automobiles carrying the Ferrari name both for the street and competition. Besides Enzo Ferrari, four others were named as Directors. These included Pinin Farina, Carlo Caracciolo, Ugo Colombo and Michael Cavallier. In essence, they would oversee the running of the street car side of the business, allowing the commendatore to concentrate almost exclusively on his beloved racing machinery. From that date, all Ferrari factory competition would be in the name of SEFAC, though that appellation will not be further referred to in this Testa Rossa story.

Von Trips came in unexpectedly on lap 22 to report that the TRI60 was beginning to overheat. As his lap times had begun to deteriorate anyway as the weather gradually became worse, Hill, Ferrari's best rain driver, was installed in his place and sent off still in the lead. Hill pushed the slowly worsening car as hard as possible, but by lap 28 had fallen back to 3rd, as Gurney drove fearlessly to surge back into the lead, closely shadowed by Bonnier. Bonnier snatched 1st place on the next lap when Gurney stopped to hand over to Moss, and shortly thereafter Hill came in to turn over the Testa Rossa to Von Trips, convinced that continued hard running would destroy the engine. Hopefully, Von Trips would be able to nurse it home to finish. But, on the 33rd lap, the Testa Rossa stopped out on the circuit for good, stranding Von Trips for the duration of the race. The severe overheating caused by a blown head gasket had resulted in several valve seats falling out, breaking valves, holing pistons and generally reducing the engine to junk.

By lap 35, Moss had regained the lead once more with two Porsches following. The sole remaining Testa Rossa piloted by Allison/Mairesse was in 4th, some 30 seconds in arrears, and ever so slowly losing ground. In hopes of a higher placed finish, the car was called in and given to Hill, who began to pound away at the Porsches, quickly moving into 3rd, and knocking a steady 30 to 40 seconds a lap off the 2nd place Porsche's initial 5-minute lead over him. Hill found that the TR59/60 seemed to handle much better than the TRI60, and as the circuit started to gradually dry out a bit, began really flinging the car about in an obviously very spirited drive. He closed to within 40 seconds on the 42nd lap, but on the last two circuits lost ground when balked on several critical occasions by slower machines, finishing just 1:12 out of 2nd place after a magnificent effort.

Though Maserati won the race, of more significance in deciding the championship was the fact that once again, for the third straight race, Porsche gained more points than Ferrari. Porsche's 2nd place finish raised their total to 26, a 4-point advantage over the Maranello forces, who gained only four more by virtue of taking 3rd.

TROUBLES AND TRIUMPH AT LE MANS

Le Mans, scheduled for June 25/26, 1960, became the critical race for Ferrari, as anything less than a 2nd-place finish, even if Porsche received no points at all, would result in a tie or loss of the championship to the German firm. Of course, Le Mans was ideally suited to the Testa Rossa, unlike the Targa Florio or Nürburgring, where smaller, more nimble machines had the advantage.

Le Mans had abandoned the very unpopular and difficult to manage minimum distance refueling regulations for the 1960 grind, replacing it with a new nightmare called the *Index Energetique*, of importance only to the tiddlers. Now, refueling would be allowed at any time, with the larger displacement entrants generally ignoring the Index, figuring they had no chance to win it anyway.

Ferrari decided to send only Testa Rossas to Le Mans, believing that the extra half liter displacement over the Dino 246 made a significant difference on the high-speed Sarthe circuit. Upon arrival for practice, the transporter disgorged a formidable array of Testa Rossas that included a pair of the normal De Dion TR59/60s and two TRI60s, one of which was the rebuilt Allison Targa Florio accident victim. Backing up this imposing force was a TR59 entered by Luigi Chinetti's NART for the Rodriguez brothers.

There is more than a little bit of confusion as to exactly which Testa Rossas actually ran at Le Mans in 1960. The car crashed by Ginther in the Targa Florio (0772) had been entered and homologated for the race along with 0770 and the two TRI60s (0780 and 0782). It appears that 0774, the other TR59/60, was switched to take the place of 0772 with the numbers changed accordingly. It has been suggested that 0772 was actually stripped and then scrapped due to the Targa Florio accident with many of its components then married to 0780, the TRI60 wrecked by Allison in practice prior to that event.

The driving situation presented a very interesting study in complexity. Only three regular team members were on hand: Hill, Von Trips, and Ginther. Allison had been extensively,

though not seriously, injured in a practice accident at Monaco on May 27, just two days before that Grand Prix was contested. He had not mended completely by Le Mans, and during his recuperation began to have serious doubts about the wisdom of continuing to drive. During the summer he quit the team, never again driving a Ferrari after the Monaco incident.

Scarfiotti and Mairesse, semi-regulars, came to Le Mans, as did Gendebien, hired specially for the occasion as he was convinced Porsche had no chance to win. Frere, who never got a chance to drive at the Targa Florio, was given another opportunity at Le Mans. Allison's absence left only seven drivers for the four team cars, with Frere recommending Andre Pilette, another experienced Belgian, as worthy of consideration as a Testa Rossa pilot. Ferrari took another tack though, asking Pedro Rodriguez to join the team, which he was most thrilled to do. Chinetti then took on Pilette as co-driver to Ricardo Rodriguez in the TR59 (0766).

Adding up the 10 Testa Rossa drivers at Le Mans that year shows a total of four Belgians, two each of Americans and Mexicans, one German and one Italian. That such a small country as Belgium could produce almost half the total driving force is more than a bit amazing.

A Respectable Birdcage

Ferrari did not lack for opposition at Le Mans in 1960, as Porsche had their 1700-cc RS60s in attendance, three privateer Aston Martin DBR1s were entered, Ecurie Ecosse produced a D-type Jaguar for Ron Flockhart/Bruce Halford, and the Cunningham "E" Jaguar that went so fast in April was to be chauffeured by Gurney/Hansgen. At the top of the list was a 3-car Camoradi Maserati Birdcage entry, headed by an imposing but ugly streamliner to be driven by Gregory/Daigh. After the Nürburgring victory, the Birdcages had suddenly taken on a long overdue aura of respectability in competitors' eyes. In total, the competition to Ferrari appeared to be very formidable, an impression more than a bit reinforced by practice results.

During practice the Maserati streamliner handled by Gregory proved to be the fastest of the entire field, with top speed on the Mulsanne Straight some 10 mph quicker, and overall lap

times 4 seconds less than anyone else. As Tavoni couldn't envision that any of the Ferraris might challenge for the lead, he issued orders to let Gregory go, and try to keep a Ferrari in 2nd spot while hoping for the Birdcage to break. After all, Le Mans was named the Grand Prix d'Endurance, and only the finishing positions counted, not who led during the early stages of the 24 hours. In most years, the contest was almost always broken into two distinct races. The first part, a sprint, seemed to last several hours, fueled by equal parts adrenaline, racing ego and euphoria, and usually ended with the first round of pit stops. By then the most exuberantly driven fast machinery had usually broken for one reason or another. At that point, the race settled down to a contest of regularity and endurance, with the leaders touring just fast enough to keep their positions safely, and everyone else struggling to catch them.

During practice, the TR59/60s were significantly faster than the TRI60s, due primarily to greater stability in high-speed turns. The independent rear suspension types were still set up for tight, twisty, relatively low-speed courses such as the Nürburgring, and even the TR59 could beat their best times. Indeed, the TRI60s posted slower times than achieved during the April test day. An immense amount of fiddling went on throughout the practice sessions with many different combinations of spring rates being tried, all to no avail.

Tavoni found himself in a real tangle when the time came to establish the driver/car pairings. Hill and Von Trips, as the two leading team members, were paired in the TR59/60 (0770) that had been fastest in practice. Gendebien and Mairesse, though fellow countrymen, and a strong dislike for each other. As Gendebien preferred to co-drive with Frere rather than Ginther, they were paired in the other TR59/60 (0772). Mairesse and Ginther drew the fastest of the two slower IRS entries (0780), with Scarfiotti and Rodriguez drawing the short straw and being assigned the other TRI60 (0782), by far the slowest of the bunch.

Gendebien Hitches A Ride

The 4:00 p.m. race start took place under overcast and threatening skies that knowledgeable observers knew would produce rain within a few hours. This forecast prompted Tavoni to abandon his previous "let Gregory go" plan, as it now would be vital to establish good field positions before the rain started. All the drivers were so instructed, with Von Trips taking the first stint in his TR59/60 shared with Hill, so that the American rain master would be ready to replace him if the precipitation came on the predicted schedule around 6:00 p.m., about the time for the initial pit stops and driver changes.

Clark got away first in an Aston Martin with most of the Ferrari drivers making slow starts, including Gendebien, who got off in 25th position, just behind Gregory. Gregory proceeded to make an astounding charge into the lead, passing 18 competitors on the Mulsanne Straight alone, with Gendebien craftily tucked in behind him. By the end of the 1st lap, Gregory came around with a 4-second lead over Gendebien, who was trying his best to keep up with the flying American. All to no avail, as Gregory pulled out an amazingly long lead over the next few laps, with Gendebien backing off when he realized the futility of attempting to stay close. Initially, Hansgen in the "E" type ran just behind Gendebien, followed by Mairesse, Ricardo Rodriguez and Von Trips, but by the end of the first hour the Jaguar had fallen out of contention with engine maladies, and Von Trips had worked his way up in the pack, passing Rodriguez and Mairesse to take over 3rd spot. Gregory enjoyed an enormous lead, to be sure, but Ferraris certainly held a very strong position at that stage, with the Testa Rossas occupying the next five positions, the last in the formation being Scarfiotti, troubled by handling instability. Three of the Testa Rossas, piloted by Von Trips, Mairesse and Rodriguez ran nose-to-tail for many laps, the combined noise of almost 1000 bhp being quite ear shattering.

"Come In Immediately"

Once the start and opening laps with their attendant confusion had been sorted out, Tavoni settled down to the task of organizing his pit staff to cope with the first round of pit stops. These were expected to begin about the 32nd lap, which would place the time between 5:30 and 6:00 p.m. Early in the second hour, Chiti, on hand as usual for the race, happened to spot the team's fuel consumption charts. He saw that they had not been modified since the April Le Mans test session. At that time, the Testa Rossas were running with a higher ratio rear end, and to get additional revs and consequently more top speed on Mulsanne, a slightly lower rear end ratio had been installed for the race. The higher revs resulted in a greater quantity of fuel being consumed, but Tavoni had assumed the rear end change would be so slight that overall consumption rates would hardly be affected.

Chiti collared Tavoni immediately, but the team manager was adamant that the difference was too trivial to worry about. Chiti thought otherwise. Hurriedly he worked out the calculations, and proved conclusively that the Testa Rossas couldn't cover more than 30 laps at their current rate of travel with the 120 liters of fuel each car carried. After a quick perusal of the figures, Tavoni realized in dismay that each of his cars had covered at least 25 laps at that point and all were in imminent danger of running out of fuel. He quickly phoned his signaling pit on the other side of the circuit and ordered the "Come In Immediately" signal for all the team cars.

Ricardo Rodriguez takes to the verge at the start, trying to outrun Scarfiotti (12) and Von Trips (9). Inset: Mairesse, Von Trips and Rodriguez thunder past a Corvette in the first hour.

Unfortunately, Von Trips and Scarfiotti went roaring past while the mechanic was preparing the signal board. After completing the lap, Von Trips was seen to slow suddenly and gradually coast to a halt near Tetre Rouge, obviously out of gas. The signal would have been too late for him in any event. The stunned driver leaped out of the car to see what had gone wrong and whipped off the hood, refusing to believe he had run out fo fuel, as several laps yet remained before his scheduled pit stop. A quick check of the empty gas tank and the merrily chattering electric fuel pump, now just sucking air, convinced him that he had indeed gone dry. After a couple of desultory kicks at the Testa Rossa's posterior, he stomped off to have a drink and take some photographs. The same fate befell Scarfiotti only moments later and he similarly abandoned his car as being too far away to push around to the pits.

The other drivers were a bit luckier. Gendebien ran out of gas approaching the pits, but had just enough speed to carry him on in the remaining distance. Mairesse, after seeing the signal and deducing what was happening, slowed to a crawl, seemingly taking forever to complete the next lap, but coming in safely with but a quart of gasoline left. The loss of half the team was a serious blow, but without Chiti's intervention, the Ferrari forces would likely have been totally wiped out.

Von Trips later admitted he suspected he was running low on fuel his last lap. This was due to a Testa Rossa characteristic that occurred on the flat-out Mulsanne Straight. The car would naturally get very light at high speed, and without a fuel load to keep the rear tires glued down sufficiently, they would start to spin. This happened to him but the German paid little attention to the cause, believing it to result from oil on the track. After all, he knew he had at least 2 to 3 laps yet to cover before coming in for his scheduled refueling. As no driver substitutions were allowed, neither Hill nor Pedro Rodriguez got to drive, particularly galling to the latter in light of subsequent events.

Von Trips glides to a halt near Tetre Rouge, raises his arm in disbelief, and then gloomily checks the gas tank to verify that he is indeed out of gas and out of the race.

In early evening, Andre Pilette peers over his windshield into the steadily worsening rain.

Maserati Exits And The Rain Arrives

Though Ferrari had suffered grievously over the fuel situation, it was minor compared to the misfortune striking Camoradi almost at the same instant, when Gregory, enjoying an obscenely long lead, came in for this first pit stop. The Maserati refused to restart, a problem eventually traced to a broken internal wire in the starter motor, requiring an hour to fix; all the Birdcages were similarly afflicted, and none would, from that point on, be a factor in the race.

With the threat of Maserati gone, Testa Rossas by 6:00 p.m. occupied the three leading positions, with Frere 1st, Ginther 2nd, and Pilette 3rd. The sprint period had ended, and the endurance session now became everything the term implies as, about that time, the promised rain began, gently at first and gradually becoming more severe in intensity, with sudden and unexpected gusts around the course. Drivers, as at the Nürburgring, found it quite impossible to see through the bug-spattered, oil-smeared high windscreens as the ineffective wipers uniformly coated the mess over the surface, leaving an almost opaque view. The rain, wheel spray and lack of vision combined to cut lap times from the 4:10 to 4:15 range to a leisurely Australian crawl of 5:25 to 5:30.

As the evening hours wore on, it became clear that Mairesse was actually racing, trying hard to catch up with Gendebien. He consistently ignored "Go Easy" signals from Tavoni, earning a severe chewing out from the team manager when he finally made his scheduled pit stop. Pilette did not find the rain and nighttime driving conditions to his liking, and remained content to circulate steadily, though slowly. Frere almost ran out of gas on one stint, bringing a stuttering Testa Rossa into the pits during the evening.

By midnight the storm had spent itself and the track began drying. Frere/Gendebien had a 2-lap lead over Mairesse/Ginther, but despite eight hours of competition, Mairesse/Ginther and the next three cars were all on the same lap. In 3rd was the Clark/Salvadori Aston Martin, which was driven very quickly all through the spell of bad weather to displace Rodriguez/Pilette, pushing their NART TR59 back to 4th. Fifth and moving up steadily was the Jaguar of Flockhart/Halford. With four cars on the same lap, and in easy striking distance of the lead, Frere/Gendebien were forced to speed up to hold their margin.

144

Fire In His Eyes

Shortly after midnight the Jaguar crew made a big push, working their way initially up into 3rd, and then into 2nd, when Ginther brought in the brakeless TR160 for a five minute pit stop while new pads were fitted. Mairesse had used the brakes rather severely during his abortive chase of Gendebien, and had not bothered to inform Ginther of the fast fading stoppers during the driver changeover. Evidently, Ginther had quite a rough time trying to fend off the Aston Martin and Jaguar, pitting with severe cramps in his right leg from practically standing on the brakes to make the Testa Rossa slow down. A fresh Mairesse charged out with fire in his eyes, taking only a few laps to regain 2nd place.

The course continued drying all through the night, with lap times gradually improving as Mairesse once more began chasing after Gendebien for the lead. At 2:30 a.m. Mairesse came in for his next pit stop and driver changeover, closely shadowed by Gendebien to do the same thing. Though Mairesse had arrived first, the mechanics ignored him to work on Gendebien's mount, ignoring his "refuel me now" pleas. The pleas quickly turned to blind rage and Mairesse pushed the waiting Ginther aside, leaped back into his car and screamed off into the darkness, leaving Tavoni, Ginther, et al., standing there in open-mouthed shock. He came in on the next lap, wherein a vastly relieved pit crew set a new Ferrari speed record in refueling the car and sending Ginther on his way.

By 5:30 a.m. the Jaguar had dropped out of the chase with a broken crankshaft. The last factory Porsche had also exited from the contest by then, none having been near contention for a top spot. The Ginther/Mairesse TR160 began to shake and shimmy with rear-end vibration problems that gradually became worse over the next few hours, caused by the pinion bearing assembly rocking in its housing. The car gradually slowed as Ginther and Mairesse tried to nurse it home, losing 2nd place to Rodriguez/ Pilette, but clinging to 3rd ahead of the Aston Martin until almost 9:00 a.m. At that stage, the driveshaft broke in half from the vicious vibration, leaving both Ginther and Mairesse more than a little relieved that it had happened at slow speed instead of on the Mulsanne Straight, where the flailing tube might have cut one or the other of them in half.

Gendebien/Frere held a 5-lap lead over Rodriguez/Pilette by that point in the morning, with the latter pair holding a similar advantage over the Clark/Salvadori Aston Martin. The next four places were occupied by a squadron of 250 GT Short Wheel Base Berlinettas, so it was hard to imagine that a Ferrari of some sort wouldn't wind up 2nd or higher, no matter what fate had in store during the concluding seven hours.

No problems ensued, however, as everything proceeded smoothly over the remaining time. On the last lap, all the Ferraris lined up in finishing formation behind Frere to take the checkered flag. Instead of the flag, all they received was a pleasant smile and a cheery wave from the clerk of the course, as it was only 3:59, forc-

Manning the signaling pits just past the Mulsanne Straight was always a demanding position.

ing them to take another full lap. An exasperated Frere stuck his foot in, as did all the others, the entire 6-car contingent roaring down the pit straight, leaving some very numbed eardrums in the mob of spectators massed for the finish celebration.

The time had more than elapsed on their next crossing of the line, Frere and Gendebien's win leading to a wild scene for the popular victory among the Belgians' fans. For Ferrari, the victory brought the championship laurels back to Italy, and the old, reliable Testa Rossa had again proven superior to the opposition—but just barely.

Le Mans: Aftermath

The 1960 racing season had been another tough year for the Ferrari forces as they managed to win only two out of five championship events outright, the first, Argentina, and the finale, Le Mans. On both circuits the greater power of the Testa Rossa more than overcame the Porsche handling advantage. Sebring

should have likewise been to the advantage of Testa Rossa, but Porsche racked up the victory. The Stuttgart forces were clearly superior at the Targa Florio and Nürburgring, both handling courses, and not suited at all for the Testa Rossas. The lightweight Maserati Birdcage had been the surprise of the 1960 season, leading every race contested, but finishing only at the Nürburgring. Of the five races, Ferrari and Porsche won two each, and Maserati one, with the championship being decided on the point totals in the five races contested. Both Ferrari and Porsche had finished 2nd only once in the remaining three races, forcing the title decision to be settled on the basis of 3rd place finishes, of which Ferrari held a two-to-one advantage. Anytime a championship has to be decided by determining who has more 3rd place finishes, the competition must be severe. The key to the championship was the 3rd place at Sebring by Nethercutt/Lovely, and without it Ferrari would have tied with Porsche. Ferrari would think twice before arbitrarily boycotting a race

in the future if competition continued to be so tough.

At the conclusion of the championship season, Ferrari sold off the TR59/60 De Dion team cars, retaining the IRS versions for further refining and possible team usage in 1961. Chinetti purchased the fastest Testa Rossa at Le Mans that year, a TR59/60 (0770), which ostensibly was to go to the Rodriguez family as a part of a very convoluted deal. Chinetti commissioned the construction of a Testa Rossa "special" during the late summer which he reasoned would be faster than 0770. His arrangement with the Rodriguez family on the whole situation is purported to be that Chinetti guaranteed to have both cars ready for Nassau in December. Pedro and Ricardo would drive them and then Papa would purchase whichever one proved to be the quickest. Chinetti also agreed to take 0766 as partial trade in the transaction.

The other TR59/60 (0774), was purchased by Eleanor Von Neumann who intended to enter it for Phil Hill in the fall West Coast races.

Paul Frere takes the winning TR home to the victory enclosure, with the second place Rodriguez/ Pilette car following behind.

OTHER RACING

Testa Rossa competitive posture changed rather dramatically between 1959 and 1960 in the U.S. as machinery became available, such as the Maserati Birdcage and Porsche RS60, which were clearly better suited to the typically twisty American circuits. Even the TR59/60s could not win against such competition, probably accounting for their sparse usage at anything other than the most important events. The situation was even more gloomy for the customer cars, as none scored so much as a single point or placing throughout the season in a major race or SCCA National. Class D Modified in 1960 was the private preserve of the Maserati Birdcage, and probably symptomatic of the rapid obsolescence of the older, front-engine racing machinery was a perusal of final 1960 SCCA results where, for the first time in many years, a Ferrari did not capture a championship in any modified class.

The customer cars by 1960 were getting pretty long in the tooth. Often belonging to second or third owners, they were frequently poorly maintained and no longer capable of performing to their theoretical limits. In addition, some of the later owners were not really first class chauffeurs or didn't possess the means or ambition to become really top contenders.

The most actively run customer car in 1960 was undoubtedly the one owned by Dick Morgensen and so successfully campaigned in 1959. He rebuilt the machine mechanically over the winter of 1959-1960, and obviously was more concerned about how it went rather than its cosmetic state. It entered the 1960 lists appearing somewhat woebegone bodywise and continued to become progressively more ratty as the season wore on. Like 1959, Morgensen confined his activities to Southwestern and California outings, primarily California Sports Car Club and SCCA Regional events, sort of racing's minor league. In the only major event outing of the year, the Riverside Examiner GP on April 3, 1960, he finished a well-beaten 4th overall, behind Pete Lovely in the Nethercutt TR59 and just ahead of Russell Cowles. Morgensen's next outing was May 8 at his hometown, Phoenix, where he finished 2nd to Bob Drake piloting a Birdcage, one of the West's most successful combinations that year. The Arizonan captured 1st the following week at Del Mar, California, finished a disappointing 6th at Continental Divide Raceway in Colorado on June 26, took 2nds at Santa Barbara on September 4 and Del Mar on September 25, and crowned his season with a victory at Tucson on November 27.

About the only other customer car to see anything approaching extensive use was the example of Jack Graham of San Jose, California, who purchased his machine (0754) from George Keck in early 1960. Apparently confining his activities to California, he recorded a 5th at Stockton on April 10, a 4th at Cotati on the 24th of the same month, 3rd at Vaca Valley on May 1, a DNF due to brake failure at Laguna Seca on June 5, 4th at Pomona on June 26, 4th at Santa Maria on July 3 and a 3rd at Santa Barbara on September 4. He failed to start at Hanford on September 18 as the bearings burned in practice, to be expected in what was by that stage of the year a well-worn machine.

Right: *Charlie Hayes in 0714 at Thompson, Connecticut.*
Below: *Indy Ace Roger Ward in a Camoradi 250TR at the Cuban Grand Prix. He ran out of brakes but Gurney was able to finish up.*

The Morgensen and Graham cars provided the bulk of 1960 customer entrants as a quick survey of the others run will show. Dick Hahn purchased 0704 from Nethercutt and employed Jerry Grant to drive it in a number of minor Pacific Northwest races. He was victorious at Arlington on June 12 and Kent on August 14, and took 2nds at Shelton on May 15 and Seafair on July 31, all Washington events. Alex Budurin brought his car (0752) to California to compete in several early season races, finishing way back in 9th at Palm Springs on January 24 with brake maladies, and the balance of the year saw him sticking closer to his Tucson base as he DNF'ed at Phoenix on May 8 and La Junta, Colorado, on May 30, the last mentioned due to bending a valve. Budurin repaired the damage but his racing effort continued to be rather discouraging as he DNF'ed once again at Midland, Texas, on September 18, suffering from lack of oil pressure, and then crowned the season on October 29 at El Paso, Texas, when he spun off the course into a lake. Not exactly a vintage year for Budurin.

Charlie Hayes of Washington, D.C., purchased the ex-Connell (0714) 1959 SCCA Class D Modified champion from Lucky Casner but seems to have recorded only a few finishes in 1960, including a 2nd at Vineland, New Jersey, on July 24, and a 5th at Marlboro, Maryland, on July 31, both Regionals. Gordon Glyer, with 0718, was bedeviled with engine and pinion bearing difficulties in 1960 and made just a few appearances; possibly the best of those was a 4th overall at Laguna Seca on June 5. Russell Cowles ran his car only once after Riverside, this begin at Santa Maria on July 3 where he finished 3rd overall. A short time later he sold it.

This brief recitation pretty much sums up the extent of Testa Rossa participation in 1960 U.S. club racing. Not much to brag about.

The Big Five In America

The Elkhart Lake 500, Riverside Times GP, and Nassau races were augmented by two additional important events in 1960, these being the Laguna Seca Examiner GP scheduled the week after Riverside, and the Havana, Cuba, GP held in February. All but Elkhart Lake were professional events and attracted first-class fields of cars and drivers and a win at any one of them was worth a tremendous amount of prestige.

Top: *Start of the Cuban Grand Prix, with Ricardo Rodriguez in the Porsche and Pedro in the TR59, the latter finishing second.* **Center:** *Jerry Grant at Riverside on October 17.* **Bottom:** *Even Hill couldn't manage to qualify Carveth's car at Laguna Seca.*

The first of the major events was the Havana race held on February 28, 1960, which attracted the poorest field of the five and was easily won by Stirling Moss piloting a Camoradi Maserati Birdcage. Following him home in 2nd place was Pedro Rodriguez, in his NART-entered TR59 (0766), though he was never anywhere near contention for the lead. Finishing way behind in 13th position were the duo of Roger Ward and Dan Gurney in another Camoradi entry, the team's pontoon fender Testa Rossa (0722). Ward drove the car until the brakes completely disappeared and brought it into the pits intending to retire for the day. Gurney, whose Camoradi Porsche had previously expired, jumped into the Ferrari and proceeded to finish out the race.

The next of the major events, the Elkhart Lake 500, was held on September 11, 1960, and retained its amateur status. It was a hotly contested affair marked by numerous leadership changes and bad weather, with the Dave Causey/Luke Stear combination in a Birdcage outlasting everyone else to capture the victory. Finishing a close 2nd were Augie Pabst and Bill Wuesthoff in Chinetti's TR59/60 (0770), which had the power to deal with the Birdcage, but not the handling. The only other Testa Rossa to compete was the customer car of Dave Biggs (0720), co-driven by Fred Van Beuren, who came in 24th overall.

The next two major American events, the California segment, were marked by struggles between the Maserati Birdcage and Lotus 19, with Ferrari never in the chase. At Riverside on October 16, for the 62-lap, 203-mile Times Grand Prix for Sports Cars, the Birdcage driven by Bill Krause bested Stirling Moss in a Lotus 19 to clinch the victory. Phil Hill was at the controls of the Von Neumann TR59/60 (0774) but could manage no better than a well-beaten 7th overall. The Testa Rossa had been suffering from clutch slipping problems during practice and, in spite of the mechanics' efforts, it continued to deteriorate in the race, collapsing completely near the end. No other Ferrari could even post a fast enough qualifying time to make the race grid, including Jerry Grant (0704) and Jack Graham (0754), the latter crashing when his steering gear broke.

The following week the racing circus moved north to the tricky 1.93-mile Laguna Seca course located near Monterey, where the Examiner GP was staged on October 23, 1960. Like Riverside, the race was strictly Lotus 19 vs. Birdcage, with the former triumphing this time. Not a single Ferrari started the race. The Von Neumann TR59/60 clutch could not be repaired in time, and Hill tried to make the race by qualifying the Rod Carveth prototype (0666) but was unable to get it around fast enough. Jack Graham, after a hasty repair job on his broken steering, also attempted to make the grid, but the fix failed to hold and he had a lurid crash, rolling over at least twice, with the car being extensively damaged, as was he. Every panel on the car was bent, battered or torn off except the passenger door. Later it would be rebodied, though not quite precisely to the original specifications.

Nassau Wrap-up

The season wrap-up was, as usual, the Nassau Speedweek, and the airport course was certainly much more suitable for Ferraris than any other of the major races run that year in America. A tremendous conglomeration of top-notch drivers and cars were entered, with the job of upholding Ferrari's honor primarily falling on the Rodriguez brothers, who brought along two of the latest Testa Rossas. Pedro had the 1960 Le Mans veteran (0770), and Ricardo was at the helm of the Chinetti commissioned TR59/60 special (0746) on its first race outing.

Both Testa Rossas were entered for the 102-mile Governor's Trophy event on December 3, sort of a tune-up for the following day's big go, and one which some of the top competitors sat out to save their machinery. For the Governor's Trophy race, the brothers shared the front row and Ricardo easily won the event. Pedro unfortunately got involved in a first lap collision with Jim Jeffords' 1960 Maserati Birdcage Le Mans streamliner, putting both out of action for the remainder of the race as well as the morrow's much more important event.

The Nassau Trophy race provided an interesting commentary about the kind of problems the classic, old style, conservative Ferrari Testa Rossas were up against as the racing revolution took hold. The primary opposition was expected to be Dan Gurney in the Arciero-owned Lotus 19, already proven to be very quick and exceedingly fragile, at least in contrast to the Ferraris. Not only was the combination potentially faster than any Ferrari, but the Lotus could go the distance without refueling, assuming it stayed together and didn't collapse on the rough circuit. The Rodriguez brothers, now down to one entry, paired up to drive 0746. They knew full well that a pit stop would be required to take on more fuel, as it would be impossible for the Testa Rossas to make the required 252 miles on one tank—but they had a plan.

The strategy of the two contenders was evident from the outset. Pedro Rodriguez blasted around at the very limit to build up a lead suf-ficient to compensate for a refueling stop, while Gurney serenely cruised along in 2nd place, close behind and ready to snatch the lead when the Testa Rossa pitted. When the inevitable pit stop occurred, Gurney smiled by into the lead and easily held it the remaining distance to the finish, totally frustrating the best efforts of Ricardo to catch up. While all eyes were riveted on the front-runner's struggle, Hap Sharp, in his first race with the newly acquired Rodriguez 1960 Le Mans 2nd place finisher (0766), took 6th overall after a trouble-free run.

Summarizing the 1960 major American races shows three victories by the Birdcage Maserati, two for the Lotus 19, and none for Ferrari. The best Testa Rossa placings were the 2nds of Augie Pabst/Bill Wuesthoff at Elkhart Lake and the Rodriguez boys at Nassau. In sprint racing, the tables had irreversibly turned, and the Testa Rossas now were outclassed machines.

Hap Sharp in his first drive in the ex-Rodriguez TR59 (0766) at Nassau, where he finished a creditable 6th.

Tubular space-frame of the new TR61.

CHAPTER 6

1961: An Era Ends

THE CSI HAD BEEN so occupied during 1960 wrangling over the new 1.5-liter Grand Prix rule that sports cars were more or less forgotten. The Gran Turismo program continued to gain favor amongst the members of the CSI, with that body leaving the impetus for a 1961 sports car championship mainly to the various race organizers. If a minimum of five races could be staged, the series would continue with much the same rules as in 1960. If the requisite number could not be organized, then a Gran Turismo championship would be promulgated to take its place. In any event, the CSI decreed that 1961 would absolutely be the last year for the sports car championship, and that in 1962, the title would be contested by the Gran Turismo type of machinery. Four definite spring-time sports car races were promised for 1961 in the sequence of: Sebring, Targa Fiorio, Nürburgring and Le Mans, with a tenuous fifth following during the summer at Pescara, Italy. On this promised schedule, championship status was approved, though Pescara continued to be a very shaky proposition throughout the season.

Into The Wind Tunnel

Ferrari experiments with Testa Rossa improvements for the 1961 campaign had started the previous summer, only one part of a comprehensive and revolutionary development program undertaken by Chiti. At his urging a small, home-built wind tunnel was installed early in 1960 for the scientific study of various body configurations. Pleased at the success of the venture, he constructed a larger, more permanent structure later in the year. Based on the experience gained with this facility, a 1960 Testa Rossa (0780) was selected to be the guinea pig in proving his theories. Initially only the rear half of the body, from the windshield aft, was affected. Chiti laid the long windshield back at a steep angle to allow air (and hopefully bugs and oil) to flow more smoothly over it. The rear body section was very high in front, meeting up with the cockpit sidescreens, which came practically straight rearward from the windshield. The tail was long and rather squared off to take advantage of the Kamm effect in reducing drag, and sported a stabilizing fin á la

Top left: *Ginther testing a doorless TR61 prototype (0780) at Modena.* **Top right:** *The cockpit, with the five-speed indirect geared transmission.* **Lower left** **and right:** *Ginther pulls in with brakes smoking in a later test. To find out why, Chiti installed mechanic Marchetti in the trunk . . . and off they went.*

D-Type Jaguar. When viewed from the side, the prototype had all the appearance of a coupe with a hole cut in the roof for driver ingress.

Testing of the completed prototype took place in October, 1960, with Chiti quickly becoming convinced that he was on the right track, as lap times at the Modena Autodrome were improved by more than a full second. The prototype car was not developed much further at that stage, as Chiti shifted his attention toward building a new 1961 model Testa Rossa, which would incorporate other changes he had in mind as well.

Two new 1961 cars were built (0792, 0794) to be known as TR61s and featuring a space-frame, all-independent chassis of 91.5-inch wheelbase. Altogether it was a bit lighter and more rigid than the 1960 version. The engines were said to produce the same 315 bhp at 7500 rpm, but the real figure is believed to have been at least 15-20 bhp more. The engine was set even lower and farther back in the chassis, and continued using the five-speed indirect-geared transmission that had been previously fitted to the TRI60s. The body style had one very noticeable change from the prototype, featuring a long, pointed twin nostril nose with horizontal brake vents on either side, a basic configuration utilized on all 1961 Ferrari sports and Grand

Prix competition vehicles. The TR61 thus marked a radical departure from the sensuous round shape of the previous Testa Rossas, now having the angularity demonstrated via wind tunnel experimentation to produce the best aerodynamic effect. The new model also appeared to be enormous, though only about six inches longer than the TRI60 and actually weighing some 110 pounds less.

In addition to the TR61, a new, rear-engined Grand Prix contender for 1961 had been designed and constructed, along with a sports car offshoot of 2.5-liters called the 246SP. The extensive (and expensive) development and testing program took longer than expected, causing Ferrari's 1961 press conference to be delayed from the customary November/December time frame until February 13, 1961, when the entire racing lineup could be displayed in final form.

The Outlook For 1961

As 1961 promised to be the last year for the Sports Car Championship, it seems somewhat puzzling that Ferrari would expend such a considerable effort in development time and cost to construct both a new Testa Rossa model and the 246 SP. Possibly he still remained dubious as to the virtues of the rear-engined cars, and

intended to hedge by once more updating the reliable and well-proven Testa Rossa. Additionally, the move could have been dictated by the inescapable fact that the Maserati Tipo 61 Birdcage had clearly proven to be the fastest competitor in 1960, and both Maserati and Porsche could be expected to improve their position before the next campaign got underway. Whatever the case, the TR61 was clearly the most revolutionary edition of the Testa Rossa, though still basically following the evolutionary approach begun back in 1957.

The new Testa Rossa was most definitely not the star of the press conference. It appeared enormous in comparison to the other two cars, with most observers considering it rather homely, though acknowledging its undoubted efficiency. Ferrari, during his remarks to the assembled onlookers, made a similar observation about the Testa Rossa's size, believing it might be too big and bulky for the Targa Florio or Nürburgring, but eminently suitable for Sebring and Le Mans. In addition, he stated that the front-engined sports car should still have another several years of successful competition life, though the point was moot, as 1961 would be the last year for the Testa Rossa as a contender for the championship, with the coming change in regulations.

Giancarlo Baghetti.

Driver Stability

For once, the Ferrari organization was spared the agonies of a major reshuffle in the driving ranks. Hill, Von Trips and Ginther all signed on once again for 1961. Gendebien, after a look around at the opposition, also inked a contract to drive sports cars only. Mairesse rejoined similarly, now on a full-time basis. His sports car performances in 1960 had been a bit less than outstanding, but his hard fought victory in the Tour de France probably was the key to winning a steady job. Allison's permanent departure from the team left one spot open, not immediately filled, but occupied on a race to race basis for most of the 1961 season by Giancarlo Baghetti, a very promising Italian newcomer. His only real experience up to that point had been in Formula Junior races during 1960, but he was highly thought of as an intelligent and cool driver, though rather sensitive. He also seemed to possess the ability to learn from others' mistakes without making his own. Baghetti, during 1961, would drive both the sports cars and Gran Turismos in the championship races, as well as crack the Grand Prix game, in a works-maintained Ferrari Formula 1 machine lent to Federazione Italiana Scuderie Automobilistiche (FISA), a sponsoring body which helped promising young Italian drivers. During the course of 1961, he received some almost hysterical publicity from the Italian motoring press, in their anxiety to proclaim him as the successor to Ascari, Musso, et al.

AN EASY WIN AT SEBRING

The first of the 1961 crop of championship races took place on the bumpy 5.2 mile Sebring airport course on March 25, in warm and sunny Florida weather. Knowledgeable pundits expected a fierce battle between Ferrari, Maserati, and defending Sebring winner, Porsche, and the publicity generated by the prospect of a three-way struggle, drew the event's largest ever crowd to the wilds of Florida. This year there would be no fuel hassle, as the CSI ruled that an event could decree the brand that must be used by all competitors, and that effectively ended the argument.

Ferrari, as always, put forth a major effort to capture the season's first event, believing that a victory provided an important psychological advantage to his forces, while fostering a discouraged outlook in competitors' minds. He shipped over two TR61s, the first of the new series (0792), and the prototype (0780) with its 1960-style front end configuration. They had not intended to send the prototype, but the other 1961 Testa Rossa (0794) was not yet completely finished. Supporting the Testa Rossas was a 246 SP.

The Spoiler Appears

All three factory entries had a new wrinkle not previously seen, a four-inch high spoiler tacked onto the top rear of their tails. Though several rather ingenuous explanations of the new feature were offered by the drivers, such as Ginther's remark that "it prevents exhaust gases from spilling up and forward into the cockpit during hard braking," the real reason for its use was to combat a tendency for the rear end to lift at high speed caused by the flat deck acting aerodynamically like a wing. This rather annoying habit had manifested itself during late February Monza testing, where the TR61 had undergone final checkout. At that time, the tail fin was discerned to be rather useless and summarily removed in favor of the spoiler.

Tail fin discarded, a spoiler adorns the rear deck of the TR61. Aerodynamic, but ugly.

The problem had first cropped up at the Modena Autodrome in February when Von Trips, during the first test of the 246 SP, executed a spectacular flip, much to everyone's puzzlement. Once the aerodynamic problem had been deduced to be the prime suspect, the TR61 was taken to Monza to effect a cure. The method of solution was quite direct. First, tack on a spoiler about one foot high and send the Testa Rossa out for high-speed runs to check the effect on top speed and rear-end lift. Then, after each session, chop an inch or so from the top of the spoiler and send the car back out again. Eventually, whacking away like this, the four-inch spoiler turned out to be the best compromise in holding the rear-end down to the pavement without inordinately inhibiting top end speed. A primitive approach, but highly indicative of the state of race car engineering at the time.

Backing up the official Maranello entry was the NART sponsored TR59/60 "special" for the Rodriguez brothers. This car, first appearing at Nassau the previous December, was constructed on chassis 0746, which is believed to have lain unused at the works since being run at the Nürburgring in 1958. During 1960, it was converted from left to right-hand drive, rebodied as a TR60, and fitted with the latest Testa Rossa mechanical components. Ginther had tested the "special" extensively and pronounced it to be a "darn good car." Before the Sebring race ended, many more would be similarly convinced.

All three TR59s were brought to Sebring by their privateer owners. Jack Nethercutt and Pete Lovely once again entered the former's car (0768), in which they had finished third in 1960. The Texas duo of Hap Sharp and Ron Hissom entered 0766, the 1960 Le Mans second place car, and George Reed came with 0770 for himself and Bill Sturgis to drive. With six Testa Rossas and one 246 SP on hand, the Ferrari sports entry could best be described as formidable.

Major competition was expected from the Maserati forces, particularly the Camoradi team, still smarting from the previous year's Sebring debacle. They entered a new Tipo 63 rear-engined Birdcage for Stirling Moss and Graham Hill, accompanied by a backup Tipo 61 for Masten Gregory and the team's guiding light, Lucky Casner. The Cunningham team entered a similar pair of Maseratis, a Tipo 63 for Walt Hansgen/Bruce McLaren and a Tipo 61 to be piloted by Dick Thompson and John Fitch. Also in attendance were the Dave Causey/Luke Stear pair in a Tipo 61 Birdcage to complete the Maserati assemblage. Porsche, hopeful of repeating their rousing 1960 Sebring success, brought two 1700-cc RS61s for Gurney/Bonnier and Herrmann/Barth, augmented by several privately entered RS61s and RS60s of varying displacements. All in all, a strong field of contenders for the top finishing spot.

The Sharp/Hissom TR59 (0766) has an add-on cover over the enlarged gas tank.

Driver Assignments

The Ferrari driving team came in full strength to Sebring, including Mairesse, on the mend from a skiing accident, and rookie Baghetti as the sixth member of the factory crew. While assignments were not fixed until the conclusion of practice, Ginther, who had extensively tested the 246 SP, preferred to pilot that car in the race. Von Trips felt much the same way, so the two of them latched onto the car during practice, literally preventing anyone else from trying it out. Gendebien had something of a rough time at Sebring that year, first garnering a speeding ticket on the way down to the track, and then hurting his left ankle as a consequence of some pit horseplay on Thursday. Though the ankle bothered him considerably, fortunately it was the left leg affected, used only on the clutch and not the right, which might have caused him to be unable to stand the strain of pushing the heavy, non-servo assisted brake pedal on the Testa Rossa. Gendebien's practice times were adversely affected by the injury, but he vowed to be ready to go for the race.

In practice, Hill cranked out a clocking of 3:13 flat with the TR61, a new course record, in spite of a lack of power in the mid-range and a mysterious affliction preventing the engine from revving as high as it should. Both problems were attended to, primarily by Ginther, seemingly more expert on carburetor jetting than any of the Ferrari team mechanics. He did manage to get in some time on the track in between this chore, and pulled out a 3:13 lap in the 246 SP, almost without effort, or so it appeared to onlookers. Later, in another practice outing, the 246 SP got away from him, executing a wild spin into the boonies, though both car and driver apparently escaped without harm. Pedro Rodriguez surprised just about everyone, including the Ferrari team, by reeling off a 3:14.5, almost a second faster than anyone could achieve with the prototype TR61. The Maseratis and Porsches were literally nowhere, none having gotten below 3:17 in practice. The new Maserati Tipo 63 evidently did not handle very well, causing Moss and G. Hill to switch to Camoradi's Tipo 61, leaving the vacated seat for Gregory and Casner. By the end of practice, the inescapable conclusion had to be that the race would be a runaway for Ferrari, based on their clear speed superiority.

Mairesse in the prototype TR61, shared with Baghetti, later taken over by Von Trips and Ginther.

Final Ferrari driver assignments were made after practice via the usual phone call to the Commendatore, with Hill/Gendebien paired in the pace setting TR61 (0792), Mairesse/Baghetti drawing the prototype (0780), and Ginther/Von Trips getting their wish to drive the 246 SP, and also winning the job of "rabbit" if any front running competition materialized, as unlikely as that prospect seemed.

The Rodriguez Boys Take Charge

At the 10 a.m. race start, Gregory stunned everyone by charging into the lead in the Maserati Tipo 63, with Pedro Rodriguez hot on his heels, followed by Lovely, Hansgen in the other Tipo 63, Hill and Ginther. Lovely coasted into the pits after the first lap trailing a gigantic cloud of smoke, caused by engine oil being pumped out the breathers onto the exhaust manifolds. Though he rejoined the race a few laps later, the car was retired for good at 12:30 after the mechanics had removed the sump pan and found the oil pump to be completely inoperative.

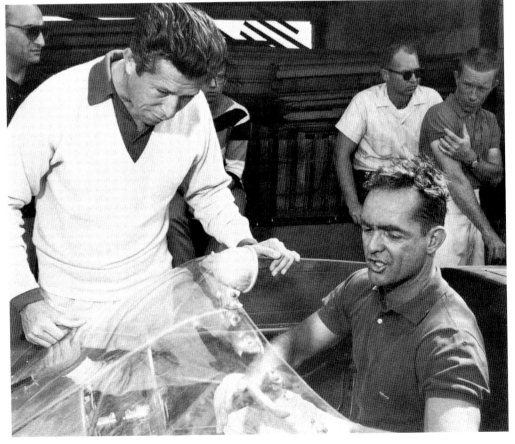

Hill explains something to the impeccable Mr. Gendebien while Ginther looks on.

158

Rodriguez grabbed the lead from Gregory on the 4th lap as the Maserati began fading from handling problems caused by cracking rear suspension tubes, a situation continually worsening and causing its retirement in the early afternoon. Ginther moved up rapidly to 2nd, passing Hill, who had worked his way by Hansgen earlier. Just past 11 a.m., Ginther got by Rodriguez into first, followed closely by Hill, who passed the Mexican shortly thereafter. Moss had lost almost six minutes at the very start, courtesy of a dead battery, and by noon had managed to carve his way up to 2nd place, pushing back Hill and Rodriguez respectively. The leaders were moving at a sprint pace with the top four continually under the Moss 1960 race lap record of 3:17.06, though the Englishman, during his rush to regain the front, set the lowest time of all at 3:13.2 or 97.4 mph.

Just after the first set of pit stops, the Moss/G. Hill Tipo 61 broke off its exhaust manifold, ending their threat to Ferrari for the day. About 1 p.m. Von Trips went into a wild looping spin on a fast left hander, winding up in the grass well off the course after mowing down numerous marker pylons. He got out to investigate the cause and discovered the lower right wishbone was bent and the tie-rod broken clean through at the inner end, possibly a result of Ginther's gyration in practice. He walked away from the 246 SP, but after going part way to the pits, thought it better not to abandon the car there, came back, and slowly drove it around to the team compound.

With the withdrawal of the 246 SP, Gendebien took over the race lead, hounded by Ricardo Rodriguez, who turned consistent 3:15-3:16 laps in pursuit, broadsliding the corners and ripping down the straights in a remarkable demonstration of ten-tenths driving. By 2 p.m., Rodriguez had re-taken the lead, closely followed by a wise Gendebien, who decided not to wear out his machine at such an early stage in the proceedings. Mairesse and Baghetti, running 5th, came in for their scheduled pit stop at 2:15, with Tavoni installing Ginther in the car. With his partner Von Trips, they kept the controls from then on. While Ginther's Testa Rossa was being serviced, Gendebien pulled in for his scheduled stop, a slip-up by team management, who should have kept him out another lap. As only one crew of mechanics was on hand, Gendebien had to wait his turn, causing the TR61

to slip further back in time behind the Rodriguez brothers. Just another example of how Ferrari could build good cars, hire topnotch drivers, put in great race performances, and then blow the advantage by poor pit work.

The sole remaining Maserati challenger, Briggs Cunningham's Tipo 63, driven by Hansgen and McLaren, stayed in 3rd place much of the afternoon, a constant threat to the two Ferraris ahead of it. Finally, at about 4 p.m., it retired with transaxle problems, and as the factory Porsches had never been contenders at all, a Ferrari victory appeared certain. The Marque occupied the top six positions, with half the race yet to go.

A Generator Brings Tears

The only issue that remained in question was whether the winner would be a factory or private Ferrari. All afternoon long the Rodriguez brothers hung onto first, even increasing their lead substantially over the TR61s when the Ferrari pit crew did their specialty act once again just before 4 p.m., as both team cars came in to be serviced almost simultaneously.

The Rodriguez boys continued to pour on the coals with consistent lapping in the 3:17-3:19 range, no matter which brother drove, gradually pulling out a two lap lead, and raising the race average speed to a point where a new distance record would likely be a certainty. At 6:30 p.m. headlights had to be turned on, and shortly afterwards trackside observers noticed the Rodriguez car seemed to have rapidly dimming beams. Pedro screeched into the pits at 6:50 p.m. with one headlight out completely, and the other very dim, due to the generator malfunctioning. Some 17 heartbreaking min-

Von Trips cleans his windshield during a pit stop. After his 246 SP retired, he and Ginther took over the Mairesse/Baghetti car.

Ricardo Rodriguez in 0746, third place finisher after a flat-out drive.

Hill at the controls of the winning TR61.

Hap Sharp in his TR59.

The eighth place Reed/Sturgis TR59.

utes were lost while the problem was traced and fixed, pushing them back to 3rd before Ricardo blasted off in vain pursuit of the factory leaders, leaving his mother in tears at the thought of how victory had been so capriciously snatched from them.

Ricardo had no intention of simply cruising around to keep a secure 3rd place. He went flat out after the leaders, turning spectacular lap times for over two hours in the 3:15-3:16 range in a fearless display of nighttime driving. He managed to make up the one lap deficiency behind Von Trips/Ginther within an hour, and squeezed by into second place only to overdo it shortly afterwards and spin violently on a fast right hander when a slower car suddenly moved over into his racing line. The incident allowed Von Trips to recapture 2nd and hold it to the end as, for once, the last Ferrari drivers' changes at 9:30 were handled smoothly.

Hill/Gendebien took the checkered flag for the victory at 10 p.m., and by virtue of the long scrap with the Rodriguez duo, set a new distance record of 1092 miles, breaking the 1958 record by more than 60 miles. Ginther and Von Trips, capturing 2nd, made it a 1-2 sweep for the TR61s, with Ginther thinking he had won for a few moments. The starter's checkered flag was thrown at him, and as Hill had been in front out of his sight, he reasoned that something must have happened to the leader, resulting in his victory instead. So Ginther motored happily into the victory enclosure only to be informed that he was mistaken, Hill and Gendebien had actually won.

The Rodriguez brothers ended up 3rd, disconsolate after so nearly snatching victory from the might of Maranello, with the Sharp/Hissom TR59 in 4th after a clean, trouble-free and well-paced twelve-hour run, giving the Testa Rossas a sweep of the top four positions. Even the Reed/Sturgis TR59/60 finished, though back in 8th place after a series of minor but annoying carburetion problems caused some extended pit stops.

For the fourth consecutive year a Testa Rossa had won the opening event of the season, proof of Ferrari's "get them built and tested" policy well in advance of the coming season. Ferrari racked up the eight points for winning, with the highest place competitor, a Porsche, far back in fifth place, garnering two points.

SURPRISE AT THE TARGA FLORIO

The next 1961 championship outing was the venerable Targa Florio held on April 30 over the same course and distance as used in 1960, but now no longer being run by the Florio family. Ferrari entered only a single Testa Rossa for the event, the prototype TR61 (0780) with the 1960-style nose, to be driven by Pedro Rodriguez and Willy Mairesse. For the first time since the introduction of the Testa Rossa series in 1958, Ferrari would rely on another model sports racer to be the big gun in its attack. On a circuit such as the Little Madonie, the V-12 Testa Rossa had clearly proven over the past few years to be inordinately heavy and unwieldy compared to its adversaries. For the 1961 edition of the event, Maranello's hopes rested on a brace of rear-engined 246 SPs with driver pairings of Hill/Gendebien and Ginther/Von Trips.

Looking for a repeat of their 1960 victory, Porsche came to Sicily with an extremely strong team of RS61s, two of which were differing 2.0-liter models for Moss/G. Hill and Bonnier/Gurney. The Italian team Serenissima, or more properly titled as Scuderia Serenissima Republica de Venezia, brought along two Maserati Tipo 63s and a 2.0-liter Tipo 60, but none were expected to be capable of fighting Ferrari or Porsche for outright victory.

Ferrari did not bother to send a hack car for practice use, requiring his team members to tour the circuit in Fiat 600 rental cars, not exactly comparable to the real thing. The last day of practice took place with the course closed to normal traffic for a meager four hours, with Moss astounding everyone by virtue of a fantastic 40:51 lap, annihilating his old 1958 record of 42:17. Bonnier also broke the old record, establishing a 42:04 timing, with Von Trips the top placed Ferrari driver at 43:31, and Gendebien following at 43:56, both in the same 246 SP. Hill seemed unable to get to grips with the course, recording slower times with the other 246 SP, although the car had some pesky carburetor problems. Ginther's lap times were exceedingly slow as he seemed to prefer working out the bugs on the 246 SP, and besides never felt comfortable on the course.

The TR61 prototype was taken out first by Mairesse and badly mangled almost immediately, when he left the road on the descent to

First lap of the Targa and Pedro Rodriguez gets two wheels airborne in the TR61 prototype, which he drove without benefit of practice.

Collesano, though not affecting it mechanically. The left rear fender was thoroughly jammed into the tire, prohibiting it from continuing and requiring that the Testa Rossa be dragged in after practice and straightened out. This happening prevented Rodriguez from getting any practice laps at all in the car, not improving his outlook on the race.

A Last Minute Adjustment

Ferrari final race assignments were made, as customary, after completion of practice. Mairesse and Rodriguez kept the TR61 prototype, with Pedro being soothed by drawing the initial driving stint. A bit of a strange decision to let him go first, without the benefit of any practice in the car, but likely done to atone for

the practice situation. The Von Trips/Ginther duo in the fastest 246 SP, and Hill/Gendebien pairings remained intact, flying in the face of all logic. Von Trips and Gendebien had clearly been the quickest in practice and should have shared the fastest car, but the Commendatore decided otherwise. Gendebien protested vigorously at what he considered a blatant attempt to cheat him out of victory, but to no avail. On the morning of the race, as car after car left the starting line, he suddenly announced to Tavoni that he would not take his first driving stint in the mount he was to share with Hill, but replace Ginther as Von Trips' co-driver. As Gendebien absolutely refused to drive, a furious Hill was forced to hurriedly prepare to take out the car himself.

In the mountain pits, mechanics refuel from churns as Pedro watches from the cockpit. He holed the gas tank on the fourth lap during an off-road excursion.

Rodriguez drives slowly to the main pits after temporary repairs.

On the first lap, Hill stormed off in the 246 SP, caught up to Von Trips, and then both spun when Hill hit him while attempting to pass. They recovered and took off again with the German wisely deciding to let him get by. On the descent to Collesano, near where Mairesse had his practice incident, Hill overdid it, got sideways, nailed a concrete marker post with the Dino's tail, spun around, hit another marker with the front end, and almost flipped. The 246 SP was too badly crippled to continue, though Hill escaped unscathed.

At the end of the first lap, Rodriguez languished in 6th place, struggling to learn just how far the Testa Rossa could be pushed, and quickly realizing its inherent unsuitability for the course. In addition to its basic unwieldiness, the car exhibited some wandering characteristics as the front end must have been slightly damaged by Mairesse.

On the fourth lap, Rodriguez also overcooked things a bit, spinning off the road into a rocky bank that rearranged the rear suspension and holed the gas tank. He continued on very slowly to the Ferrari mountain depot, where the mechanics made temporary repairs sufficient to get him back to the main pit area, though fast motoring was completely out of the question. On the way around, Rodriguez stopped to pick up the spectating Hill and the pair leisurely toured back to the pits.

A New Lap Record

With the TR61 prototype relegated to the dead car park and Hill's mount similarly out of action, only the Von Trips/Gendebien driven 246 SP remained to carry the Maranello fortunes in a see-saw battle for first place against the Moss/G. Hill Porsche. Moss set a new lap record of 40:41 on the 7th lap to regain the lead,

extending it to over a minute by the end of the 8th lap when Von Trips took over the final driving spell from Gendebien. Von Trips went like the wind to catch up, setting a new course record in the process of 40:03, though not needed as the unfortunate Moss suffered a broken ring and pinion only a few kilometers away from the finish line and certain victory, handing the laurels to Ferrari. Along with it went eight points, running Ferrari's total to sixteen, with Porsche garnering six for second place in the event and making their total for the year to date of eight. Maserati finally made the points board, picking up three.

Ferrari had been proven right, winning the Targa Florio for the first time since 1958, with the new 246 SP as the leader of the attack. Still, a great deal of life was left in the Testa Rossas, as subsequent events would prove.

162

A FULL BAG OF TRICKS AT NÜRBURGRING

Following the Targa Florio by a three-week gap instead of the normal fortnight, was the 1000-kilometer Nürburgring race held on May 28, 1961. Ferrari again led with his rear-engined Dino 246s, entered with pairings of Hill/Von Trips and Ginther/Gendebien. Supporting them was the TR61 prototype (0780) loaned to NART and entered for the Rodriguez brothers with factory supplied mechanics on hand to prepare the car and perform the pit stop chores. This was the Mairesse/Rodriguez Targa Florio mount, now repaired and repainted. A 1961-style nose had been grafted on, replacing the original 1960 front, but the TR59/60 style body side vents were retained. A further private Testa Rossa entry by Gachnang/Caillet was a 1958 customer's left-hand-drive pontoon fender live-axle car (0742) that had been extensively reworked to appear somewhat akin to a 1961 model and featured a home-built independent rear suspension.

The usual competitors were in attendance, including three 1700-cc RS61 Porsches for Moss/G. Hill, Bonnier/Gurney and Barth/Herrmann. The Camoradi team, in deep financial trouble, appeared only with a Tipo 61 Maserati for Casner and Gregory, while Serenissima fielded two Tipo 63 rear-engined Maseratis for Trintignant/Maglioli and Vaccarella/Scarfiotti. A thin field to be sure, with Ferrari clearly the race favorite, a feeling reinforced during the first practice session on the Thursday before the race when Hill knocked off a lap time of 9:33.7, with Moss recording the next fastest mark of 9:37.1, closely followed by Ginther and Pedro Rodriguez.

While Thursday's weather conditions were sunny and hot, overnight it turned to rain and cold, preventing any rapid motoring, a condition continuing into Saturday before it began to improve. Race day dawned clear and sunny, though cold, but appearances can be deceiving, as rain had been forecast to begin shortly after the 9 a.m. start. Hill had been handed the "rabbit baton" on the Ferrari team, not only for his excellent practice clockings, but also as he was determined to make up for the Targa Florio incident, and prove once again he was the team's best driver. The Rodriguez brothers had been extensively coached by Chinetti on the race strategy they were to follow, one that emphasized cautious driving in the early laps before stepping up the pace.

Hill Makes His Point

At the start of the race, Pedro got off very well, and following Chinetti's instructions let the sprinters do their thing, though keeping in range of the leaders. Moss held the lead at the end of the first lap, followed by Hill and Ginther, Clark in an Aston-Martin DBR1, then Rodriguez 5th, just ahead of Gregory. Hill took the lead on the next lap, setting a new sports car record of 9:31.9 in the process, and continued to pour it on, steadily lowering the mark to a rousing 9:15.8 on the 10th lap, in a truly memorable effort. Rodriguez, hounded constantly by Gregory, had moved up to 4th by that point in the proceedings, turning steady laps in the 9:35-9:37 range, and impressing everyone with his smooth driving manner.

By this stage of the race, the sun had disappeared and it began to get really cold, and just kept getting colder as the laps reeled by. The regular pit stop activity beginning around lap 15 enabled Rodriguez to briefly move up to 2nd overall, but after his own stop to turn over the controls to brother Ricardo a lap later, the prototype slipped back to 5th, and at about the same time, it began to snow and sleet, a new surprise in the Nürburgring's bag of tricks. This caused a general slowdown as the drivers adjusted to the suddenly hazardous conditions. A number of the front runners, including the rear-engined Ferraris and Maseratis, suffered from water entering the carburetor air intakes, causing them to run very rough. Meanwhile, the Testa Rossa continued to tick steadily along, though Ricardo, following caution orders, finally had to let the Gregory/Casner Birdcage by, after numerous rounds of jousting with them for sole possession of 4th place.

By lap 25 of the 44-lap race, the whole complexion of the affair changed. The Moss/G. Hill Porsche broke its engine, and Phil Hill aboard his 246 SP went off the road, the car catching fire, though quickly quelled. Hill was uninjured but remained stranded out on the course until the race ended. These incidents allowed the Gregory/Casner Maserati to take over the leader's position, with the Rodriguez brothers close behind, and Maranello's only hope for victory, as the stuttering Ginther/Gendebien 246 SP was in 7th place, far behind and totally out of contention for victory.

Top: *The Rodriguez TR61 prototype temporarily leads the Casner/Gregory Birdcage. The latter went on to win after Phil Hill crashed and Moss/G. Hill lost the engine on their Porsche.* **Bottom:** *Pedro shows a bit of opposite lock negotiating a turn.*

With a broken wheel jammed under the front fender, Ricardo Rodriguez drags into the pits on the 42nd lap. After quick repairs he held off six other cars to finish second.

Chinetti Holds Firm

On lap 28, Ricardo came in for a long pit stop, both to change over to Pedro and effect repairs to the throttle pedal linkage. Tavoni had previously tried to convince Chinetti to allow Von Trips to take over the Testa Rossa but he refused, feeling the Rodriguez boys were going just as fast as conditions would permit. As the prototype was not a factory entry, Tavoni could not order Chinetti to follow his wishes, so he installed Von Trips in the remaining 246 SP in an attempt to improve its position.

As the race ground on with the weather gradually improving to sunny conditions once more, the pace picked up with Ricardo gradually closing in on the Maserati, though slipping back further during the last pit stop. This last stop was very rapid by Ferrari standards, but the

Maserati made a super-short stop only to take on gas. Camoradi didn't change to new tires because they had no spares whatsoever, and actually ran the entire race on one set of rubber!

Ricardo began to really close in on the Maserati during lap 41, but on the next circuit had the misfortune to break the right front wheel entering the Karussel. The spokes shattered and the wheel collapsed, tearing the tire to shreds and jamming the whole mess under the brake disk. He limped around to the pits, trailing a streak of rubber and got a new wheel fitted before charging out again to protect his 2nd place against six other cars now on the same lap as he, headed by Von Trips, burning up the course in the 246 SP that was once again running properly.

Though hampered by erratic front braking caused by the collapsed wheel incident, Ricardo completed the final two laps in very respectable

times, to finish 2nd overall, less than a minute behind the Maserati, and more than two minutes ahead of Von Trips.

As in 1960, Maserati once more triumphed at the Nürburgring, with an old reliable Testa Rossa just behind, and not even a factory car at that. Under Chinetti's tutelage, the Rodriguez brothers had driven a fine, heads-up race, never once putting a wheel out of line, and appearing thoroughly at home in the Testa Rossa.

The points standing now showed Ferrari with twenty-two, Maserati at eleven, and Porsche still at eight, not placing in the top six in the only race of the year before the home folks. Ferrari's points advantage meant that to beat them out of the title one of the two competitors must win both remaining races, with the Maranello forces being practically blanked. Not exactly an encouraging prospect in view of the Ferrari dominance expected to come at Le Mans.

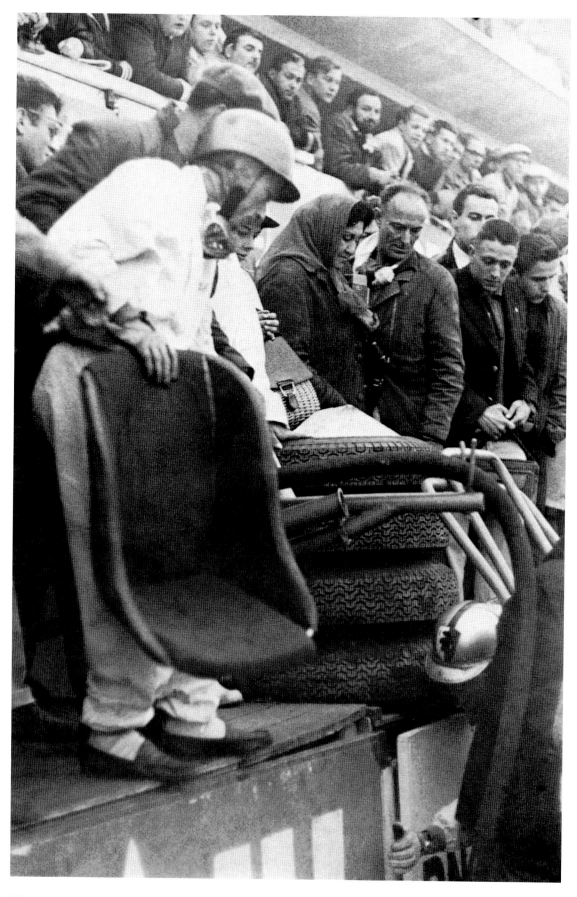

CLINCHING THE TITLE AT LE MANS

The fourth championship event of 1961, and the most prestigious, took place at Le Mans on June 10/11, with absolutely everyone expecting an easy Ferrari victory, not only based on race results to date, but also when considering the springtime practice performances. At the practice days held on April 8/9, Ferrari sent up a TR61 (0794) and a 246 SP for Hill, Mairesse and Ginther to try out, and both cars easily bested the previous fastest times ever recorded on the Sarthe circuit, though Mairesse, living up to his wild man reputation, bent the TR61 more than a little bit on Saturday in an incident at Tetre Rouge. The Belgian, before his off-course excursion, posted a 3:55 flat in the TR61, being pipped by the 246 SP at 3:54.6, both eclipsing Fangio's 1957 practice time in a Maserati 450S of 3:58.1, and Musso's 1957 race record clocking of 3:58.7. No other competitor was even in the same ballpark as the Ferraris, so the race conclusion seemed foregone, even at that early date.

Ferrari entered two TR61s, the first (0794) to be handled by Hill and Gendebien after strenuous efforts by the Commendatore to get them to patch up their differences. Though not exactly very cordial to each other, they managed to work together, without actually communicating directly, Tavoni taking on the chore of inter-communication between the two. The Rodriguez-driven Nürburgring TR61 prototype, (0780) was entrusted to Mairesse and a newcomer to the Ferrari ranks, Mike Parkes, an Englishman who had driven Gran Turismos most effectively in the past few seasons, and was deemed capable of better performances in the future. Normally, Baghetti would have been partnering Mairesse, but he opted for a Ferrari GT factory entry instead.

*Mairesse locks up the brakes in the wet and skids
helplessly toward the sand bank . . . which he luckily
bangs into at just the right angle, so that he's able to
bump along and swerve back onto the track.*

Stopwatch in hand, Papa Rodriguez watches intently at 2 p.m. with son Pedro, their faces etched with worry for the overdue Ricardo, whose engine had just blown out on the course. A few moments later he coasted into view, to their great relief.

Gendebien in the race-winning TR61 late in the day.

Enzo Keeps The Pot Boiling

Ferrari loaned the other TR61 (0792) to the NART organization to be driven by the Rodriguez brothers, but remaining in custody of the factory pit staff, much to the disgust of Papa Rodriguez. The Commendatore had been quite impressed by the brothers' performances at Sebring and the Nürburgring, particularly as they were hard chargers and never gave up. Ferrari always preferred to have drivers of this sort on hand, partly to spur everyone else to greater efforts by increased competitiveness in the driving team, and also to ensure seasoned replacements in case of driver defections or injuries.

Tavoni was most unhappy about this situation, as he feared the Rodriguez brothers could likely contest the lead, and in the ensuing battle with the regulars, all the cars might be worn out. Enzo Ferrari's final dictum on the matter satisfied neither Chinetti nor the Rodriguez family, who desired to compete strictly as an independent entry to push for the victory, or Tavoni, who wanted some means to control them. The Rodriguezs were free to go after the win with Tavoni managing their signaling, refueling, and other pit activity. Typical of Ferrari's management style, neither side got all it wanted, and most of the team drivers were left more than a bit disgruntled over the unnecessary challenge certain to come. A 24-hour race,

with all its attendant hazards, plus the competitors in other makes, were already enough to cope with. Encouraging an internal battle made little sense to them, though they all realized it was just the Commendatores way of keeping the pot boiling.

Practice turned out to be rather desultory, as the Ferraris had no need to prove anything, and besides it rained off and on, making conditions a bit tricky. This did not apply to the Rodriguez brothers, who tore around the course constantly before Pedro lodged the Testa Rossa most firmly in the sand bank at Arnage, though apparently without damage.

Race day dawned cool and cloudy followed by a late morning rain, fortunately stopping in the early afternoon and allowing the course to dry out almost completely before the 4 p.m. start.

At the start, both Ginther and Gendebien moved off smartly, but Pedro Rodriguez and Mairesse had difficulty in getting underway. Ginther took the first lap lead and then dropped behind Gendebien on the next lap to take up his station as blocker against competition, while both circulated in close company in the 4:06-4:07 range. Pedro had no intention of waiting around for misfortune to strike the leaders, and quickly elbowed his way up to 4th spot, snatched 3rd on the 5th lap, and proceeded to

steadily reel in Ginther and Gendebien. He clocked continuous times 4:01 or faster over the next few laps, taking over the lead on the 9th lap by virtue of a charge down the Mulsanne Straight, overhauling both factory cars in one swoop.

Gendebien, not content to be shown up so easily, fought it out with Pedro, retaking the lead on the 11th lap, though losing the top spot once again on the next circuit when the Mexican lad decided the issue in his favor by cranking out a clocking of 3:59.9 for a 125.4-mph average. This was the first ever below four minute race lap at Le Mans for a 3.0-liter machine. Pedro continued forging on with lap speeds of 4:00 to 4:02, picking up 4-6 seconds per lap over Gendebien, who was closely shadowed by Ginther, with Mairesse in 4th place, well ahead of the leading non-Ferrari competitor, Hansgen in a Cunningham entered Maserati Tipo 63.

Hill (10) and Rodriguez (17) sandwich a 246 SP. The two TRs battled fiercely, almost nose-to-tail for 12 hours.

Nose-To-Tail In The Dark

The leading order became somewhat confused after the initial spate of pit stops, though the battle for first place between the Rodriguez brothers and Hill/Gendebien continued unabated, not withstanding heavy rain that fell for some two hours before darkness enveloped the circuit. All evening the struggle continued, with the leaders regularly swapping positions due to pit stops, but otherwise often running nose-to-tail. The Ginther/Von Trips and Mairesse/ Parkes partnerships held 3rd and 4th respectively, content to wait out the struggle for first,

assuming that sooner or later one or both of them would drop out at the sprint pace still being maintained. After all, even Ferraris couldn't be flogged flat out for twenty-four hours. Oddly enough, three of the leading Ferraris could have been wiped out at one moment when Rodriguez, closely shadowed by Gendebien, lapped Mairesse and clipped the nose of the latter in his haste, nearly causing a disastrous situation for all concerned.

As the battle for first place continued, tempers began flaring in the Ferrari pits, as the Rodriguez boys consistently ignored the "Go Easy"

signals hung out at Tavoni's orders. Their father wanted the victory as badly as his sons, urging the youngsters to continue pressing on, a fact all too apparent to Tavoni, who wanted them to ease up and stop forcing the pace so much. After all, the goal was a Ferrari victory and, as Tavoni carefully pointed out to Papa Rodriguez, they had been lent the TR61 with the implied understanding that they would support the team to fend off competition, not try to beat it if none materialized. Papa wouldn't hear of it, however, vowing to press on for the victory he so desperately desired.

The Mairesse/Parkes TR61 prototype.

A Faulty Condenser

Tavoni, never exactly a fool, decided not to contest the issue further with the obstinate elder Rodriguez, but simply wait for an opportunity to arise where he could justifiably enable the Hill/Gendebien mount to take a solid, uncontested lead. His patience was rewarded just past 4 a.m. when the leading Rodriguez Testa Rossa came spluttering into the pits with an ignition problem. The mechanics, coached to go slow by Tavoni, made a very leisurely study of the problem, whilst the Rodriguez clan clamored for them to hurry up. All the spark plugs were changed, as was the coil, before the mechanics decided it must really all be caused by a faulty condenser, casually studied and unhurriedly replaced. The Rodriguez car re-entered the

"Piano! Piano!" Gaetano Florini signals Hill around 7:00 a.m. from the Ferrari pit just past Mulsanne Corner. Florini is today manager of Customer Relations.

Manager Tavoni's eyes slip shut in the early morning hours.

The Rodriguez brothers' TR61 demonstrates how close to take a corner.

chase some 20 minutes later and almost five laps down in 4th place behind Hill/Gendebien, Ginther/Von Trips and Mairesse/Parkes. The Rodriguez forces vented their full fury on Tavoni, but he smugly and very calmly insisted to them that the pit crew did the job just as fast as humanly possible. So, Tavoni got what he wanted, his first place team car secure in the lead and finally an end to the destructive sprint race, certainly the longest ever seen up to then at Le Mans.

The never-say-die Rodriguez brothers charged on nonetheless all morning, easily getting by the Mairesse/Parkes Testa Rossa, which suffered from grabby brakes, and then moved up to 2nd when, through a pit signaling mixup, Von Trips ran out of gas on the Mulsanne Straight. He tried to get the 246 SP around to the pits using the starter motor, but the battery gave out after a few hundred yards, ending its bid for good. Even though some brief rain showers occurred late in the morning, temporarily slowing them down, the Mexicans pounded away in the Testa Rossa with many 4:02-4:05 laps, and several at 4:00 even. Though gaining

on Hill/Gendebien, they would never catch up by 4 p.m. unless the fates adversely struck the leading duo.

After twenty-two hours of non-stop flogging, the Rodriguez Testa Rossa finally blew up at White House, coming into the pits trailing a vast cloud of oily smoke. A quick inspection of the engine compartment showed oil everywhere, and rocking the car back and forth in gear produced a clonking sound from its innards, a sure sign of a broken piston. A later removal of the belly pans revealed a large hole in the side of the block where a rod had exited, but whatever the case, it would run no more that day.

Hill Keeps His Seat

Hill and Gendebien slowed drastically afterwards, content to cruise around sedately the remaining two hours to take the checked flag, though all was not entirely peaceful as Gendebien wanted the honor of taking the Testa Rossa across the finish line, with Hill insistent that as he had the last driving spell, it was his right. Hill pitted at 3 p.m. and refused to vacate his seat, leading to some unkind words on all

sides, before he casually motored off to kill the remaining time. Hill took the checker at 4 p.m., the Testa Rossa setting new records of 2778 miles (4476 kilometers) at an average speed of 115.8 mph, handily beating the previous mark of 2731 miles (4439 kilometers) set in 1957 by the Flockhart/Bueb Jaguar. For Hill it was the 2nd time he had won at Le Mans, while Gendebien now claimed a total of three. However, as far as the crowd was concerned, the non-finishing Rodriguez brothers were the moral victors. The Mairesse/Parkes prototype finished 2nd for a one-two sweep by the factory Testa Rossas, both running faultlessly for the twenty-four hours, except for some minor but annoying brake grabbing problems in the latter car, which were remedied by pad changes.

The point totals now read Ferrari 30, Maserati 14, and Porsche 10. Even though only the best four race finishes counted, Ferrari had won the championship no matter what happened at Pescara. Still, the Pescara event had to take place, or there would be no championship to win, a problem yet remaining to be solved.

All smiles on the victory stand are Hill and Gendebien, though things were definitely not that friendly earlier. To their left are Mairesse and Parkes.

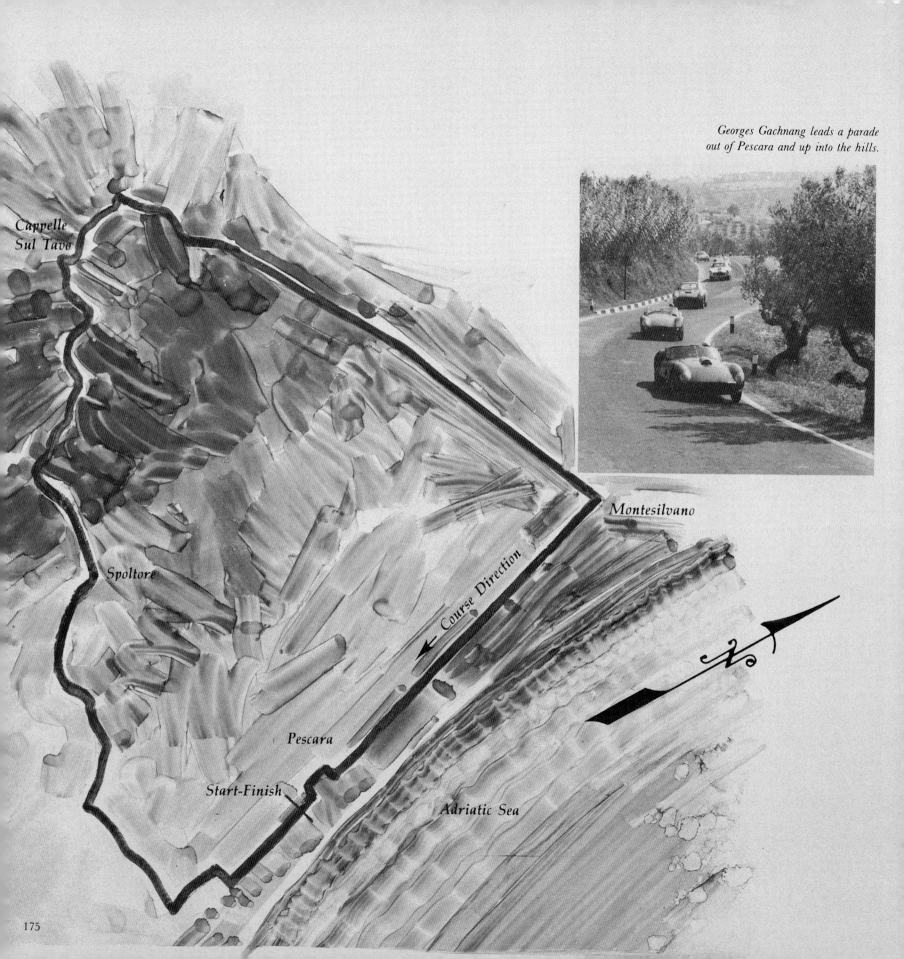

Georges Gachnang leads a parade out of Pescara and up into the hills.

Cappelle Sul Tavo

Spoltore

Montesilvano

Course Direction

Pescara

Start-Finish

Adriatic Sea

N

HOLIDAY IN PESCARA

The last championship event had long been scheduled to take place at Pescara on August 15, 1961. The promoters had a never-ending problem of obtaining the necessary financing to stage the event, compounded by early suspicions within the Porsche camp that if an Italian marque was not in the hunt for the championship, then the race would be cancelled. As five events were required, and if Porsche had wrapped up the title in terms of an unbeatable points lead at the conclusion of Le Mans, they feared the event wouldn't be run, nullifying the championship, as the minimum number of races would not have been staged. Their worries were unfounded as exactly the reverse took place, and Ferrari now needed the Pescara event to officially confirm their title for the glory of Italy, etc., etc.

After Le Mans, personal efforts by the Commendatore to line up the requisite financial support eliminated any blocks in holding the event, though it would not cover the minimum distance prescribed by the FIA. As the weather is unbearably hot in Italy at that time of the year, the FIA agreed to go along with a four-hour event, though ruling it would only be worth half the normal points. Not that Enzo Ferrari cared a hoot for the points involved, all he wanted was for the race to happen.

Through The Olive Groves

Pescara, located about midway on the Adriatic coast, is a medium-size city and rather dirty by Italian standards, but boasts one of the finest and toughest road circuits anywhere. It dated back to the pre-World War II days, though infrequently used since the mid-1950s as the organizers always had trouble raising the necessary capital to stage events. Prior to 1961, the last contest to be held on the circuit was a 1957 Formula 1 race won by Moss in a Vanwall. The same course, all roads in daily use, would be used again in 1961.

The circuit, some 15.5 miles (25.5 kilometers) around, is roughly triangular in shape. The starting point is just on the outskirts of Pescara, the first leg of the triangle being composed of a bit of straightaway followed by a long, twisty climb past farms, olive groves and vineyards to the villages of Spoltore and Cappelle sul Tavo. Just before the latter town, the highest point of the circuit is reached, some 800-plus feet (250 meters) above the starting level, and a series of snaking downhill curves begins the second part of the course, with the tight corners gradually opening up to gentler bends, becoming ever more quickly negotiable. These lead to a long downhill straight heading toward the Adriatic, and normally the fastest part of the course. At Montesilvano, on the coast, there is a ninety-degree bend heading onto another long straight paralleling the sea front and leading to the start-finish line. To slow the speeds through Pescara, a chicane had been installed just before the finish line. The Pescara circuit was a good test of cars and drivers, though in general, the big-displacement machinery had a definite advantage.

Ferrari sent only a single factory entry, in the form of 246 SP for Baghetti and Ginther, though he also lent the TR61 prototype (0780) to Mimo Dei's Centro Sud racing team for Lorenzo Bandini and Giorgio Scarlatti to pilot.

In support were the plodding pair of Gachnang/Caillet in their TR61-like special (0742). Competition consisted of Lucky Casner in the Nürburgring-winning Tipo 61 Maserati, two Serenissima Tipo 63s and a gaggle of semi-official Porsches.

The race was contested on a Tuesday, the date of August 15th being a holiday in Italy known as Ferragosto, with practice on the two preceding days. Practice sessions began at 9 a.m. and ended at noon, and the race would start at the same early morning hour in an attempt to mitigate the effects of the stifling Italian heat, that would surely rise to over 100 degrees by midday. Baghetti enlivened the initial practice period both by clocking the fastest lap of 9:49.4, equivalent to an 94 mph (155 km/h) average, and also just afterwards bending the 246 SP in a head-on crash into a stone wall. The mechanics spent all Sunday night beating out the panels, but the timings the following day were considerably slower as the suspension seemed to have been affected in some mysterious manner, and one not readily resolvable.

Bandini and Scarlatti were much more cautious in the Testa Rossa loaner, achieving a best clocking on Sunday of 10:17.1, though recording a rousing 174 mph on the Cappelle-Montesilvano straight. On Monday, Bandini turned in a 10:03.7 lap, and later reported that another 10-15 seconds could be pared if the necessity arose. All the other competitors were far behind these two Ferrari times, including the Gachnang/Caillet duo, who could only post a best showing of 11:29, actually slower than several Alfa 1300-cc coupes. The only unresolved question in observers' minds was which Ferrari would win, with Baghetti the popular choice. Ginther, the co-driver, seemed to be completely ignored by all the Italians, leading him to remark at one point that he felt like a non-person.

Bandini Becomes 37th

By the time the 9 a.m. start was to occur, the temperature had already climbed into the 90s with promise of higher readings yet to come. The Le Mans start got underway after a fifteen-minute delay, with Casner jumping into an immediate lead, though quickly passed by Ginther with Bandini hot on his heels. Bandini screeched into his pit at the end of the first lap with the cockpit inundated in oil and gas. The gas tank was overfull and the oil tank had worked itself loose. By the time these problems were corrected, a disconsolate Bandini found himself reentering the fray in 37th position, but not to remain there for very long.

Lorenzo Bandini, one of the new generation of Italian drivers, who drove from 37th place to capture Pescara.

Top: *Bandini leaving Pescara in the TR61.* **Center:** *Georges Gachnang in the heart of Pescara.* **Bottom:** *Bandini waves to the spectators on his way to the checkered flag.*

On the 3rd lap Casner retook the lead when Ginther pitted to have the mechanics study the 246 SP's suspension problems, rejoining the race in 4th place and recapturing the lead several tours later. Bandini, not wasting any time, had climbed back up to 10th place by the end of lap three and continued charging around the course to such effect that he lay 3rd overall by the end of the 9th lap, behind Ginther and Casner. On the next lap, Ginther pitted and Baghetti took over, but shortly after his departure the wounded front suspension finally collapsed, ending his drive before he could begin to show the folks what his publicity was all about. The go fast signal was given to Bandini, now 2nd, though he needed little additional urging to press on. Bandini was handling the Testa Rossa rather like a Formula Junior, tossing it around the tight corners with great elan, and taking the faster curves in long, nerve wrenching opposite-lock power slides, continually gaining on Casner, before coming in for refueling and handing over to Scarlatti on the 13th lap. Scarlatti, considerably slower than Bandini, only was allowed two laps before being called in and replaced by a refreshed and fully recharged Bandini.

The haste in calling in Scarlatti became a bit redundant, as on the same lap, Casner crashed the Birdcage while inadvisedly attempting to pass a slower competitor on the outside of a curve. Bandini inherited a substantial lead with Casner's exit, as his closest pursuer, the Barth/ Orthuber Porsche RS61 was more than ten minutes behind. The heat took its toll of many drivers and Bandini, feeling faint at one point, came into the pits for a long drink of cold water, with a couple of buckets more of the wet stuff thrown at his perspiring body for good measure.

Bandini continued slogging around the remaining time, completing the necessary fourth hour on his 23rd lap, after covering a total of 572.878 kilometers at an average speed of 143.219 km/h. The victory gave Ferrari a 1961 record of four wins and a 2nd out of five starts, and a 34 point total score, more than the combined sum of Porsche and Maserati.

The Le Mans winning TR61 (0794) was hastily rebuilt at Maranello and shipped to Chinetti in New York, who had purchased the car for the Rodriguez family, with the brothers anxious to campaign it in the major 1961 fall American races. Count Volpi's Serenissima team bought the other TR61 (0792), while the TR61 prototype (0780) was retained for further experiments.

THE RECORD

Even though the emphasis of Ferrari design and development had shifted toward the rear-engined cars, the Testa Rossa accounted for the bulk of 1961 points, with victories at Sebring, Le Mans and Pescara, and a second at the Nürburgring. The point total gained by the Testa Rossas alone would have been sufficient to win the championship. In view of the results, Enzo Ferrari had obviously made the right decision when he expended the necessary effort to produce the 1961 variant of the Testa Rossa, as the rear-engined 246 SP performances would have been insufficient to capture the title.

In the 1958-61 period, the Testa Rossas had won the championship three out of the four years, and only missed the title by two points on the other occasion. This is a superlative record, and an excellent example of how to initially design a winning machine and then develop it in an evolutionary manner to remain competitive over a long period of time. Of particular interest is the fact that the substantial improvements did not overstress any components or reduce the tremendous reliability of the Testa Rossa.

Looking At Statistics

A study of the four years of championship racing reveals some interesting statistics. Official Ferrari Testa Rossa entries participated in 19 of the 20 races contested over the 1958-61 period (1960 Sebring not counted), and won 10 of them. Their losses were to Aston-Martin (4), Porsche (2), Maserati (2), and a rear-engined Ferrari (1).

In total, 48 individual factory Testa Rossas started in these 19 events and 29 finished. In addition to the 10 victories, they recorded 9 seconds, 5 thirds, 2 fourths, and 3 fifths. Of the 19 that didn't finish, 12 were the victims of mechanical failure, 5 dropped out due directly or indirectly from accidents, and 2 just ran out of gas. The bulk of the mechanical failures, 8 out of the total 12, or 75%, occurred during the disaster year of 1959. The 1959 problem involved only two major maladies, ring and pinion or blown head gaskets. The remaining 4 mechanical failures were split between 1958 (clutch, generator) and 1960 (blown head gasket, ring and pinion leading to broken driveshaft). In 1961 there were no mechanical failures and only one accident.

The accidents, while sometimes severe enough to reduce the Testa Rossas to junk, never resulted in a single serious driver injury. This fact must be partly attributed to Ferrari's policy of building the Testa Rossas strong and then carefully maintaining and rebuilding them.

The finishing record of privateers in the international races over the same period is much less notable, though hardly a reflection on the factory. As private entrants, they are unlikely to have been prepared or maintained as well as the works' entries. In the case of ex-team cars, before they were sold, it was standard procedure to undertake a complete factory rebuild before customer delivery. What happened later was not the factory's doing, as they generally left Maranello in fine fettle.

The Best Sports Racer?

It is an arguable premise to state that the Testa Rossa was the best sports racer throughout the 1958-61 period. A good case could be made if quantities of championships and victories are the sole measurement criteria. However, looking at the broader view, it is also clear that Ferrari and Porsche were the only competitors to seriously contest the World Sports Car Championship over the entire time frame. The long term commitment on Ferrari's part probably had much to do with the successes gained. The Aston-Martin DBR1, in 1958 and 1959, was equal to or marginally faster than the Testa Rossa, and in 1960 the Tipo 61 Maserati enjoyed a distinct advantage. Both makes could conceivably have won more often and perhaps captured additional championships, if they had taken a more serious and better organized approach with the proper level of funding.

The automobile itself is only one part of the total package, and all the other ingredients must be present to produce victory. Ferrari took the right tack by expending the money and effort necessary to support the endeavor properly, and won, while the others failed (excepting 1959 and the odd race) because they did not. It takes more than a good car to win and Ferrari was the only firm who did the entire job.

Viewed only in the narrow context of a racing machine compared to its competitors, the Testa Rossa should probably be rated as an excellent, but not great, package. Its success was partly a case of shortcomings in performance being more than counter-balanced by the other supporting elements in the totality of the Ferrari racing effort.

George Reed at Nassau in his TR59/60 (0770) now powered by 3.5-liter 290 MM engine. He ran eighth in the Governor's Trophy Race.

OTHER RACING

A review of 1961 non-championship Testa Rossa activity again indicates relatively few successes were gained at anything other than minor events. The customer versions continued to show diminishing usage, being generally worn out at this stage, and uncompetitive. By the conclusion of the 1961 racing season they were but rarely seen, even at minor club races, and almost all the better results were achieved by ex-team cars.

Looking around at the regional events, Jerry Grant had another successful year with Dick Hahn's car (0704) at Northwestern contests, notching a string of seven consecutive wins in the Spring and early Summer of 1961 against some very mediocre competition. He later made the mistake of straying off his home turf to Vacaville, California, on August 20, and was soundly beaten by Chuck Parsons in a Birdcage. The balance of the year Grant spent in the much safer Northwest, excepting a go at Riverside in October.

Rod Carveth made only a few appearances in 1961 with 0666, on one occasion teaming with the aforementioned Mr. Parsons to take first place at the Cotati, California, three-hour endurance race on July 16 before selling the car to Lew Florence. Gordon Glyer (0718) captured a first at Sacramento on May 14, then DNF'd at Laguna Seca on June 11 from an accident caused when he spun in another's oil deposit and bent the front suspension beyond immediate repair. Later that year, Glyer removed the engine from his car with the intention of installing it in the ex-Kunstle, Parsons Lotus 15 which already boasted a four-cylinder Testa Rossa motor. The now engineless TR fell victim to the eventual fate of most of the U.S. Testa Rossas, having a Chevrolet engine dropped into the chassis.

In the Midwest, several Testa Rossas were active competitors in addition to George Reed with his TR59/60. These included Owen Coon in the ex-Reed TR58 (0728), who ran in a number of 1961 events and gained one win at Wilmot Hills, Michigan, on August 27, beating his car's previous owner. Dave Deubles' ex-Cowles customer car (0732) also appeared regularly as did Wayne Burnett in the ex-Hayes (0714) machine, though he often seemed more out for a lark than serious competition, normally content to cruise along keeping out of trouble.

Just A Parts Car

The following story might help illustrate just how little value the customers' Testa Rossas had in 1961 as competitors. Alan Connell had switched to campaigning Birdcage Maseratis that year, but felt they needed more power to be a sure winner. He settled on the V12 Testa Rossa engine as being the most suitable 3.0-liter unit available and bought Gary Laughlin's complete car (0748) in the early summer of 1961. He then pulled out the engine and somehow managed to shoehorn it into the Maserati. Unfortunately, the Laughlin engine was none too healthy, having a cracked crankshaft and several bad connecting rods. Connell called up Chinetti in August to purchase another engine, but the latter had none available for sale. However, he did have a complete Testa Rossa on hand (0724), not run in some time but reputed to be in good condition, which Connell promptly bought. As time was of the essence if the Texan were to be able to make the major fall races with his hybrid, the car was air-freighted from New York to Dallas. Upon arrival, the engine and transmission were jerked out and the carcass sold to a local competitor, Willis Murphey, who installed a Chevrolet engine and transmission and took to the race track. Connell dropped in the Testa Rossa engine and also went racing, quite successfully, it should be noted, though the handling characteristics of the conglomeration must have been rather unique.

A number of the Testa Rossas, primarily the customer versions, acquired Chevrolet or other American engines during this time frame in an attempt to keep them running. Ferrari parts were expensive and sometimes difficult to get in a hurry, while American engines were cheap, easily installed, and produced considerably

more horsepower. Further, most of the Testa Rossa owners by 1961 were operating with meager budgets and simply could not afford the expense required to keep their Testa Rossas all Ferrari, especially when knowing full well that they would be uncompetitive at best.

By the end of 1961, most of the customer cars had been retired from active competition, or were bastardized with non-original engines. In any case, they were hardly capable of winning anywhere, and at that time there was very little worth less than a racing car no longer competitive. They did continue to occasionally show up at the track, generally occupying the back of the grid, and appearing far down in the final results list. Gradually most faded away to street use or, more commonly, languished as derelicts.

The Ex-Team Cars

The only Testa Rossas to have any measure of success were the 1959 and newer team cars, now all in private hands. Rarely seen in the minor events, they did make forays into the SCCA National circuit and the major professional races.

In the Nationals, the most successful venture was organized by John Bunch of New Canaan, Connecticut, who purchased the Rodriguez TR59/60 "special" after their 3rd place 1961 Sebring finish. Bunch engaged George Constantine to be his driver, the combination starting slowly with a 4th overall behind three Birdcages at Bridgehampton, New York, on August 6. Constantine improved to 2nd at Thompson, Connecticut, on September 4, and then scored an overall victory at Watkins Glen on September 22. The Glen win came at the expense of Walt Hansgen piloting a Cunningham entered Tipo 63 Maserati, who, after leading most of the race, was forced to slow with transaxle trouble in the closing stages. The Testa Rossa win at the Glen marked the first occasion where a Ferrari had ever won the historic event, America's oldest sports car race. It was also Ferrari's first Nationals modified class victory in two years and the last to come for another several. Also at the Glen were George Reed in his TR59/60 (0770), who came in 7th, and Bob Hurt in the ex-Sharp TR59 (0766) finishing in 11th position.

Two weeks prior to that date, Reed had teamed with Ed Hugus to bring the TR59/60 into 2nd overall at the Elkhart Lake 500 mile

race on September 9, being beaten only by Hansgen and marking two years in a row that the TR59/60 finished second. Three other Testa Rossas started at Elkhart but none finished. These included the customer car (0732) purchased by Dave Deuble of Glenview, Illinois, from Russell Cowles. It was driven by Ted Baumgartner and Buzz Hahn, and crashed by the former during the event. Also dropping out was the Owen Coon TR58 (0728) partnered by Bob Major (broken valve), and the customer car (0714) of Wayne Burnett/Charlie Hayes, who exited with burned bearings.

Canada and California

The balance of the most important 1961 North American contests were all professional events taking place in the fall of the year.

The lead-off race was the 240-mile Canadian Grand Prix held at the Mosport circuit near Toronto on September 30, where Pedro Rodriguez finished 2nd in the unhealthy-sounding 1961 Le Mans winning Testa Rossa (0794). Following him home in TR59/60s were George Constantine (0746) in 4th and George Reed (0770) in 5th.

The east coast contingent then made the long trek out West to contest the October California races held on consecutive weekends at Riverside and Laguna Seca. Starting positions in both races were determined by qualifying, and as there were more entrants than the maximum allowed, many aspirants would be left to spectate. At Riverside, Constantine managed to qualify in the middle of the pack with John Bunch's car (0746), which looked decidedly the worse for wear with body damage fore and aft sustained when it fell off the truck loading ramp at the Los Angeles airport after being flown in from New York.

Constantine qualified 13th fastest with a respectable 2:07.7, but felt his car was somewhat misgeared for the course, and if that had been rectified, he might have achieved a time in the 2:05 range. To establish the proper perspective however, Jack Brabham held the pole with a 2:01 clocking in a Cooper Monaco, and four other competitors were within a second of his time.

None of the other Testa Rossas managed to qualify, all being forced to run in a Consolation race to make the rear of the main grid. Ricardo Rodriguez had all kinds of problems with the

George Constantine passes a fading Walt Hansgen on his way to winning Watkins Glen, the first time a Ferrari captured America's oldest sports car race.

Bob Hurt at the Glen in 0766.

TR61 (0794), which seemed to have been rather poorly rebuilt at the factory before shipment to Chinetti. He missed making the main go by a bare 7/10 of a second, the Testa Rossa having definite steering and breathing problems. He tried to make the main event via the Consolation race but dropped out on only the 2nd lap with rear end difficulties.

Jerry Grant (0704) did manage to make the starting grid via the consolation race, but Bob Hurt (0766) was unable to qualify due to rear main bearing seal problems caused by improper thrust washer installation. In the 203-mile race on October 15, neither of the two Testa Rossas starting were ever anywhere near contention for a top spot, Grant finishing 14th and Constantine, whose engine destroyed its rear main bearing seal near the midpoint of the race, was credited with the 15th position.

At the conclusion of the race, Constantine commented to an observer that he had "made a good start and ran in about the second group of leaders, where the car belonged. It could not keep pace with the leading Lotuses and Coopers, but through the Esses it was as fast as any car. About the 100-mile point, it started throwing oil into the cockpit and once at turn 7 I missed a shift because of oil on the pedals and almost hit a photographer. I pitted; we found out there wasn't a thing could be done to fix it, so I just stroked to finish."

Laguna Seca and Nassau

At Laguna Seca the following weekend, only Bob Hurt appeared in a Ferrari, the rest of the Testa Rossa squad having packed up and headed home in the interim. The Rodriguez and Constantine cars went back East to be readied for Nassau, and Grant took his car north to Washington. In spite of stiff competition, Hurt qualified the TR59 for the main event grid by recording a 1:19.3, a highly respectable time for a Testa Rossa, but quite a bit off Gurney's pole winning clocking of 1:14.8 in the Frank Arciero owned Lotus 19. During the race, run in two heats on October 22, Hurt charged around determinedly, but the combination was totally outclassed, finishing the sessions 15th and 16th, respectively.

Nassau capped the American racing season the first week of December, 1961, attracting an enormous entry for the plethora of races and parties. The tuneup for the main event was, as customary, the 102-mile Governor's Trophy run

Top: *The imperturbable Graham Hill in the Serenissima TR61. He finished fifth.* **Center:** *Pedro Rodriguez in a TR61. He finished third.* **Bottom:** *Bob Hurt, who finished third overall in the Governor's Trophy Race.*

183

Top: *Owen Coon bends his TR58 around a Nassau turn.*
Center: *Wayne Burnett in 250 TR No. 0714.*
Bottom: *Spencer Litchie gets it wrong in No. 0730.*

held on December 9, consisting of 25 laps around the suspension and tire murdering Oakes Field course. The race was a Ferrari TR parade with Pedro Rodriguez easily capturing first place with the TR61 (0794), George Reed 2nd in the TR59/60 (0770) now powered by a 3.5-liter 290 MM engine, and Bob Hurt taking 3rd in his TR59 (0766). As usual, many of the hot shoes sat out the race in order to save their equipment for the 252-mile main event and the big buck payoff that went with it.

In that race, Gurney repeated his mastery of the Oakes Field course, winning with the same Lotus he used in 1960, followed home at a distance by Roger Penske in a Cooper Monaco. Far behind in 3rd was Pedro Rodriguez in the TR61 (0794), the highest placed Ferrari that day and leading home a crowd of other Testa Rossas. The group included Graham Hill, piloting a Ferrari for the first time, in the Serenissima TR 61 (0792) taking 5th, with Constantine (0746) 6th, Reed (0770) 8th, and Spencer Litchie 12th in his customer car (0730) ex-Martin, Harrison. Bob Hurt (0766), after a fine run in the top five for most of the grind, dropped out late in the proceedings with a broken halfshaft, a rare Testa Rossa failure.

So ended the 1961 American racing season, another rather disappointing year for Ferrari as even the TR61s could not best the competition in sprint races.

Though it may be hard to understand the reasoning, the Serenissima team shipped their TR61 from Nassau to England to compete in a very minor 15-lap race at Brands Hatch, held on December 26, 1961. The weather was seasonably cold as might be expected, and the morning of the event found parts of the circuit covered with ice. The track management threw rock salt on the affected areas and then sent out a number of race cars to circulate for an hour or so to spread it around, grind it in and help melt the ice more completely. The surface remained slippery all day, causing traction problems for the TR61 and resulted in quite a struggle for Graham Hill before he managed to take the victory over a field composed mostly of 1100-cc small fry. Chris Ashmore in a 1100-cc Lola Mark 1 clung tenaciously to the big Ferrari's tail most of the race, before Hill lengthened the gap and finished with a six-second advantage. From England, the Serenissima crew reshipped their by now well-traveled Testa Rossa to Florida for the 1962 Sebring race.

184

TRIUMPH & TROUBLE

The competition year of 1961 was a great triumph for Ferrari as the Maranello forces scored a neat triple by capturing all three major championship series—Grand Prix, Sports Car and Gran Turismo. Phil Hill became the first American to win the Grand Prix World Champion Driver's title, though the achievement was marred by the death of his closest rival and friend, Von Trips, in the final race of the season at Monza.

Much of the satisfaction that Enzo Ferrari should have derived from the splendid 1961 competition record must have been destroyed by the major upheaval that erupted within his organization late that year. Discontent amongst some of the key personnel had long been a festering wound. They were bitter about their penurious pay scales and difficult working conditions; upset by interference from Signora Ferrari, and in general felt their hard work in making the Ferrari firm successful was unappreciated by the Commendatore. Certainly he gave them no public credit, a state of affairs everyone had to learn how to adjust to at Ferrari, but still it was reasonable to expect some kind of recognition from the boss, and none ever came.

Led by Chiti and Tavoni, eight of the key players presented a package of requests to Ferrari, including wage increases, more staff to ease the workload, improved working conditions in general, and more decision-making power. Ferrari refused to acquiesce to the modest request and the respective positions rapidly hardened when the rebellious eight, convinced that the firm couldn't manage without them, changed their requests to demands. Ferrari would not negotiate at all, leading the rebels to threaten to quit en masse rather than continue working in the future as they had in the past. Eventually, it all boiled down to one side or the other surrendering and losing face in the process, an unthinkable act for Enzo Ferrari. In spite of frantic negotiating efforts by many people, particularly Luigi Chinetti, who tried to function as a mediator and intermediary, any possibility of resolving the situation disappeared when Enzo absolutely refused to throw even the most modest of crumbs to his unhappy managers. After all the avenues of graceful reconciliation had been blocked, the group's honor and pride dictated quitting the company en masse.

The opportunity to leave proudly came to fruition in early December when Count Giovanni Volpi hired most of them to form the management nucleus of a new automobile racing and construction organization to be known as ATS, the initials of Automobili Turismo Sport.

Confusion reigned supreme at Ferrari for some months afterwards, as a patchwork reorganization was effected to compensate for the departed key people. The competition lineup for 1962 was in good shape, thanks to Chiti's efforts, and presented no real problems as far as the initial season openers were concerned. Naturally, detail improvements would be required over the course of the year, as well as major new enhancements to remain competitive, in addition to rebuilding the depleted design staff so that the necessary development activity to handle future needs could be undertaken. Only two rather junior engineers were left to form the design nucleus, but one of them was Mauro Forghieri, who later would become the Chief Engineer.

So ended 1961 for the Ferrari firm. Not a joyful conclusion, as should have been the case after such a successful year.

CHAPTER 7
1962: There's Life In The Old Girl Yet

A
S LONG PROMISED, the 1962 Constructors
Championship was restricted to Gran
Turismos, with 12 races on the schedule. The
reign of the sports cars was officially at an end.
However, all was not as it seemed, thanks to
some backing and filling that occurred during
the 1961 negotiations between the CSI and
race organizers. Promoters of the three key
events in the 1962 schedule—Sebring, Nürburgring and Le Mans—were very leery about the
prospects of drawing large crowds with GTs as
the sole attraction.

the "Organizers Cup." The regulations for cars contesting this award were basically the same as those for the "Sports Car Cup" excepting that the maximum displacement allowance increased from 3000cc to 4000cc. To be eligible for the title a constructor would have to compete in all four events. The intention of the award was to foster development by the manufacturers of more exotic machinery, which led to the class being called "Experimental."

A Contradiction In Classes

The result was rather incongruous. For some years the FIA had wanted to change the emphasis from the all-out sports racers toward Gran Turismo cars, as they were more akin to normal passenger-carrying road cars, the speeds would be lowered, and a wider range of manufacturers might be enticed to enter the lists. After achieving this ideal for 1962, they then threw the results out the window, not only by allowing the sports cars to run simultaneously, but by additionally promulgating an even more potent class with the Experimentals. It's hard to imagine how a more confusing conglomeration could be derived.

The Experimentals and Prototypes would always be faster than the GT cars. While GT placings would determine the championship, outright race wins most likely would be achieved by the two faster types. The glory and publicity have always gone to the overall winner at the major events, not to class winners, even considering the latter's importance in gaining championship points. Enzo Ferrari realized this fact of life as well as anyone. He decided to produce an Experimental 4.0-liter machine for that class, and campaign his 1961 sports racers in the prototype class, updated only in minor ways for 1962. Thus, the Testa Rossa saga did not end in 1961, as the TR61 and its Experimental derivative would play an important role in Ferrari racing fortunes in 1962.

Though Ferrari might have desired to update the Testa Rossas for 1962, a comprehensive program could not be considered because of the problems engendered by the walkout of key personnel the preceding fall. Very few changes were made to any of the racing cars because of this situation, but this was not as bad as it might sound, due to clear Ferrari superiority with the Sports and GT cars at the end of 1961. As no significant competition improvements seemed to be on the horizon for 1962, the Maranello organization gained something of a breathing spell to once again get its house in order.

Ginther Leaves

On the driver side, Richie Ginther quit at the end of the year, moving to BRM for 1962. He had become disenchanted with the low wages and infrequent opportunities to pilot Grand Prix machinery, always his primary goal. BRM had undertaken an extensive development program and his skills as mechanic, test driver and competitor fit their needs exactly. Willy Mairesse took over Ginther's role as test driver, solely in hopes of earning more frequent Grand Prix drives. However, he lacked Ginther's testing and mechanical expertise, causing the cars to be incorrectly set up and prepared at many of the 1962 races. This is not to imply that he was stupid, as the reverse was true. The problems were essentially between him and the engineers and mechanics, i.e., an inability to communicate with each other about problems and their resolutions. In addition, his driving style was unlike anyone else's, causing the other team members to run the mechanics ragged with wholesale suspension changes at races. As the racing season progressed, the testing program atrophied, as everyone just went through the motions, certain that the results would almost always have to be revised by race day.

Oliver Gendebien announced his retirement at the end of 1961, but apparently had second thoughts about his decision, and soon signed on once again with Ferrari for 1962, but only for a limited program of races.

Phil Hill, now the defending World Champion, at last won the accolade as number one driver at Ferrari, though his reign would be short lived and marked by rapidly deteriorating relations with the Commendatore.

Giancarlo Baghetti now became a regular, as did Lorenzo Bandini and Ricardo Rodriguez, with his elder brother Pedro and Mike Parkes being invited to run factory entries in certain races.

The discussions resulted in the formation of the "Sports Car Cup," to be contested in seven races by up to 3.0-liter "Prototypes." The rules were identical to those in force for the sports cars in 1961, except that a lower windshield height of just over 6 inches was allowed. These prototypes could run in selected races in concert with the Gran Turismos and win the events, but not garner any championship points for their make, those going instead to the highest placed Gran Turismo finishers.

In addition, led by the Le Mans-promoting Automobile Club de l'Ouest, a new award was established by the Sebring, Targa Florio, Nürburgring and Le Mans' organizers, grandiosely titled as the "Challenge Mondial de Vitesse et d'Endurance," otherwise commonly known as

Contrasting corner techniques at Daytona: **At left** *George Constantine in John Bunch's TR59/60;* **at right** *Peter Ryan in the NART TR61.*

Enter The Dragon

Eugenio Dragoni was appointed team manager to replace Tavoni, and came to Ferrari with considerable background experience running the Scuderia St. Ambroeus, where Baghetti got his start. Dragoni, colloquially known as the "Dragon," was the diametric opposite of Tavoni. He was imperious, opinionated, uncommunicative and unreasoning with everyone except the Italian pilots, whom he promoted in every possible way. The other drivers, particularly Hill, were constantly embroiled in battles with Dragoni, especially on the Grand Prix side, where Ferrari's 1962 campaign fell to pieces rather quickly. The Prototype and Gran Turismo arenas were much more successful, primarily as both were being contested in the name of the factory by independents, not subject to Dragoni's machinations and further, Ferrari had no real opposition in either class. Ferrari captured both the GT Championship and the Sports Car Cup, with the Testa Rossas playing an important role in the latter. Inherent reliability brought them success, even though, in the case of NART and Serenissima, they were no longer being maintained by factory personnel.

Testa Rossas did not take part in all of the 1962 events for which they were eligible. Of the four major events, Testa Rossas were important factors at Sebring, Nürburgring and Le Mans.

None were entered at the Targa Florio. Other than these three events, Testa Rossas were only on hand at the season opener held at Daytona, Florida, and the Bridgehampton, New York, Double 400 event that took place in the late summer.

On The Banking At Daytona

The Daytona 3 hour race was run on February 11, utilizing a combination of the high speed banked oval and flat road course in the track's infield. Ferrari was represented by NART with a 246 SP for Phil Hill, the 1961 Le Mans-winning TR61 (0794) to be driven by Ricardo Rodriguez, and George Constantine at the wheel of the John Bunch owned TR59/60 special (0746). Their principal opposition consisted of Dan Gurney in a Lotus 19, Chaparrals for Jim Hall and Dick Rathmann, and Roger Penske's Cooper.

Both the 246 SP and TR61 were controlled by the Rodriguez family, with Ricardo electing to use the TR61, as he calculated its extra power would be an advantage on the Daytona circuit. Hill got to drive the 246 SP with the understanding that Ricardo could take over the controls at any point in the race, if he so desired.

The early stages of the race witnessed a close duel for the lead between Hill, Rodriguez, and Gurney, after Penske retired. Gurney soon made

it by both Ferraris and gradually built up a substantial lead. About the 1-hour mark, Ricardo blew out the left front tire of the TR61 while at top speed on the steep banking and barely made it back into the pits. Replacing the wheel and tire was no great problem, but the brake line had been severed, requiring a new line to be fitted, brake fluid added and the system bled to remove the air. This of necessity took some 20 odd minutes, dropping the car out of contention. The decision was made to let Peter Ryan take over the car, and have Rodriguez replace Hill, when the latter made his scheduled pit stop still clinging to 2nd place, though far back of the flying Gurney.

This was duly done, though Rodriguez only spent a few laps out on the track before diving into the pits to correct a cockpit overheating problem, as contemporary journalists delicately reported it. The line to the oil pressure gauge had sprung a leak, and as luck would have it, the hot oil was being sprayed directly at Ricardo's crotch. A little tape resolved that difficulty and he quickly roared off in pursuit of Gurney.

At the very end of the three hours, Gurney's Lotus 19 blew up, but he cleverly halted some 10 feet or so from the finish line and at the appropriate moment used the starter to take the checkered flag. In this way he followed the dic-

PRIVATEERS COME THROUGH AT SEBRING

Joakim Bonnier in the winning TR61 at Sebring.

tum that says "to be ruled as finisher, a car must cross the line under its own power." Rodriguez finished 2nd, with George Constantine 5th, and Peter Ryan way back in 15th place.

It is conceivable that Constantine might have finished as high as 3rd had it not been for an early race incident that was stopped just short of becoming a major disaster. His crew had installed an auxiliary gas tank plumbed to the main supply to allow the TR59/60 to run the race nonstop, but had never tested the whole package under fully loaded racing conditions. Shortly after the start, gas began spilling out of the tank onto the exhaust pipes and ignited. Constantine, unaware of the conflagration raging three feet aft of his body, continued pressing on. It took a tremendous effort by Phil Hill, just behind at that point, to pass the TR59/60 and alert the driver to the imminent disaster. As soon as Constantine caught on to what was happening, he promptly dived off the track and made a mad dash directly to a fire truck parked on the verge, whose crew quickly doused the rapidly growing blaze. He then motored on to the pits, where the errant gas cap was sealed before he rejoined the race now well back in the pack.

Three Testa Rossas were entered for the 1962 edition of the 12 hours held on March 23, as part of an overwhelming onslaught by Ferrari. The factory did not actually participate officially, leaving that burden to Luigi Chinetti's NART, and Count Volpi's Scuderia Serenissima, with a supplementary contingent of privateers. Chinetti entered the 1961 Le Mans-winning TR61 (0794) for Buck Fulp and Peter Ryan, though his team's real primary candidates for the overall win were considered to be a 246 SP in the hands of the Rodriguez brothers, and Ireland/Moss piloting a new 248 SP. When practice commenced, the 248 SP was quickly determined to be rather ill-prepared and in dire need of further refinement. Ireland and Moss promptly switched to the TR61, leaving the vacated 248 SP seat for Fulp and Ryan.

Serenissima also entered their TR61 (0792) for Graham Hill and Joakim Bonnier. Keeping a foot in both Modenese camps, they also brought along a Tipo 64 Maserati and several GT Ferraris. Volpi's organization was being directed by Nello Ugolini, the former team manager for Maserati during their golden racing years and a renowned strategist.

Additionally, the ex-Rodriguez brothers TR59/60 special (0746) that had proven to be so quick at Sebring the previous year, was once more on hand, chauffeured by George Con-

stantine and Gaston Andrey. Other contenders included Cunningham entries of a Tipo 64 Maserati and a Cooper-Maserati, and a long-shot in the NART organization's front-engine Dino 246 to be piloted by Bob Grossman and Alan Connell.

Ferrari certainly seemed to be in a dominating position to win Sebring outright with one of its Prototypes, but domination in this area was nothing compared to the sure thing they appeared to enjoy in the Gran Turismo Class. The Ferrari GTOs were the stars of GT racing in 1962, and Hill and Gendebien were on hand in one of these models to lead the attack in garnering the all-important championship points.

Serenissima's race weekend took a decidedly wrong turn when Graham Hill suffered a slipped disc on Thursday, the consequence of lugging some heavy parts around the pits. This sent him on a trip to the local hospital, where he was held for overnight observation and fitting of a back brace. Though he was released the following day, the brace made driving impossible, so Ugolini switched Lucien Bianchi to take his place in the Testa Rossa.

Practice times among the prototypes were rather inconclusive, as no one seemed willing to push his car to the limit, though the Tipo 64 Maseratis did not appear to handle particularly well.

Innes Ireland in front with a hungry Corvette on his tail.

Moss Sidesteps An Early Duel

The race start produced another surprise. Moss, heretofore always Number One in the Le Mans type start, instead decided to let Ireland go first to attempt avoiding a suicidal early duel with Pedro Rodriguez. Ireland's instructions were to set his own pace and let Rodriguez do whatever he wished.

The first lap saw the usual confusion as the faster cars weaved and charged their way through the hordes of slower machinery. Constantine and Ireland fought out the lead side by side down the long back straight and tried to outbrake each other at the end with almost disastrous results, as both spun wildly onto the grass. Neither hit anything and Ireland did a full circle before reentering the track broadside, still in command of the lead.

At the end of the first lap, Ireland just barely clung to first, followed by Hansgen in a Tipo 64 Maserati, Jim Hall in his Chaparral, Constantine, Vaccarella in the other Tipo 64, and Rodriguez. Pedro was really flying and rapidly began picking off the front runners, setting a new lap record of 3:12.4 (97.2 mph) in the process before getting by Ireland into the lead on the 10th lap. At about the same time, Bonnier, after an exceedingly slow start finally moved up into the top 10.

Soon after the first round of pit stops, the TR59/60 of Constantine and Andrey went out with a broken halfshaft while running in 4th place. Such an incident was a real rarity for a Ferrari, as they just never seemed to break halfshafts. Freak occurrence or not, the TR59/60 was through for the day.

By the initial round of pit stops, the Maserati threat had evaporated, though Bruce McLaren enjoyed a momentary lead in the Cooper-Maserati, as some of the faster, more thirsty cars were in the pits being refueled. The NART pit stops were unbelievably chaotic as no one seemed to be in control and, further, it appeared that lap charts were not being kept by the team, with the mechanics calculating the proper time to call their cars in by figuring how long it would take to run X laps at the speeds being maintained.

Gus Andrey chases Bianchi after the first round of pit stops. The TR59 was a DNF with a broken half-shaft.

Adding to NART's problems, Ireland came charging into the pits at speed, incurring the displeasure of the race stewards, who promptly slapped the car with a time penalty. Conceivably, the penalty might have only been a reprimand, but Ireland and Chinetti took violent exception to the steward's warning, engaging him in a heated argument. He retaliated with the time penalty to teach them a lesson. Sometimes it's better to keep your mouth shut when dealing with officialdom.

The contrast between the NART pit operation and Serenissima's could hardly have been more pronounced. Ugolini ran the operation with a sure hand, everyone staying calm, doing the necessary tasks efficiently and carefully controlling their drivers' activities. Even though their highest placed car, the TR61, was still well behind the front runners, insiders began to suspect that when the race finished, the car would be very well placed indeed.

At quarter distance, the leading quartet was all Prototypes, the Rodriguez brothers still clung to first place with a decreasing lead over Moss/Ireland, both on the same lap. Two laps behind were the McLaren/Penske Cooper-Maserati and the Bianchi/Bonnier Testa Rossa, which had been steadily marching up through the field.

Ugolini Counts To 20

Shortly thereafter, a highly aggravated Moss pulled in to hand over the Testa Rossa to Ireland, complaining loudly about fading brakes, which he claimed to have unknowingly inherited from Ireland on the last switch. Rather than waste the time to find and install replacement pads on the spot, Ireland was told to go out and do 20 easy laps to conserve the brakes.

Ireland makes his displeasure known to Chief Steward John Baus over time penalty assessed for his high speed pit entry.

This would enable the pit crew to become properly organized for a speedy pad change when he brought in the car to turn over to Moss. Unfortunately for Ireland, the brakes went away altogether during his tenure at the wheel and he came in after 18 laps, with the NART organization unaware of that fact as they weren't keeping a lap chart. The "plombeur," similarly unaware that the Testa Rossa had not covered the required minimum of 20 laps before refueling was allowed, broke the gas tank seal. A mechanic, seeing the cap open, promptly slung in enough gas to top up the tank. After the fitting of pads and refueling, Moss leaped in and tore off.

However, Ugolini's crew, keeping accurate lap charts, knew that NART had broken the rules, and Ugolini promptly lodged a protest with Chief Steward John Baus. After a check of the charts, Baus informed Chinetti that the premature refueling constituted a violation. Chinetti reposted that the "plombeur" should not have broken the seal if the 20 lap minimum had not been covered, and that his mechanic assumed it was proper to refuel if the seal were cut. Baus replied that it was Chinetti's job to make sure the 20 lap minimum was observed, not the "plombeur." The argument got fiercer and fiercer as time went on, enlivened by appropriate arm waving and shouting which drew a

large crowd to the scene in front of the NART pit.

Blown Engine and Black Flag

The argument became even more intense at 3:30 p.m., when the leading Rodriguez car blew up just before the pit straight, handing Ireland/Moss a two lap lead over Bianchi/Bonnier, now lying 2nd, and a comfortable four laps in front of the next car. If the Ireland/Moss Testa Rossa were disqualified, then the Serenissima machine would automatically take command of the race. Finally, at 5:00 p.m., almost three hours after the incident took place, the stewards ordered out the black flag for Moss and Ireland, disqualifying the car.

In early evening Bianchi leaps aboard as Bonnier watches from pit wall. On the last stop he refused to vacate the cockpit for Bonnier, wanting to savor the checkered flag himself.

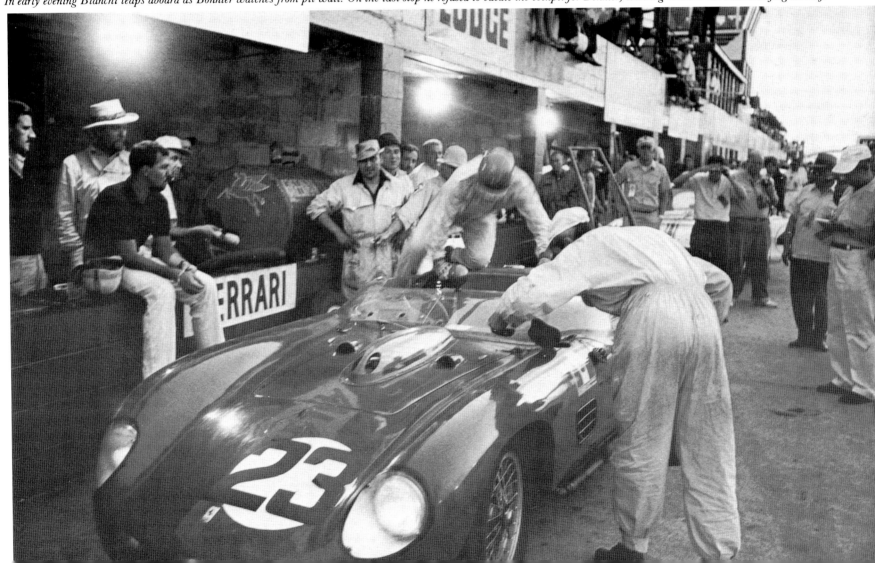

Bianchi (top) and Bonnier hoist the first place trophy, as Bonnier chats with well-wisher Hill.

Bianchi and Bonnier inherited a cushy six lap lead at that stage and had only to stroke the Testa Rossa around the remaining five hours to win. Ugolini, exercising extreme caution, slowed his drivers' natural instincts to press on by wisely showing lap time signals 3 seconds faster than the real time, forcing them to adopt a more reasonable pace.

Bianchi, always hyper, was so worked up over the impending prospect of his first major victory, that he refused to vacate the driver's seat to Bonnier during their last scheduled pit stop. Entreaties in at least two languages, and arguments in several others impressed the Belgian not one whit. It was his first chance to grab some glory and he wasn't about to miss any of the thrill.

So he kept the controls to the end, with the Testa Rossa completing 206 laps totaling 1071 miles at an average speed of 89.1 mph, all marks well off the previous year's record. No one could fault Ugolini's management of the Serenissima operation, as they captured the most significant win of the team's career.

The rear-engine Ferraris once again proved to be incapable of running the distance, seemingly a parody of Ferrari long-time reliability attributes. Stamina counts for a great deal in long grinds such as Sebring, and the Testa Rossa certainly had that attribute in abundance.

A SHORT RUN AT
THE NÜRBURGRING

Somewhat surprisingly, Serenissima entered their Sebring-winning TR61 for the 1000 kilometers of Nürburgring, held on May 27, 1962. Surprising is the right word as the car would clearly be at a disadvantage on the twisty course and could not reasonably expect to win. Bringing the Testa Rossa may have been a last-minute decision on the team's part, as they originally intended to enter a Tipo 64 Maserati, which unluckily caught fire during a Modena test session and could not be repaired in time to make the German grind. The TR was entrusted to Carlo Abate and Nino Vaccarella, neither of whom could be characterized as overjoyed at the assignment.

Carlo Abate in the TR61 during the opening laps. He drove very hard, only to crash into a spinning Alfa.

The ever hopeful Georges Gachnang entered his customized Testa Rossa (0742) with Ernst Grog as co-driver, but they were not expected to figure prominently in the end results.

The winners were expected to come from a pack including Gurney in a 2.0-liter Porsche coupe, Hill and Gendebien piloting a 246 SP, a 268 SP for the Rodriguez brothers, and a GTO for Mairesse/Parkes stuffed full of a 4.0-liter Superamerica engine. The dark horse entry was a diminutive 100-bhp Lotus 23 for Jim Clark and Trevor Taylor.

Clark stunned everyone by rocketing into an early lead, leaving Gurney, Mairesse, Hill, Ricardo Rodriguez and Abate panting along behind and losing ground steadily. Rodriguez and Abate began really charging after the uncertainties of the first few laps were overcome, both storming by Hill as they fought out possession of 4th place. The Italian and Mexican waged a ding-dong battle on the 3rd lap with each trying to feint the other into the weeds. On the 4th tour, Abate simultaneously outbraked Rodriguez and forced him to the outside coming into the Karussel to take on undisputed 4th place.

Rodriguez, with fire in his eyes, tore after Abate to get his position back, and overdid it on the downhill Aremberg right-hander, spinning off smartly into the underbrush. Abate continued blasting on, determined now to snatch 3rd from Mairesse. On the next lap he tried to pass an Alfa in the Schwalbenschwanz with the latter picking that most inopportune moment to spin. The Testa Rossa and the Alfa collided and both went off the road, winding up in the woods upside down and rather badly bent. Fortunately, neither driver was seriously injured. It is said that Abate had to be physically restrained from attacking the Alfa pilot, and was forced to expend his rage on the Alfa by virtue of a few kicks at the offending car's posterior.

The Serenissima TR61 was clearly through for the day, leaving only the Gachnang/Grog duo to uphold Testa Rossa honor. They actually finished the grind, though way back in 17th place, and whether that constitutes upholding Testa Rossa honor is debatable.

Georges Gachnang in his modified customer's car, 0742. With co-driver Ernst Grog they finished 17th.

Stuffed inside a stretched TR61 chassis, the 4-liter Superamerica engine developed 360 bhp at 7200 rpm. It is seen here in 3-carburetor version on Le Mans Test Day, April 10.

LE MANS: THE LAST TESTA ROSSA

After studying the 4.0-liter Experimental classification as defined by the CSI, Ferrari decided to field an entry for that group. Due to problems emanating from the walkout late in 1961 by some of his key people, the new car (0808) could not be finished in time for Sebring, and made its maiden appearance at the Le Mans test days held in early April, 1962.

The experimental car consisted primarily of an assemblage of tried and true components rather than breaking any significant new or exciting technical ground. It retained the front engine form of propulsion, the last sports racing Ferrari to employ that configuration. The chassis used was that of the TR61 prototype (0780), double wishbone front and rear suspension, but the rear brakes were now mounted inboard, differing from normal Testa Rossa practice. The engine was a breathed-on version

of the 4.0-liter Superamerica powerplant of 77mm bore by 71mm stroke, displacing 3968 cc and fitted with three Weber carburetors that produced at 360 bhp at 7200 rpm.

As the Superamerica engine was four inches longer than the 3.0-liter Testa Rossa, the chassis had to be stretched sufficiently to accommodate the extra bulk, resulting in a wheelbase of 95.2 inches. The frame tubes were also strengthened slightly to cope with the extra weight and power, though the standard 5-speed rear-mounted indirect Testa Rossa transmission was retained, albeit with somewhat beefier internals.

The body appeared to be very similar to the TR61, though of necessity some four inches longer, and continued the 1961 rear spoiler practice. Ferrari fitted a horizontal stabilizer just behind the cockpit, which was intended to smooth the flow of turbulent air over the tail and enhance the effectiveness of the rear spoiler in holding the car's back end more firmly to the pavement at very high speeds. Though this new experimental projectile was always referred to as a Prototype, either as the 330 TRI/LM or 330 TRI62, rather than a Testa Rossa by the factory, it certainly is an evolutionary derivation of that family.

The First Trial

The van carrying the Ferraris for Le Mans practice on April 9/10, 1962, unfortunately became delayed in a snow storm blocking the Alpine passes and arrived at the Sarthe circuit after the first day's activities had concluded. The following day it rained off and on throughout the practice session, preventing any really rapid motoring by the team pilots who put the car through its paces. Mairesse, Rodriguez and Parkes took turns trundling it around, with Mairesse recording the fastest lap time for the car of 4.10:8, which also turned out to be the day's best clocking by any entrant.

The 330 TRI did not appear for the Targa Florio or Nürburgring, being viewed as rather unsuitable for either venue. Instead, it underwent some further development work and testing in preparation for Le Mans, where it was considered to be the perfect weapon. Satisfied with the basic design of the car, the changes were strictly oriented toward two goals, gaining more power and improving visibility.

The cylinder heads were redesigned to become more Testa Rossa like, being stretched as necessary to fit the larger 4.0-liter block and fitted with bigger valves and more radically profiled camshafts. The three carburetor setup was replaced by six 42-mm Webers, and in this revised form the engine now produced 390 bhp at 7500 rpm.

It always seemed to rain at Le Mans during some stage of the 24 hour grind, and the plexiglass windscreens would become practically opaque as the windshield wipers smeared bugs, oil and grime into a uniform coating. Ferrari had experimented with glass inserts in several of the sports racer windshields, usually covering only the surface area immediately in front of the driver, but for the 330 TRI they constructed a complete glass windshield running across the width of the body and framed within a 2- to 3-inch border of plexiglass.

Pre-Race Speculation

When the 330 TRI made its appearance at Le Mans, most observers felt that the effort resulted in something of an overkill on Ferrari's part. Pre-race speculation concluded that no serious competition would be on hand to challenge Ferrari domination of the race in either the Experimental and Gran Turismo categories. Le Mans in 1962 had done away with the 3.0-liter sports car Prototype classification entirely, simply lumping all the formerly described sports racers into the Experimental class.

The 330 TRI/LM, assigned to Hill and Gendebien, was assumed by everyone as a sure bet to win the grind. The factory backed them up with a 246 SP for the Rodriguez brothers, a 248 SP for Baghetti/Scarfiotti and a GTO-based coupe for Parkes/Bandini. The coupe, seen previously at the Nürburgring a month earlier, used a 4.0-liter Superamerica engine also just rebuilt to the same specifications as the 330 TRI, and competed in the Experimental class, though at a definite disadvantage as it weighed some 250 pounds more than the roadster. Also included in this category were both TR61s, one (0794) belonging to NART that sported a ludicrous rollbar, to be driven by Peter Ryan/Buck Fulp, and the other the Serenissima car (0792) which had been hastily rebuilt after its Nürburgring shunt, and now would be piloted by Bonnier/Gurney.

Other competition in the Experimental class, with some potential of going for an outright win, was restricted to four brand new and previously untried cars. Aston Martin entered a 4.0-liter, 6-cylinder coupe for G. Hill/Ginther, and three examples of a new Maserati, the Tipo 151, were on hand. Two were owned and entered by Briggs Cunningham with pairings of Bill Kimberly/Dick Thompson and Bruce McLaren/Walt Hansgen, and the third example, belonging to Maserati France, was to be driven by Trintignant/Bianchi. The Maseratis, all coupes, were based on 450S components, the engine being reduced in size as necessary to meet the 4.0-liter limitation.

Pre-race practice proved conclusively that the new Maseratis and Aston Martin, while more than the equal of the 330 TRI/LM down the Mulsanne Straight, could not come within 4 seconds of the Ferraris' lap times. Phil Hill served notice early in practice that the 330 TRI was surely in a class by itself when he broke the official course record with a sparkling 3:55.1 clocking in the big roadster. By the end of practice, only three other entrants managed to slip under the 4 minute mark, the quickest of the lot being Parkes in the 4.0-liter GTO at 3:58.6. Dick Thompson managed to wrestle around one of the Maseratis in 3:59.1, while Graham Hill pulled out a 3:59.8 lap in the Aston Martin.

Both TR61s recorded rather disappointing times. The NART car seemed to be in rather ragged mechanical fettle with severe oversteering characteristics, leading to considerable fiddling with spring changes and camber adjustments. Further confusing the issue was an apparent significant difference in Ryan and Fulp driving styles. Ryan preferred an oversteering slider, while Fulp felt more comfortable in a neutral handling machine. The result was a compromise in handling that pleased neither pilot.

The Serenissima TR61 exhibited not only traces of the Nürburgring accident, but appeared very tatty around the edges, as though it was a very tired machine in need of a total rebuild. Neither Bonnier nor Gurney were terribly optimistic about the prospects of finishing the 24 hour grind, and their concerns were oriented more toward resolving high-speed wandering urges, particularly severe when encountering air turbulence in passing other cars, and trying to get at the bottom of the feeling that something was bent or binding in the drivetrain.

Mellow and Bellow

An area of contrast quite noticeable to spectators was the complete difference in the exhaust notes of the TR61s and 330 TRI. The TR61s sounded as Testa Rossas always had; mellow, full throated, with the expected V-12 song at high rpm, and the ripping canvas noise as they revved up under full load. The 330 TRI just bellowed, certainly full throated, but distinctly flatter and deeper sounding. Even at top rpm it retained the deeper exhaust note, as though it were turning over much slower than the 3.0-liter machines. Parkes remarked at one point that when Chiti, Tavoni, et al., left Ferrari the previous fall, they must have taken the "song of the V-12 with them," as since then the organization's cars all seemed to sound differently.

Gendebien drew the first driving stint in the 330 TRI, when the race commenced at 4:00 p.m., and he got off rather hesitantly well back in the pack. The Mulsanne Straight on the first lap witnessed the usual chaotic struggles as the faster cars charged around and through the smaller fry, weaving and darting, pushing and shoving, flashing lights and raising fists, in an effort to get up to the front. Gendebien used the power of the 330 TRI to good advantage in barging by everyone on the long straight to snatch the lead and complete the first lap with a several second advantage over his closest pursuer, Graham Hill in the Aston Martin. The Belgian steadily increased his lead in the opening laps, and excepting occasional moments when the 330 TRI lost the front-runner's position by virtue of routine pit stops, it kept a firm grip on first place all throughout the remainder of the 24 hours.

Gurney driving the Serenissima TR61. He was initially slowed by an oil-covered windscreen, still visible here.

By the end of the first hour, Gendebien, lapping in the 4:05 to 4:07 range, had pulled out more than a 3 minute lead over Graham Hill, but the Belgian could certainly not be accused of flogging the roadster with those lap times. Third through 5th places were occupied by the thunderous Maserati coupes, while Rodriguez held 6th, after an uncharacteristically slow start, though moving up on the Maseratis steadily. Gurney, in 7th place with the Serenissima TR61, had also made a poor start, but was now traveling at a tremendous rate and threatening to overtake Rodriguez.

By The Leg of His Pants

The cause of Gurney's initial slowness was an inability to see where he was going. On the first lap the American came up behind one of the Tipo 151 Maseratis which must have had an overfull oil tank as it threw a great quantity of the stuff onto the Testa Rossa's windscreen. The seat on the TR61 had been lowered to keep the driver's head out of airstream, and consequently Gurney could not see over or through the liberally coated windscreen, and due to an oversight on his part he had forgotten to bring along the customary rag to deal with such a contingency. Gurney's solution was to rip off a pant leg from his new driving suit and wipe up the worst of the oil, getting it all over himself, the steering wheel and shift lever in the process. All this activity took a while to perform, and the time lost dropped him well behind the leaders before he could begin racing seriously.

Ryan was well back in the NART TR61, though trying hard to catch up via some spectacular power sliding which, however, did not pay off in worthwhile lap times. Meanwhile, Parkes had managed to bury the 4.0-liter coupe in the infamous Mulsanne Corner sandbank on the very first lap. He labored mightily and eventually extricated the coupe, but the radiator had sprung a leak from the excursion. Unable to add water before 30 laps had passed, the engine eventually seized in spite of Bandini's efforts to nurse it around for the minimum number of circuits.

After the first driver change, Phil Hill must have felt the need to get some additional distance between the 330 TRI and its immediate pursuers, as he promptly reeled off a series of quick laps, the penultimate of which was a 3:57.6 timing (126.849 mph), a new official race

record. Once he'd shown his stuff, thoroughly discouraging the competition in the process, he settled down to the more prosaic task of competing in a 24-hour endurance grind. Hill rumbled around the course, going just fast enough to retain first place, both he and competitors fully aware that more speed was easily available if anyone should dare to challenge the 330 TRI's primacy.

All the non-Ferrari contenders for the top spot eventually fell out of the running with the never-say-die Rodriguez brothers slowly moving up to 2nd place. The Serenissima TR61 dropped out soon after the first driver change-over while in 4th place, when a rear hub carrier began to disintegrate on Graham Hill, something of a strange malady on a billiard table course such as Le Mans, but quite possibly an uncorrected problem resulting from the Nürburgring accident and unnoticed by the mechanics during repairs.

The endurance contest proceeded throughout the night with Hill and Gendebien stroking the 330 TRI along in first place, displaced from the top spot only for short periods while in the pits for routine stops. The Rodriguez brothers, as was their wont, pounded away in the 246 SP flat out all the time in an exhausting and futile effort to keep in contention with the Testa Rossa. Unlike 1961, Hill and Gendebien would have no trouble in dealing with a Rodriguez threat and could easily cruise along, waiting for the Mexican's machine to eventually break.

Ricardo Takes A Hike

Break it did, and very strangely at that. At about 4:00 a.m., the 246 SP underwent a routine pit stop and when they tried to restart, the starting mechanism became bound up in the flywheel and refused to disengage, emitting terrible noises. The engine was turned off, and the mechanics hammered away at the offending unit for a very long while. They started the engine again, but the problem remained, sounding like someone trying to cut bricks with a meat slicer. The engine was revved up and down to try to clear the problem, all to no avail, and incredibly, Ricardo was installed in the car and sent off. It's a bit difficult to understand the reasoning behind such a move, and suffice to say the car only made about two miles before the

starter and clutch assembly exploded in a shower of sparks, tearing apart the engine. Ricardo got to walk back to the pits.

With the Rodriguez effort finished, the race was for all intents and purposes also finished, even though 12 hours remained to be yet completed. The 330 TRI enjoyed well over a 50-mile lead and had only to cruise around sedately the remaining time to post the third consecutive victory at Le Mans by a Testa Rossa. Cruise around they did, but amazingly, Hill and Gendebien lost no time at all to pursuers, and in fact continued to steadily increase their lead as the sun came up and the morning hours slowly crept by.

At one point during the morning Hill came through Arnage and almost lost control due to a large quantity of oil dumped on the corner by some luckless competitor. As no flag waving marshal was on the scene to warn drivers of the danger, and no work crew seemed to be in evidence spreading lime dust to sop up the oil, Hill assumed that the corner marshal was unaware of the problem. He practically came to a halt and half stood up in the TR, while shouting to the marshals and pointing back to the corner, before storming off again. On his next lap, Hill found the problem still existed, so this time he brought the Testa Rossa to a complete halt in front of the marshal and told him in no uncertain terms to get with it. When a driver can afford to take the time to do such a thing, you can readily assume that his lead must indeed have been imposing.

The NART TR61 had had a rough time of it all night. Ryan's power sliding antics had caused the tires to overheat far beyond their intended limits, resulting in chunking and tread throwing on at least two occasions. The additional pit stops to fit new tires kept the car well back in the field most of the night, never getting much higher than 12th for any considerable period. About 7:00 a.m. Ryan overshot the corner at the end of the Mulsanne Straight trying to get by a slower car, and buried the TR61 in Parkes' private sandbank. In spite of much frantic shoveling, bracing and pushing he was eventually forced to leave the car there, ending a frustrating Le Mans venture for NART, seemingly doomed to failure from the very outset.

330 TRI booms along in the sunshine toward victory... and a barrage of milk cartons.

FUN AT THE BRIDGE

Barrage For The Babysitters

The 330 TRI continued to grind on, but the run to the flag was not entirely peaceful, even with a lack of any serious competition. Hill came in for a scheduled pit stop around 11 a.m. to report that he had begun experiencing clutch slippage in the last few laps. This could not be considered surprising in view of the fact that the 4.0-liter engine put out much more power than the normal Testa Rossa clutch had been designed to accept. Hill and Gendebien discussed the matter at great length with Mauro Forghieri, now installed as Ferrari's chief engineer after Chiti's departure, who decided not to make any changes, but simply have the drivers exercise extreme care in shifting.

Fortunately for Ferrari, probably the two most skilled nurses in racing were piloting the car, both capable of attaining the longest life possible from the deteriorating clutch, which continued to weaken inexorably over the remaining five hours. In addition to the clutch problem the 330 TRI began to sound very rough near the end of the grind as the engine went off song. This was due to running for so many hours at less than the planned rpm, causing

several plugs to foul. As the condition soon stabilized, Dragoni and Forghieri decided to let the car continue on, rather than bring it in for a plug change. In spite of the clutch and plug difficulties the 330 TRI had continued to forge out an ever longer lead, and with more than a 100-mile advantage in hand, there wasn't much sense in panicking about a threat that didn't exist.

Phil Hill took the checkered flag at 4:00 p.m. in a decidedly dirty Testa Rossa and stopped to pick up Gendebien on the way to the winner's circle, the car also acquiring a crust of happy mechanics in the process. The winner's circle was even more chaotic than normal, even for Le Mans. Perhaps some of the spectators were bored with no real racing for some 12 hours. Instead of the usual applause and throwing of roses at the happy winners, they got a barrage of open milk cartons and containers of half-melted ice cream.

It was Hill's third Le Mans victory. Gendebien recorded his fourth win, a new record for any driver, and retired for good just afterward. Ferrari now owned six Sarthe wins, eclipsing both the Jaguar and Bentley marks of five each.

The organizers at the Bridgehampton, New York circuit managed to secure championship status for their Gran Turismo races held on September 15/16. The track, located in the sandy far eastern extremity of Long Island, about 80 miles from New York City, put together a very ambitious program. The Double 400, as the event was titled, consisted of two 400-kilometer races on the willowy 2.8-mile circuit, each covering 248.5 miles. The smaller GT cars ran their 400 kilometers on the 15th, while the larger displacement machines competed on the 16th. Included with the latter group were sports racers over 1000 cc which could run for victory and position, but not gain any points.

The field for the event was somewhat mediocre as Ferrari had long since sewed up the GT championship, and only a few good sports/racers made an appearance. The unquestioned star was Pedro Rodriguez at the controls of the Le Mans-winning 330 TRI. As usual, Luigi Chinetti had purchased the car just after the event, entering it for Pedro in the name of NART. The car had been modified slightly since Le Mans, the chief changes were restricted to removal of the horizontal air stabilizer and addition of a rollbar. Chinetti had decided that the horizontal spoiler actually caused the rear end to lift at high speed, contrary to what Forghieri had deduced. It's interesting to note that Forghieri continued to use that device over the next few years on the 250/330P family, and that whenever any were purchased by Chinetti, he summarily removed them. Nothing like a difference of opinion.

With the horizontal air stabilizer removed and a rollbar added, the 330 TRI and Pedro Rodriguez blew everybody away at the Bridge.

The Bridgehampton race was a foregone conclusion from the very outset of practice, as Pedro promptly broke the course record by clocking 1:49 (93.6 mph), and hit a solid 170 mph plus on the long straightaway. He also managed to scare the flag crews half to death by his shortcuts through the corners, spraying sand and rocks in every direction.

The next fastest qualifier was Alan Connell in his Cooper Monaco, one second behind Pedro. Connell planned to run the race nonstop, whereas Rodriguez would have to refuel at some point because of a much higher gas consumption rate. Therefore, Pedro's race strategy was to get way out in front and build up a big enough cushion to negate the time lost during refueling.

The race turned out to be a runaway for Pedro, as he charged around spectacularly for a few laps to establish an insurmountable lead over Connell and Augie Pabst in a Cunningham Maserati Tipo 151 coupe. The Connell challenge ended for good on the 16th of the 87 laps when his ring gear disintegrated. Rodriguez continued to increase his lead by leaps and bounds, such that by midpoint in the race he had lapped every competitor at least once. Pabst, then in 2nd spot, decided to follow Pedro around after being lapped, but the exertion caused the bit Maserati to spin, and shortly after retire with a holed piston.

Pedro continued pounding around the remaining laps thoroughly enjoying his drive, waving to the crowd and blowing off lesser fry in flat-out blasts down the straightaway. Not much of a race, but a victory is a victory.

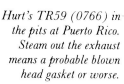

Bob Hurt at the Puerto Rican Grand Prix on November 11.

OTHER RACING

As in 1961, the 1962 non-championship racing season record shows very few Testa Rossa successes. Only a few customer cars continued to compete in fully original Ferrari form, i.e., still running Ferrari engines. Most frequently seen were the ex-team cars, almost all of which had come to the U.S. Some of them, such as Owen Coon's TR58 (0728) now sported a Chevrolet engine, and others were not run for various reasons, examples being the TR59 (0746) special of John Bunch, which he retired after George Constantine's heart attack in May, 1962, or the Von Neumann TR59/60 (0774) which lay around for several years before being sold to Team Rosebud in Victoria, Texas who wanted the engine to install in another car.

Only two customer cars were used much in 1962. Dave Biggs (0720) finished 2nd overall at a Lawrenceville, Illinois Regional on April 8, followed by 8th at the Stuttgart, Arkansas National on May 27, and 14th at the Elkhart Lake National on June 16. Subsequently, the car seems to have been used but little. Wayne Burnett ran a full program of races in 1962 with

0714, starting on May 20 at a Wilmot Hills, Michigan Regional, where he finished 2nd. His record then shows an 11th overall at the Elkhart Lake National on June 16, and another 2nd at a Regional meet on July 29 at Minneapolis, Minnesota, held in the parking lot of the Minneapolis Twins baseball stadium. At the Meadowdale, Illinois National on August 5, he finished 6th, and a week later Burnett scored an outright win at a Regional event run at Lawrenceville, Illinois. The last minor event he participated in during 1962 was back at Wilmot Hills on October 7, where he came home in 3rd place. Burnett also competed in several of the major races in 1962, to be discussed separately, but his and Biggs' customer cars were the last of their kind to be seen actively racing.

In the Pacific Northwest, Dick Hahn of Yakima, Washington had purchased the Nethercutt TR59 (0768) in 1961, selling off his previous Testa Rossa, a TR58 (0704) to Art True of Seattle. Jerry Grant piloted the Hahn machine, and one of their first races was a venture far afield to the Mosport track near Toronto, Can-

ada on June 9, 1962, where Grant finished 9th overall in the 2-heat Players 200 event. The next several races were much less successful, both ending in DNF's. These were on July 29 at Seafair, Washington, when the brakes gave out, and September 30 at Kent, Washington for the Northwest Grand Prix race, when the clutch quit. Later in the year, Hahn sold the TR59 to Bob Lampman of Seattle to make room for his newly acquired TR61 (0794), purchased from Chinetti. Art True ran the TR58 only infrequently in 1962, lending it to Jerry Grant on June 17, where he won a Pro race at Portland, Oregon. Appearances by True include a 4th at Kent, Washington on July 8 and a 5th at the same venue on October 14, but otherwise the car ran rarely.

Probably the most active Testa Rossa competitor in 1962 was Bob Hurt of Bethesda, Maryland, who campaigned his TR59 (0766) at numerous events, both amateur and professional. Included was a 4th at a Formula Libre race held at Bossier City, Louisiana on April 1, 4th at Connellsville, Penna. on August 26, and first in a preliminary race on November 4 at the Autopista Caguas, Puerto Rico track, this being a tuneup event before the Puerto Rican Grand Prix to be run a week later. During the prelim, Hurt's transmission broke and couldn't be repaired on the spot. His solution was to remove it from the chassis, and hold it on his lap while flying from San Juan to New York in hopes that Chinetti could repair it in time for the November 11 race. The repairs were effected, Hurt retraced his path, reinstalled the transmission and finished 11th in the race, but a better finish was prevented by the unit falling ill once again. In the only Nationals race of the year for Hurt, at Meadowdale on August 5, he didn't finish because of a severe case of food poisoning. Most of his other appearances in 1962 were at the major events.

The remaining frequent campaigner during 1962 was George Reed, whose TR59 (0770) got progressively rattier as the season progressed, though appearances can be deceiving as it seemed to always be in excellent mechanical shape. His record included winning the May 20 Wilmot Hills Regional, 8th at Mosport on June 9, a did-not-start at Wilmot on October 7 caused by brake failure during practice, and active participation at a number of the season's major races.

At Mosport in the Canadian Grand Prix, Pedro Rodriguez finished second in the 330 TRI.

—Masten Gregory during the Nassau Trophy Race in the NART 330 TRI.

THE MAJORS

The major Western Hemisphere races followed the customary pattern set in prior years by beginning with the Elkhart Lake 500-mile event in September, followed by a West Coast duo at Riverside and Laguna Seca in October, and capped by the Nassau Speed Week in December.

At Elkhart Lake on September 8, the only Testa Rossa to complete the grind was Burnett's machine in 10th place, co-driven by Luke Stear. George Reed entered his TR59/60 at the event, but with a new engine installed in the car taken from a 4.5-liter 375 MM Ferrari. He expected this to provide much more power than the 3.5-liter 290 MM unit which in turn replaced the original TR59 3.0-liter mill (whew!). Reed's co-driver was intended to be Bob Hurt, who brought along his TR59 as a practice and backup car. The night before the race, Reed became ill and was unable to drive, forcing Hurt to run most of the grind by his lonesome, being spelled for an hour by Alan Ross. At one point in the proceedings a brake caliper broke, but they yanked a unit from Hurt's car to replace it and continued on. He ran in 4th place right up to the very end until the pinion shaft fractured, preventing the hard-fought struggle from being fruitful.

Two weeks later, the 240-mile Canadian Grand Prix for sports cars was staged at Mosport, an event taking on major status for the first time. Pedro Rodriguez finished 2nd in the 330TR, with Hurt 8th in his TR59.

At Riverside, only Hurt attempted to qualify a Ferrari, but failed to make the grid for the race, run on October 14. The following week he tried once again at Laguna Seca, made the grid, but finished last in the two-heat affair.

The American racing season ended at Nassau, with the chief Ferrari threat being Masten Gregory at the controls of the 330 TRI. Normally, Pedro Rodriguez would have been the driver, but he was still in mourning for his brother Ricardo, killed in a Lotus during a practice session before the Mexican Grand Prix on November 1, 1962. Gregory ran in a preliminary event at Nassau on December 7, but retired when the car caught fire from a leaking fuel line. The problem was cured in time for him to run the Nassau Trophy event on December 9, where he finished 4th overall. Also competing and finishing the 252-mile race were George Reed in the 4.5-liter engined TR59/60 and Wayne Burnett with 0714, who came in 10th and 13th respectively.

CHAPTER 8
Twilight and Rebirth

THE 330 TRI, AS EXPECTED, was the last expression of the Testa Rossa family and the final derivation of Ferrari's long line of front-engine sports racing machinery. The CSI declared the sports car as officially obsolete in 1963, with only two basic classes now allowed in championship racing, Gran Turismo and Prototype. The latter class was natural heir to the sports car, but now unencumbered by any requirement or pretense for utilization beyond competition.

Championship racing was not improved one iota by the new rules, and 1963 produced some of the dullest events ever seen from the standpoint of intermake competition. In most races, the winner came from a pack of Ferraris, the only make to fully support both championship series. As in 1962, Ferrari captured both championship titles, and failed miserably in the **Grand Prix game**, where numerous competitors were ready, willing and able to fight for victory. Ferrari actually cut back his firm's direct racing involvement in 1963, usually entering only two cars in Grand Prix events, and a similar number of Prototypes in the long distance races, leaving customer-owned GTOs to gain the Gran Turismo title for his firm on their own volition.

Exit Phil Hill

Phil Hill and Ferrari parted company late in 1962, the former World Champion having lasted as a works driver for six years, perhaps the longest ever in the firm's history. His departure was mostly a case of mutual unhappiness; Ferrari felt Hill had become too cautious and lost the aggressiveness needed to win, while the American was convinced that Dragoni was doing everything possible to make him look bad and, additionally, the Grand Prix cars were not competitive. As the time came due for negotiating the 1963 contract, neither Ferrari nor Hill would take the initiative and approach the other to get discussions underway.

Ferrari announced in November 1962 that his 1963 Grand Prix driving team would consist of Willy Mairesse and the ex-world motorcycle champion, John Surtees, with Mike Parkes handling the test driving chores and taking the third car on those occasions when an additional entry would be fielded. They would be joined in the long distance Prototype races by Nino Vaccarella, Lodovico Scarfiotti and Lorenzo Bandini. During the announcement, Ferrari stated that Hill evidently wanted to retire as he had not shown any interest in initiating discussions for a 1963 contract. Hill, well aware and men-tally prepared for what had happened, waited several months before signing with ATS to drive their Grand Prix cars, and piloted Prototypes in the endurance races for a number of manufacturers in 1963.

Ferrari had originally intended to include Ricardo Rodriguez as part of his team, but the youngster, still not even 21 years old, was killed driving a Lotus in practice for the Mexican Grand Prix on November 1, 1962.

The 330 TRI (0808) prepared by NART and the Serenissima TR61 (0792) were entered in a number of the 1963 championship races, and about the only members of the once dominating Testa Rossa family to see much action during the year. Most of the others had faded away into retirement by then as a period of neglect and obscurity enveloped them. It seems as though hardly anything had less value in those days than an obsolete and no longer competitive front-engine racing car. Still, the two Testa Rossas provided some very exciting and competitive racing in 1963 against the newer machinery, as a review of their activities will show.

*Smiling World Champion
Graham Hill doesn't know
what lies in store for
him at Sebring.*

STRUGGLE AT SEBRING

At the 1963 edition of Sebring, staged on March 23, only one lonesome Testa Rossa was on hand, the 4.0-liter 330 TRI, entered by NART for Pedro Rodriguez and Graham Hill, the latter replacing Phil Hill in 1962 as the Grand Prix driving champion. In spite of the expected severe competition from the Ferrari factory-entered new rear-engine 3.0-liter 250 P prototypes, the Testa Rossa was reckoned by many race pundits to be the co-favorite for overall Sebring laurels. It had proven to be extremely durable and very strong, and would be running on a course well-suited to its characteristics. The 330 TRI was certainly the sentimental favorite at Sebring in 1963 among the spectators, as to them it represented the last remaining link to the good old days. Unfortunately, and in spite of an all out effort by the NART team, the Rodriguez Sebring gremlin was once more lurking in the nighttime hours to foil their hopes for victory.

During practice the 330 TRI proved to be the equal of the 250 P prototypes entered for Surtees/Scarfiotti and Mairesse/Vaccarella, all three recording times in the 3:10 range, some two seconds faster than Pedro's record 1962 race clocking of 3:12.4. No one else was even close to their times.

Rumpled rear fender is only sign of Rodriguez's earlier incident as Hill takes over after first pit stop.

At the 10:00 a.m. race start, Rodriguez got off the mark very well and snatched the lead away from Phil Hill, now at the controls of a Shelby Cobra, on the 2nd lap. Thus began an epic effort that would witness the big roadster holding onto first place for the next nine hours, while the car gradually deteriorated around the intrepid drivers. Pedro managed an off-course excursion in the first hour while attempting to dodge a spinning smaller competitor, with the Testa Rossa seemingly not adversely affected, and he continued tearing around the remainder of his first driving stint to build up more than a lap lead on the closest competitor. When Rodriguez came in for refueling and to turn over the driving chores to Graham Hill, he reported that the tachometer had quit functioning, but that otherwise the TR was behaving perfectly.

Shortly after Hill took to the course the right side exhaust manifold began to split, possibly resulting from the earlier Rodriguez incident, and funneling the deadly gases directly into the cockpit. The NART mechanics could not resolve the problem, forcing the drivers to fight off drowsiness and asphyxiation as best they could throughout the balance of the grind. In spite of this severe handicap, Rodriguez and Hill succeeded in steadily increasing their lead over the pursuing 250 Ps throughout the afternoon hours, and at one point enjoyed almost a 3-lap advantage.

The Rodriguez Gremlin Strikes

Problems continually erupted with the 330 TRI throughout the daytime hours, including a tire blowout during Pedro's second

turn at the wheel. Later, the engine began to seriously overheat and electrical failures spasmodically occurred, all causing additional grief for the thoroughly harassed NART mechanics. However, these problems were but minor nits compared to the disaster yet to come during the nighttime segment of the race.

As darkness enveloped the circuit, the Testa Rossa still clung to first place with a gradually decreasing but sufficient lead to carry on to victory if the race pattern did not change drastically to the benefit of the pursuing 250 Ps. Practically as soon as the lights had to be turned on the waiting Rodriguez spook leaped out to strike the 330 TRI with a vengeance as everything seemingly went wrong almost at once. First, it burned out a headlight, then, a bit later, the generator went kaput, accompanied by the

A nighttime pit stop and signs of the Rodriguez gremlin steams from the engine compartment of the overheating 330 TRI.

engine going sour almost simultaneously, and making like Old Faithful at every pit stop.
A 2-lap halt to effect a modicum of repairs, coupled with a slightly later stop to wire up a dragging exhaust pipe and dump more water in the radiator finally cost Rodriguez and Hill the lead.

The two drivers desperately fought on to regain the lead as the engine continued to weaken and lose power. The blown head gasket that caused the overheating problem was now joined by failing oil pressure as the gauge dropped to zero every time a driver hit the brakes hard. Pedro, behind the wheel at this stage, could perform no magic to hold his position as the Surtees/Scarfiotti 250 P pulled out a steadily longer lead, and the 3rd place Mairesse/Vaccarella 250 P gradually closed in on him.

Driving By Braille

Hill took over from an almost totally numb Rodriguez for the final push to the finish, and kept their 2nd place into the 12th hour, when the generator failed completely. He struggled on as the battery quickly drained down to a point where the lights shone but feebly, certainly not enough to see with and making it impossible for him to prevent Mairesse from getting by into 2nd place. Hill continued running, though technically the Testa Rossa should have been disqualified, but the stewards, possibly out of compassion for the disaster-plagued team, allowed him to continue to the 10:00 p.m. finish. Lights or not, a very determined Hill charged around the course trying to regain 2nd, attempting to stay in front of faster machinery by using their beams, or clinging to their posteriors, if passed. All this in the dark at speeds up to 160 mph!

At one point near the finish, Hill found himself entering the Esses all alone in the pitch black at 100 mph plus and suddenly felt the road becoming exceedingly bumpy. Realizing he'd strayed off the course, and without a clue where he was, Graham prudently slammed on the brakes and came to a complete halt enveloped in darkness. He engaged reverse and backed up until once again reaching smooth pavement, then waited until another competitor came past and fell in behind him. Notwithstanding the delay caused by this bizarre off-course excursion (it's not often one gets lost on a race track), Hill managed to hold on to 3rd position till the end, capping a heroic struggle over the entire 12-hour grind by both drivers.

Umberto Maglioli cleans the windscreen while Carlo Abate puts in his own seat cushion during a pit stop for the Serenissima TR61.

Serenissima At The Nürburgring

Count Volpi had rebult his TR61 (0792) between the 1962 and 1963 racing seasons and entered it for the Nürburgring 100-kilometer event held on May 19, 1963. The formal entrant was actually Juan-Manual Bordeu, a onetime protege of Fangio, and the drivers were Carlo Abate and Umberto Maglioli.

The TR61 was not reckoned to have much of a chance against a trio of SEFAC-entered 250 P roadsters, though the odds were improved slightly when Vaccarella wrote one off for all intents and purposes in a crash just past the Flugplatz in practice. About the only competition expected to worry Ferrari even a tiny bit were a pair of 2.0-liter flat-8 Porsches fresh from

a heartening Targa Florio victory, but not within 12 seconds of the 250 P practice times at the 'Ring.

The TR61 got off rather hesitantly at the race start, eventually settling into 7th place. It was troubled thoughout the 621-mile run by grabbing brakes and abrupt understeering changing to oversteering on the slower turns, that required both Abate and Maglioli to exercise extreme caution and mind their manners. Nonetheless, the Testa Rossa marched up steadily in the standings as both Porsches were eliminated, one courtesy of a broken halfshaft while the other, driven by Phil Hill and leading the contest near the midpoint of the proceedings, took

an off-course excursion and became stuck in a ditch. Also coming to grief was Mike Parkes, who demolished one of the 250 Ps in an earlier incident. By the end of the race mechanical failures and accidents had eliminated almost all of the front-runners, but not quite enough to allow the Testa Rossa to clinch a victory. Abate and Maglioli finished in 3rd place, far behind the winners, Mairesse and Surtees, in the sole surviving 250 P, but quite close to the 2nd place pair, Noblet/Guichet, in a GTO which had slipped by the erratically handling TR61 in the closing stages of the race.

Maglioli **(above)** *and Abate* **(below)** *brought the re-bodied Serenissima TR61 home third overall at Nurburgring.*

The Curtain Comes Down At Le Mans

The 31st edition of the 24 Heures du Mans took place on June 15/16, 1963, with the NART team bringing the 330 TRI back to the scene of its previous year's triumph. Completely rebuilt after Sebring and now sporting wider tires, it looked to be very competitive at Le Mans once again. Pedro Rodriguez was joined by Roger Penske as a co-driver for the grind and NART hopes for victory were high. Pedro confirmed the Testa Rossa's potential by posting a 3:50.9 practice lap, eclipsing the old course record by a solid 4 seconds. Certainly the wider tires were a major factor in this somewhat surprising performance, but additionally it appears that Rodriguez had acquired some smoother and much faster driving skills and that the NART mechanics had put the 330 TRI into really first-class condition.

Competition, all clocking practice times within a few seconds of Rodriguez's best, included the factory Ferrari 3.0-liter 250 P roadsters driven by Mairesse/Surtees and Scarfiotti/Bandini, the 4.0-liter Aston Martin of Phil Hill/Bruce McLaren and the 5.0-liter Maserati of Andre Simon/Lucky Casner, both of the latter cars in coupe form. The stage was set for an exciting race, with the NART forces quietly confident they had the right package to pull out the victory.

The 4:00 p.m. race start witnessed the usual confusion till the leading order became established. After a few laps it was clarified, with Simon out front in the thunderous Maserati, closely shadowed by Rodriguez in the always intimidating 330 TRI. Both were charging along at under-4-minute laps, followed at a discreet distance by the 250 Ps. The strategies of the leading quartet were apparent almost from the outset. The Maserati had superior acceleration and top speed, and simply couldn't be passed unless Simon made a mistake or something broke, which the hounding Rodriguez hoped to force. The 250 P strategy was simply to hang in reasonably close and wait for both of the leaders to fall out.

For the Ferrari forces, the hoped-for Maserati failure took place shortly after the initial round of pit stops when Casner exited with rear-end problems. What happened subsequently was not exactly what NART had intended to be the result. Penske, relieving Rodriguez at the controls, now held the lead, but by virtue of more conservative driving techniques quickly lost first place to the menacing 250 P contingent. They consistently lapped 2 to 4 seconds quicker than Penske could manage, and he seemed unable to narrow the gap in spite of frantic "GO" signals from the NART pit. The Rodriguez family was none too happy with Penske's performance, nor the pattern established as the day wore into evening. Rodriguez would charge around forcefully to regain some of the lost time, and Penske would take over and lose what had been gained,

plus more. The leading 250 Ps steadily increased their lead, though the Testa Rossa held a very secure 3rd place.

The TRI's race ended with a bang shortly after midnight, and for once a Rodriguez wasn't on board when it happened. Penske had the terrifying experience of blowing up the engine at full throttle between the Mulsanne and Indianapolis corners. Completely blinded by the smoke and covered with oil, he shot off the road into a clump of trees. The poor machine was rather badly treated by the trees but a very lucky Penske escaped almost totally unscathed.

Winding Down

Le Mans in 1963 was the last major international championship event to witness a Testa Rossa in contention for overall honors. Afterward, Chinetti sent the very wounded 330 TR to Modena for a thorough mechanical rebuild and re-bodying. Fantuzzi was commissioned to reconstruct it as a streetable coupe and the engine, reduced to rubbish by the explosion, was replaced by a more streetable 3.0-liter based unit. Upon completion, the car was shipped to the U.S. and passed into honored retirement from the racing wars as the last of the breed.

Count Volpi continued to occasionally campaign his TR61 in 1963 races, carefully picking events where the competition wouldn't be overly severe. Examples of its use include the sports car race held at Reims, France, on June 30, 1963, as

Roger Penske shared the NART 330 TRI with Pedro Rodriguez, but not too well as far as Rodriguez was concerned.

The Serenissima TR61 at Reims.

a curtain raiser before the French Grand Prix. This event, sort of a run-what-you-brung affair was roughly equivalent to the normal American minor race where all manner of strange vehicles would come to the starting line. Competition included Jo Schlesser in a Le Mans 4.0-liter Aston Martin coupe, Andre Simon in the 5.0-liter Tipo 151 Maserati coupe, Mike Parkes in a Ferrari hot rod composed of a 4.0-liter engine crammed into a 250 P, Roy Salvadori with a Cooper Monaco, Lucky Casner in his rebodied ex-1961 Nürburgring-winning Maserati Tipo 61, and assorted other luminaries, including Carlo Abate in the Serenissima machine.

The race was something of a joke as Parkes wrecked his clutch at the start, Schlesser led until he overrevved and dropped a valve, Simon swatted a bank with the Maserati, Salvadori took the lead and blew up and Casner's mount got sick. Abate just took it easy as everyone fell to pieces, and romped home to an easy victory.

A week later, on July 7, Volpi entered his Testa Rossa for Lorenzo Bandini at a 3-Hour Race held on the Charade circuit at Auvergne, France, near Clermont-Ferrand. Bandini, with no competition capable of contesting the issue, breezed to a very casual victory.

In early August, Volpi entered the TR61 at Brands Hatch for the Bank Holiday Meeting, which combined Prototype, Sports and GT machines in one race. Carlo Abate was at the controls but the venture ended in failure when a

wire wheel collapsed. After a few further outings, Volpi retired the Testa Rossa from further active competition, retaining it for occasional personal road usage.

U.S. Appearances Few

In the U.S., Testa Rossa activity was also winding down. Late in 1962, Dick Hahn of Yakima, Washington, sold off his ex-Nethercutt TR59 (0768), purchased Chinetti's TR61 (0794), and engaged Stan Burnett to handle the driving chores. Among his 1963 appearances were a 2nd at Westwood, British Columbia, Canada, on April 21, and on May 4 at the same track he finished the two heats of the 108-mile Players Pacific Race 6th and 5th, respectively. Later in the year, on September 28, Burnett finished 3rd overall in the Northwest Grand Prix, a 2-heat affair totaling 202 miles at the Kent, Washington, course.

Art True made a few appearances with 0704 during the year, his best showing probably being 6th overall and 1st in class at Kent, Washington, on June 2.

About the only other Testa Rossa to appear in 1963 American events was the customer car (0714) of Wayne Burnett. In late 1962 or early 1963, the engine from George Reed's TR59 (0770) was installed in Burnett's machine to provide extra oomph. Reed's car shortly thereafter acquired a Ford stock car motor, but race participation proved it to be a rather unwieldy

combination. Burnett finished 8th overall and first in class with 0714 at the Elkhart Lake June Sprints, an SCCA National held on June 23, and came back to the same venue to contest the annual 500-mile grind on September 8, and finished 12th overall, partnered by Luke Stear. Burnett occasionally would appear at minor events such as Wilmot Hills, Michigan on July 21, 1963, where he finished 7th overall and 1st in class, and at Meadowdale, Wisconsin, on September 22, coming in 2nd overall. A casual perusal of the racing activities of this particular car seems to indicate that it enjoyed a remarkably long competition life, and may hold the honor of being the most-raced Ferrari ever.

By late 1963, a race appearance of a Testa Rossa or any Ferrari with a Ferrari engine still installed for that matter, was a real novelty in American racing. Compared to the Lotus 23 and 19, Cooper Monaco and other assorted rear-engined machinery, they were truly dinosaurs from another age on the verge of extinction. Wide tires, aerodynamic devices, sophisticated chassis construction, suspension tuning and increasingly scientific approaches to make racing cars to ever faster, made the rather simplistic Testa Rossa appear ever more primitive. The competition life of the Testa Rossa was over.

Bev Spencer's car.

LIMBO & REBIRTH

Gone but not entirely forgotten is probably the most accurate description of what happened to the Testa Rossas during the mid-sixties. At that time, the racing fraternity considered them to be nothing more than old-fashioned, worn out and totally uncompetitive machines of little or no value. For a time during that period complete, running examples had difficulty fetching as much as $2,000, and cases are known where some of the rougher machines sold for less than $500.

As racing became increasingly scientific and ever more remote from the principles and practices of the front-engine days, it created a feeling in some people that the olden times were somehow more interesting and enjoyable. It was this breed of romantic, frustrated, driver/enthusiast who picked up Testa Rossas as the frequently battered or butchered cars came on the market, in many cases for the proverbial song. At the time it was definitely grounds for divorce. There was almost nothing a Testa Rossa could really be used for, excepting ice-cream runs on the street, and even for that many were engineless or had acquired American drivetrain components. A number were rebodied as coupes, or otherwise modified out of character such that they were almost unrecognizable as having once been Testa Rossas. Most just languished, awaiting the day when their worthiness would once again be recognized and appreciated.

No matter what their monetary value during the mid-sixties implied, the Testa Rossas were historically significant machines and they possessed all the necessary collectible attributes: the last truly successful front-engine sports racing cars, mechanically interesting, body styling pleasing to the eye, and one of the key machines in the promotion of the ever-growing Ferrari legend.

Keeping up with the latest trends in racing began to bore many enthusiasts during the mid-sixties. The rear-engine machines came into absolute dominance, with aesthetically artful body shapes totally replaced by angularity, wings and other ugly but no doubt effective aerodynamic appendages. The changes made the cars go faster, but increased complexity to a point where many lost interest. They often turned to playing with the old front-engine racing cars, and were joined by a small but growing cadre of enthusiasts who also enjoyed tinkering with this type of machinery. Gradually, and almost imperceptibly, interest picked up in collecting and preserving the front-engine racing heritage with the attraction to Ferraris an important factor in the fledgling movement.

Vintage Racing Brings Changes

Several Ferrari and other vintage car clubs were started that promoted the collecting, restoring and low-key track usage of old racing machines, providing even more incentive for acquiring Testa Rossas. Additionally, several books came forth in the late sixties that were an important catalyst in further enhancing the historical significance of the cars and did much to ballyhoo the Ferrari legend and mystique, all vital ingredients in attracting new converts to "vintage" racing machines. A few very astute dealers took advantage of the profit potential by trading in old racing cars, and their promotion of the long-range investment possibilities of the breed to enthusiasts started a rise in prices that attracted an ever widening circle of interest. The Testa Rossa model, as the last representative of the Ferrari front-engine racing line, was soon to be become one of the most sought-after cars, and as the supply was limited, prices began to rise, slowly at first and then by leaps and bounds.

By 1970, the going figure for complete, running examples had risen into the $4,000 to $5,000 range, quite a change from the $2,000 or less of only a few years before. Prices continued to move up in 1971 to $7,500 or thereabouts, doubled in 1972 to $15,000 and just kept right on climbing. The rise in value encouraged collectors to ferret out and restore even the most badly mutilated Testa Rossas. A large percentage are now restored to as-good-as or better-than-new condition. For some of the rougher examples the restoration and resurrection process continues apace, but within a few years just about all the survivors will have been put back into a more or less original configuration.

The Price of Fame

Since 1972, the collectible value of the V-12 Testa Rossa family members has risen to astounding levels and evidences no sign of not continuing upward. Prices of $50,000 to $75,000 are now spoken of as being eminently reasonable for restored to original condition examples. Where the market value will rise to in the future is an open question, but the tremendously inflated prices are tending to adversely affect their usage. In the mid-sixties a Testa Rossa had such little value monetarily that it often had rather casual and sometimes hard use. An accident or mechanical misfortune was not of particular concern due to its modest worth and the ease of obtaining cheap spare parts. Parts can be a problem these days as most of the engines, transmissions, etc., formerly lying about have been snapped up and installed in Testa Rossas missing those components. Hence, parts are scarce, and their ready availability can no longer be taken for granted. A further inhibitor is the reluctance of many current Testa Rossa owners to race their cars very hard or extensively; being worried about what might happen to the value of their rolling bank vaults if involved in an incident.

There were only a limited number of Testa Rossas originally built, and most enthusiasts will probably never be able to own one. Because so few are being used these days, enthusiasts only rarely get the opportunity to see one at close range or ripping around a race track, where they rightfully belong. Not a very desirable situation by any means, and likely caused almost entirely by the astronomical rise in their collectible value. The ground swell of interest in collecting vintage racing cars tends to produce somewhat mixed feelings among observers. It's a pleasure to see so many of the Testa Rossas restored to their original glory, but discouraging that so few see action on the track. After all is said and done, they were built to race, and the measure of their goodness can only be evaluated by going fast.

It's a shame more don't see active use, as they are a very forgiving machine to drive, solid as a block of granite, easy for almost any driver to quickly come to terms with, and a definite confidence builder. Additionally, they are powerful but tractable, melodious sounding, feature predictable handling, and can be quite easily maintained. Coupled with the attributes of being a great racing machine and winner of the world championship three out of four years, the Testa Rossa has to be one of the most collectible and desirable competition cars ever built.

DRIVER UPDATE

Even though the subsequent activities of a number of the team Testa Rossa drivers have been noted within the story, it is interesting to study what has happened to them as a group since those halcyon days. More than half are dead, though it must be noted that no team pilot ever suffered so much as a serious injury in a Testa Rossa. The only driver known to have died from an accident in a Testa Rossa was Erik Bauer, who succumbed to his injuries at the Nürburgring in 1958. The structural strength of the Testa Rossa probably had much to do with this fine record, notwithstanding the non-existence of driver protection features taken for granted today, such as roll cages, fuel cells, on-board fire extinguishing systems, etc. In the championship races of the 1958-1961 period, factory-entered Testa Rossas started 48 times and only five were unable to finish due directly to accidents.

The Lost Ones

A number of the Testa Rossa team members were killed within the time span of their active use. As mentioned during the scenario, Luigi Musso and Peter Collins died in the summer of 1958 from accidents while driving Ferrari Grand Prix cars. Also killed in a Ferrari Grand Prix mishap was Wolfgang Von Trips, his disaster coming at the 1961 Italian Grand Prix held at Monza. Mike Hawthorn died in an English road crash in January, 1959, after his retirement from racing, while Jean Behra was fatally injured in a Porsche at Avus in August of the same year, after being fired by Ferrari. Lastly, Ricardo Rodriguez perished after crashing a Lotus in practice for the Mexican Grand Prix in November, 1962, just before his 21st birthday.

His brother, Pedro, also came to a violent end in a racing car, though much later. He continued to race after Ricardo's death, but gradually over the next few years began tapering off as he seemed to find it more difficult to get truly competitive machinery. Additionally, he found it necessary to concentrate on his Mexican commercial activities that included several automobile dealerships, as well as involvement with his father in the family construction business. In 1967, evidently growing restless, Pedro made a spectacular re-debut in the motor racing world by virtue of winning the South African Grand Prix at the controls of a Maserati-engined Cooper. He raced more or less regularly thereafter in a wide range of cars, scoring a number of successes, the most significant being a long elusive Le Mans victory. This came in 1968, when he and Lucien Bianchi won with a Ford GT40. The Rodriguez driving style never changed much over the years. He would go just as fast as he could, no matter what the track or weather conditions dictated. He always remained quiet and calm, was never fussy or complained, and the worse the conditions the more likely he was to be at the front. In many respects, Pedro could be characterized as being utterly at peace with himself, doing exactly what he liked to do, and furthermore, enjoying every moment to the fullest. The end for Pedro came on July 11, 1971, at the Norisring in Germany during a minor Interserie (Group 7) race, when he was killed in a 512M Ferrari. Typically for him, he was leading the race. At the time, he was 3rd in the 1971 Grand Prix point standings and appeared to be well on the way to a very successful year. He was only 31 years old.

Another of the drivers now gone, though not caused by a racing accident, is Willy Mairesse. Wild Willy continued on with Ferrari in 1963 but serious crashes were almost a constant occurrence, some his fault and some not. He had a horrendous crackup in the German Grand Prix at the Nürburgring later the same year, which resulted in extensive injuries and a lengthy recovery period. His Grand Prix driving career ended for good after that incident, as did his Ferrari employment when the Commendatore refused to renew his contract after Mairesse's recovery. After healing, he returned to sports and prototype racing in a variety of machines and actually did quite well for several years. The Nürburgring accident must have somehow affected his driving style, which became much smoother and probably faster than previously. After several years of behaving himself, he got into another major accident on the first lap at Le Mans in 1968 when he forgot to fully close the door on his GT40 at the start and it opened while at top speed on the Mulsanne Straight. Afterward Mairesse could no longer get good drives and, as he lived only for racing and literally knew nothing else, he gradually sank into despair. Finally, in the awful realization that his racing career was irrevocably over, he committed suicide at Ostend, Belgium, in September, 1969.

The Survivors

More happily, all of the other drivers, now retired from racing, are in more pleasant situations.

Phil Hill's move to ATS was completely unrewarding. He stuck with their floundering Grand Prix program for several years before leaving the firm and went on to drive for a number of other concerns. Later, he hooked up with Jim Hall on the Chaparral project, the highlight of the association being a splendid victory at the Nürburgring in 1966. By that stage, the rigors of racing had begun to pall on Hill and he finally quit completely in 1967, returning to Santa Monica, California, where he concentrated initially on restoring some of his antique and classic cars. Currently he is involved in a car restoration business and pursues many other activities, including articles in *Road & Track* magazine on tests of old racing cars. Hill is still as intense and voluble as ever and can probably articulate his racing experiences more vividly than any other racing driver alive.

Ferrari in late 1959, came back to drive Coopers in several Grand Prix races in the second half of 1960. He switched to BRM in 1961, but retired for good at the end of that year after a mediocre season. Since that time he has concentrated on operating a thriving automotive dealership south of London.

Allison took a long time to recover from his practice crash at Monaco in 1960, not returning to racing until 1961 with the Grand Prix team of UDT Laystall. He was injured once again at Spa, Belgium, during practice in a Lotus before the 1961 Belgian Grand Prix, and quit completely afterward.

The remaining driver, Giancarlo Baghetti, left Ferrari at the end of 1962, feeling that he was being overshadowed by the new favorite, Lorenzo Bandini. He moved to ATS and after an unrewarding year there signed on for 1964 with Centro Sud to pilot one of their BRMs, but once again only failures seemed to occur. Nothing really seemed to go right for Baghetti afterward, as cars just seemed to consistently fall apart under him. His racing career gradually tapered off as good rides became more difficult to get, and he finally gave in to the inevitable by retiring completely in late 1968. In spite of the obviously very painful decline in his racing fortunes, the quiet and uncomplaining Milanese always kept his own counsel and was never less than a perfect gentleman.

Generalizations are always dangerous, but an analysis of the careers of the Testa Rossa team drivers seems to indicate that the most rewarding years for the vast majority in sports car competition came in that period. With the exception of Dan Gurney and an occasional triumph by the others, very few consistent successes can be found in their records after the Testa Rossa days. It appears that Ferrari had the right combination to win in long distance sports car racing, with the drivers an integral part of the package. In the 1957-62 period, Ferrari's overall strategizing, driver selection and baiting tactics, coupled with Chiti engineering and Tavoni team management, created a single-minded and totally dedicated effort to winning that produced victories consistently. Whatever the case, it was a unique situation where all the ingredients for success were present in the required quantity and a set of characteristics very few of the drivers were ever to subsequently enjoy.

Gurney and Ginther

Dan Gurney had a long and varied racing career before finally retiring as an active competitor at the conclusion of the 1970 season. He won in just about every class of racing, including Sports, Grand Prix, stock cars and on Indianapolis-type circuits. Gurney finished in 2nd place behind Hill in the 1961 Grand Prix drivers' title stakes and over the years accumulated more points in that form of racing than any other American driver. He founded All-American Racers in partnership with Carroll Shelby in 1964, building Eagle Grand Prix cars, and took over sole control in 1967, expanding operations to include F5000 and Indianapolis-type machines. In 1967, Gurney won the Belgian Grand Prix at the wheel of an Eagle, the first American car and driver combination to win a Formula One event in more than 40 years. Since 1970 he has concentrated on his constructor activities, now primarily focused on Indianapolis-type machinery, and is based in Costa Mesa, California, south of Los Angeles.

The last of the American trio, Richie Ginther, stayed with BRM through 1964, compiling a very successful record. In 1963 he tied for 2nd in the Grand Prix drivers' title, compiling a record that may never be equaled, at least in one respect, as that year he finished every event started. Ginther switched to Honda in 1965 and with them won his only Grand Prix, the Mexican race, in the same year. The 3.0-liter Formula that began in 1966 seemed to be more than he was willing to cope with, and he retired from active racing. Later, Ginther moved back to Southern California and has become something of a wandering free spirit in recent years.

Brooks, Allison and Baghetti

Several of the team drivers quit during the Testa Rossa period, including Tony Brooks and Cliff Allison. Brooks, after his departure from

STILL THE LEADER

Enzo Ferrari continues to this day to be the dominant force at his namesake firm, though outright ownership of the company passed to FIAT in 1969 on a deal that left the Commendatore in total control of all racing activities. He still personally directs the competition program on a full-time basis, though it is now restricted to Grand Prix racing only, as all other sports car or prototype activity was abandoned in the early seventies. As of this writing, Ferrari is 80 years old, apparently in full command of his mental faculties, and as dedicated as ever to achieving victory, though he is reported to be suffering from deteriorating health which is said to inhibit his activities to some extent.

His goals for himself, and the policies and procedures adopted so many years ago to bring them to fruition, appear to have remained very consistent over time. Ferrari racing cars are even today stronger and heavier than any other competitors, produce more power and seem to stay together longer. One area of change is more frequent adoption of state of the art techniques, almost a necessity to stay abreast or ahead of the always severe Grand Prix competition. In almost every other way, Enzo Ferrari remains a constant and never changing force in the motor racing world. He still treats subordinates, customers, suppliers and drivers in the same imperious manner, engendering almost invariably a mixture of awe and fear that they might accidentally do something to arouse his displeasure in any way. Within his own company he seems to be revered as a god, with every word and nuance emanating from him being treated as a command.

While Ferrari may not have succeeded in reaching every goal he set for himself, he certainly has achieved an aura of immortality, and is already a living legend. No one else in automotive history has spent as long, or dedicated himself so totally to racing, or gained anywhere near his vast array of triumphs. In this respect, his record may never be eclipsed.

Unfortunately, he has no heir to carry on his tradition. Current Ferrari automobiles produced under the auspices of FIAT are already beginning to lose the unique character his involvement has always imbued them with, and

Enzo Ferrari with his 1979 World Champion Formula 1 driver Jody Scheckter.

even now, the street cars are mere vestiges of their former distinctiveness, very much emasculated and featuring an almost insipid personality. During the Testa Rossa days his street cars displayed a close and clearly recognizable kinship to their racing brethren, but no longer is there even the remotest relationship.

Ferrari stature in the world at large is primarily based on the long term success of the competition machinery. It is the respect for these machines and the man behind them, reinforced

by the outstanding results gained over the years that accounts for the present and continually growing Ferrari mystique. This has engendered the growth of an enormous body of admirers thoroughly convinced the old man is the living embodiment of all that racing is about.

Whatever the case, we can only hope he will continue to field his Prancing Horse machines for years to come, as they can always be counted on to be competitive, interesting and singularly different.

Drawing by Clarence O. LaTourette, foremost U.S. cutaway
artist of the late fifties and early sixties.

ferrari testa rossa V-12

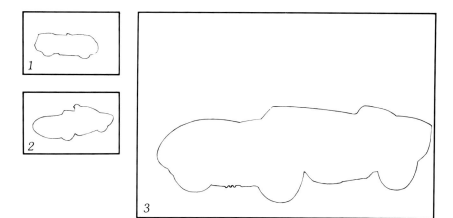

1 and 3.   A resplendent Testa Rossa, chassis no. 0710, the first
customer car with left hand drive, live axle, pontoon fenders and
inside door hinges. Unique to all TR's, it has a detachable nose
and angled cooling fins on the front brake drums.
Photos by J.E. Finn.

2.   Dan Gurney in TR 59 number 0774 at Le Mans in 1959. Car
led the race, and with Behra driving set new 3.0-liter lap record, but
retired soon after midnight with engine failure from over-heating.
Photo by Jesse Alexander.

APPENDIX I
Testa Rossa Specifications

Each of the Testa Rossa variants has been previously described within the pertinent chapter in terms of their basic body, chassis, and mechanical characteristics. In addition to these general descriptors there are the much more detailed specifications pertaining to all the mechanical components that made up each car. In the case of Ferrari this information is contained in a set of documents known as Assembly Sheets.

When a Testa Rossa was sold by Ferrari, either by being constructed directly to a customer order, or as a rebuilt ex-team car, a set of Assembly Sheets were created that listed all the components fitted. When the car was completed, it and the pertinent Assembly Sheets were transferred from the racing department to the customer sales group. In the case of ex-team machines, the Assembly Sheets detail the configuration at the time of sale. The team cars may have been rebuilt several times before actual sale, but no significant paperwork regarding their original state or points in between seems to have been created, or if created, passed on to the customer sales department.

Following are several examples of Testa Rossa Assembly Sheets which record the actual component makeup on the particular chassis at the time of sale to a customer. These examples include the first prototype (0666), the first customer's car (0710), a 1958 TR58 (0728), a TR59 (0766), and the 330TR/LM (0808).

THE FIRST PROTOTYPE: CHASSIS NO. 0666

Telaio tipo / Chassis type	525	matricola / serial No. 0666
Motore tipo / Engine type	128/LM	matricola / serial No. 0666
Cambio tipo / Gearbox type	525/B	matricola / serial No. 6
Ponte tipo / Rear axle type	525	matricola / serial No. 6/TRB
Collaudo il / Tested on		Consegnato il / Delivered on
CLIENTE / CLIENT	Sig. LUIGI CHINETTI	

Autoleleio Tipo / Chessy type **525** **Motore tipo** / Engine type **128/LM/Ges.** **Matricola N.** / Serial No. **0666/**

FOGLIO MONTAGGIO MOTORE
ENGINE ASSEMBLING FORM

Basamenti / Crankcase **128/LM/10612** **Coppa olio** / Sump **128/C/11987** **Filtri** / Filters

Albero motore / Crankshaft **128/C/12261**

Pistone / Piston **Borgo.rif.3761.** **Rapp.** / Compression ratio **8.7** **Peso** / Weight **228**

Anello tenuta / Compression ring **ACT + ACC. ⌀ 73** **Raschiaolio** / Oil scraper ring **1.Rof/B. da mm.3.4**

Bielle / Connecting rods **128/14509** **Peso** / Weight **469** **Pompa acqua** / Water pump **128/C26449**

Teste cilindri / Cylinder heads **128/LM/17265 Canne Trione al cr/ni** **Coperchi** / Covers **128/LM/17271**

Guarnizioni teste / Head gaskets **128/10622 Klingherite - Anelli rame amianto. 250/10420.**

Valvola asp. tipo / Inlet valve type **128/LM/17406** **Valvola scarico tipo** / Exhaust valve type **128/LM/17267**

Molle valvola diam. / Valve spring diam. **128/C/17281/82** **Alberi distr.** / Camshafts **130/17229/230** **Alzata** / Lift

Scatola distribuzione / Distribution housing **128/22404 supporto spinterogeni 126/30556**

Pompa mand. olio / Oil pressure pump **128/B/24551** **Pompa di ricupero** / Scavenging pump **no**

Pompa benzina / Fuel pump **FIMAC. 375/34225** **Filtro benzina** / Fuel Filter

Carburatore tipo / Carburetor type **WEBER.38/DCN3** **N.6 con ⌀ 12** / No.

Presa d'aria / Air intake

Accension con / Ignition by **2.Spinterogeni** **Tipo** / Type **ST.207/DTEM/A**

Frizione tipo / Clutch type **F.&S** **Carico** / Load

	Fase: R	IO AA 46/75	L	IO AA 46/73
Timing:	D	CS EC 73/41	S	CS EC 73/41

Giuochi albero - motore / Main bearings clearance **0.06** **Punteria** / Tappet **0.2 = 0.25**

OSSERVAZIONI / NOTES **Dinamo S.0973/B- da 300/12 - Motorino avviamento MT.21/F -18/12.D.9**

Carburante / Fuel **98/100.NO** **Carburatore** / Carburetor **6.WEBER.36/DCN3** **Lubrificante** / Lubricant **X.100.SAE.40**

Candele / Spark plugs **Marchal.34.HF** **Taratura: Diff.** / Tuning: Choke **33** **Getto** / Main jet **115** **Minimo** / Idling jet **50** **Getto pompa** / Pump jet **40X6**

Centratori / Starting air screw **4.5** **Freno aria** / Air adjusting screw **140** **Tappo-Spillo** / Needle seat **175**

Pozzetto / Bowl

Fori di progressione / Progression ports **2** **Livello a m/m.** / Level at m/m. **6**

Pressione olio / Oil pressure **Temper. olio** / Oil temp.

Rodaggio ore / Running in hours

NOTE / NOTES

FOGLIO MONTAGGIO CAMBIO
GEARBOX ASSEMBLING FORM

Cambio tipo / Gearbox type **512G/B** **Matricola N.** / Serial No. **LM.6**

Scatola e coperchi / Gearbox housing and covers **508/C/54932/933**

Marce / Speeds **4 con ingranaggi tipo 526/B.**

Sincronizzatore / Sinchronyzer **513.PORSCHE**

Albero rinvio / Layshaft **508B20/53904**

Rinvio ad angolo per contachilometri / Speedometer drive gear **NO** **Rapporto** / Ratio

Pompa lubrificazione / Lubrication pump **SI**

Comando marce / Gear lever **centrale arretrato**

Giunto / Universal joint **Fabbri ⌀ 80**

Prova al banco / Bench test **buona**

NOTE / NOTES

FOGLIO MONTAGGIO PONTE
REAR AXLE ASSEMBLING FORM

Ponte Tipo / Rear axle type **525** **Matricola N.** / Serial No. **TRB.2**

Coppia conica / Crownwheel and pinion

Planetari / Planet pinions **Scatola differenziale** / Differential housing **520/B**

Satelliti / Sun gears **Cuscinetti** / Bearings

Autobloccante / Limited slip **520/B** **Ceppi** / Shoes

Semiassi / Halfshafts **520/B/con 9 sfere** **Portaceppi** / Back plates **tipo 525**

Bracci laterali / Reaction arms **Cilindretti** / Wheel cyl. **⌀ 25.**

Guarnizioni freni / Brake linings **Fren-Do 553**

Scatola del ponte / Axle casing **525 con coppa olio** **Tamburi** / Drums **508/C/69410 per mozzi grandi.**

Giunto / Flexible joint **Saga**

NOTE / NOTES **Chiavette differenziale mm.27.5**

Assale DD tipo 520.

Telaio matricola N. 0666/
Chassis serial No.

FOGLIO MONTAGGIO AUTOTELAIO
CHASSIS ASSEMBLING FORM

Passo
Wheelbase

Trasmissione 525/514 con giunto ant.Fabbri ∅ 80 e posteriore Saga.
Transmission

Freni ant. 508/C/548 suole Fren-Do 553 Tamburi 508/C/69410.   cil. diametro ∅ 28
Front brakes   Cyl. diameter

Freni post. 508/C/481 con portaceppi   cil. diametro ∅ 25
Rear brakes   Cyl. diameter

Mozzi ant. 166/70856/857   post. 520/61283/284
Front hubs   Rear hubs

Pneumatici e ruote Ant.RW.3077   – Post.RW.3019?
Wheels and tires

Ammortizzatori ant. 508/64457   post. 520/B/61521
Front shockabsorbers   rear sh.

Sterzo tipo Ferrari   Scatola guida 102 – R= 1/15 destra
Steering mechanism   Steering box

Radiatore acqua ~~e olio~~ 8.CL.in rame   h== Olio 526/B/81107
Oil and water radiator

Serbatoio carburante tipo 525/820200 Durall   capacità lt. 145
Fuel tank type   capacity l.

Indicatore del livello no
Level indicator

Marmitta di scarico tubi con finta marmitta   Prolunghe diametro
Muffler   Exhaust diameter

Batteria Baroclem. 28.Amp/h.
Batte

Filtro benzina Mona e pompa elettrica FISPA.
Fuel filter

Frizione Fichtel & Sachs.
Clutch

Pedaliera 520/B   N. pompe 1   diam. 32   tipo FB
Pedal system   pumps No.   diam.   type

Sospensioni ant. 526/B. con barra stabilizzatrice ∅ 14.
Front suspension

Molle ant. 525/64   Carico Kg. 315   fless. 17%
Front springs   Load Kg.   flex.

Balestra post. dis. 520/61371   Carico Kg. 400 N. foglie 6X4 fless. 45%
Rear leaf springs   Load Kg.   Leaves No.   flex.

Carrozzeria Scaglietti
Body

Strumenti di bordo
Instruments

NOTE Serbatoio alimentazione freni SABIF a pressione.
NOTES
Squotimento post.superiore mm.80 con tamponi 520/61429.

"   " inferiore mm.45 "   " 250/58583 Shore 35 tagliato

Finito il 3/7/58
Deliberated on

THE FIRST CUSTOMERS CAR: CHASSIS NO. 0710

Telaio tipo	526 B	matricola	0710 TR
Motore tipo	128 LM	matricola	0710 TR
Cambio tipo	526 B	matricola	4 LM
Ponte tipo	526 B	matricola	2 B
Collaudo il		Consegnato il	
Cliente			

Rezzaghi ?   Hollywood   25/11/57

Autotelaio tipo 526 B   Motore tipo 128 LM   Matricola N. 0710 TR   N. interno LM 1

FOGLIO MONTAGGIO MOTORE

Basamento 128LM/10612   Coppa olio 128C/11987   Filtri

Albero motore 128C/12261

Pistone 128LM/14505   Rapp. 9   Peso gr. 232

Anello tenuta 1 conico + 1 torsionale   Raschiaolio 1 con ∮ 3,4

Bielle 128/14509   Peso gr. 470   Pompa acqua 128C/26449

Teste cilindri 128LM/17265   Coperchi 128LM/17271 elel.

Guarnizioni teste H Klingerite 1000 ∮ 0,9, anelli rame amianto.

Valvola asp. tipo 128LM/17266   Valvola scarico tipo 128LM/17267

Molla richiamo valvola diametro 128C/17281/2   Alberi distribuzione 180/17229/30 Alzata

Scatola distribuzione 128/22404

Pompa mand. olio 128B/24451   Pompa di ricupero NO

Pompa benzina FIMAC 375/34225   Filtro benzina NO   Pres. aria

Carburatore tipo WEBER 38 DCN   N. 6

Presa d'aria trombetta 128C/18688

Accensione con 2 spinterogeni Tipo ST 100 DTEM/A   Fase: $D = \frac{AA6/78}{CS2/45}$ $s = \frac{AA45/79}{CS/5/43}$

Frizione tipo F. & S. 526   Carico 526/50720

Giuochi albero-motore 0,06   Punteria 0,2   0,25

PRIMO MONTAGGIO

Data inizio montaggio   Data fine montaggio   Montatori { Guorzoni Baschieri

OSSERVAZIONI

Pistoni esperimento.

Data 12/11/57   Il Capo Reparto Franchini

OSSERVAZIONI DEL PRIMO RODAGGIO

Sta bene sotto carico, non fuma pressione nel carter 40 % H2O.
Potenza buona. MOTORE DELIBERATO.

Il Capo Reparto Taddei

SECONDO MONTAGGIO

Data inizio lavoro   Data fine lavoro   Montatori {

OSSERVAZIONI

Data   Il Capo Reparto

Autotelaio tipo 526 B   Motore matricola 0710 TR   Telaio matricola N 0710 TR

FOGLIO MONTAGGIO AUTOTELAIO

Passo   N. interno

Trasmissione 526/57019 con giunto Fabbri ø 80 ant. e post.

Freni ant. 508C/548 con surpressore suola 553   cil. diametro 28 F-B.

Freni post. 508C/481 con suola 553 e tamburi AZ   cil. diametro 25

Mozzi ant. 166/70856/857   post. 52E/70936/937

Pneumatici e ruote RW 3077 ant.   RW 3019 16x5,50 L post.

Ammortizzatori ant. 508/64457   post. 518/61298

Sterzo 526B/549 con scatola Z/F R=1/17 508C/75043

Radiatore acqua e olio 526/81103   olio 526B/81107

Serbatoio carburante tipo 526B/820179   capacità lt. 140

Indicatore di livello NO

Marmitta di scarico tubo unico con finta marmitta prolunghe diametro

Batteria BAROCLEM 1200 AS

Motore N. 1 LM

Cambio N 4 LM

Ponte N. 2 B   R=8x32

Frizione Fischtel & Sachs 526/50720

Pedaliera con 2 pompe 508B/67225

Sospens. anter. 508C con barra stabilizzatrice 518/64524

Molle anter. XXXXXXXXXX Kg. 320 FLESS. 0,22 %. 525/64/03

Molle Balestre poster. dis. 526B/2116   Carico Kg. 250   N. foglie   fless 0,53 %.

Carrozzeria Scaglietti

Strumenti di bordo contagiri Corbetta rimanente SACMA

Quadretto

NOTE

Inviato in carrozzeria il

Finito il 26/11/57   Il Capo Reparto Franchini

Telaio matricola N.   0766/
Chassis serial No.

FOGLIO MONTAGGIO AUTOTELAIO
CHASSIS ASSEMBLING FORM

Passo   2280
Wheelbase

Trasmissione   532/D/57119 con giunto ant.Fabbri ∅ 70 e post.SAGA/508/56894
Transmission

Freni ant.   disco DUNLOP.VB.1057/AB. disco VBM.3562   cil. diametro 2"1/8.
Front brakes   Cyl. diameter

Freni post.   3   3   3 1063/AB   "   " 3563   cil. diametro 1"9/16
Rear brakes   Cyl. diameter

Mozzi ant.   528/B/70981/982   post.   532/70972/973
Front hubs   Rear hubs

Pneumatici e ruote   Ant. RW.3513 - Posteriore 3519.
Wheels and tires

Ammortizzatori ant. KONI. 82.AA n° 9   post. KONI. 82.AA.n° 17
Front shockabsorbers   rear sh.

Sterzo   estremità Ehrenreich   Scatola guida Gemmer France n° 1 R= 1/13. destra
Steering mechanism   Steering box

Radiatore acqua e olio 532/C/81137 in rame - 526/B/81117 rame
Oil and water radiator

Serbatoio carburante tipo   532/C/820253   capacità lt.   155
Fuel tank type   capacity l.

Imp̶̶̶̶̶̶̶̶̶̶̶̶ Serbatoio olio 532/D/830030 Lt. 10 con ricupero .
Level indicator . . . .

Marmitta di scarico   ∅ 32X34   Prolunghe diametro   ∅ 44X42
Muffler   Exhaust diameter

Batteria   Baroclem. 28.Amp/h.
Batte

Filtro benzina
Fuel filter

Frizione   Fichetel & Sachs con disco senza parastrappi e cuscinetto 1812. 107000
Clutch

Pedaliera   532/C/rapporto 220/52   N. pompe   1   diam.   7/8"   tipo   Dunlop.
Pedal system   pumps No.   diam.   type

Sospensioni ant.   532/B/597 - Barra stab. 532/B ∅12.
Front suspension

Molle ant. 525/64829   Carico Kg320. spessore ∅ 10.mm   fless. 13.7/%
Front springs . .   Load Kg.   flex.

. Molla   Carico Kg. 218.Spessore foglie 30.mm   fless. 66.%
Balestra post. dis. 532/B/61763   Load Kg.   Leaves No.   flex.
. Rear.leaf springs

Carrozzeria   Scaglietti con volante Nardi
Body

Strumenti di bordo   Sacma. illuminati con contagiri a 10.000. Rapp.1/4.
Instruments

NOTE
NOTES

Finito il   30/9/59
Deliberated on

228

A 1958 TR58:
CHASSIS NO. 0728

Telaio tipo	**525**	matricola	**0728/**
Motore tipo	**128/LM**	matricola	**0728/**
Cambio tipo	**525**	matricola	**1**
Ponte tipo		matricola	
Collaudo il		Consegnato il	
Cliente	**Rodriguez.**		

Autotelaio tipo **525**   Motore tipo **128/LM/GES**   Matricola N. **0728/**   N. interno **5/GES.**

FOGLIO MONTAGGIO MOTORE

Basamento **128/LM/10612**   Coppa olio **128/D/111001-Elek.**   Filtri

Albero motore **128/C/12261**

Pistone **Borgo.rif.3784**   Rapp. **9.65**   Peso **gr.235**

Anello tenuta **1 ACT.-+ 1.ACC Ø 73**   Raschiaolio **1 Rof/B. Ø 73X4X3.4**

Bielle **128/14509**   Peso **gr.464**   Pompa acqua **128/C/26449**

Teste cilindri **128/LM/17265** -Canne Trione al Cr/Ni   Coperchi **128LM/17271**

Guarnizioni teste **128/10622-Klingherite 1000; anelli rame amianto 250/10420.**

Valvola asp. tipo **128/LM/17406**   Valvola scarico tipo **128/LM/17267**

Molla richiamo valvola diametro **128/C/17281/82**   Alberi distribuzione **130/17229/239** Alzata

Scatola distribuzione **128/22404 supp.spinterogeni 126/30556.**

Pompa mand. olio **128B/24551**   Pompa di ricupero **no**

Pompa benzina **FIMAC-375/34225**   Filtro benzina   Pres. aria

Carburatore tipo **Weber.38/DCN3**   N. **6 - spessore Ø 12.**

Presa d'aria

Accensione con **2.spinterogeni** Tipo **ST.100/DTEM/E**   Fase: D = $\frac{AA45/76}{CS71/42}$ S = $\frac{AA\ 45/75}{CS\ 74/42}$

Frizione tipo **F & S**   Carico

Giuochi albero-motore **0.06**   Punteria **0.2 - 0.25**

PRIMO MONTAGGIO

Data inizio montaggio   Data fine montaggio   Montatori }

OSSERVAZIONI

Dinamo S.0973/B.300/12 - Motorino avviamento MT.21/F.D./9.
Coppa olio con livello meccanico.
I Pistoni sono stati ritoccati sulla cuppola asportandone mm/0.3.
all'esterno eseguendo un piano a 16° questo per avere gioco fra pistone e testa
Tendicatena tipo 128.

Data   Il Capo Reparto

OSSERVAZIONI DEL PRIMO RODAGGIO

Il Capo Reparto

SECONDO MONTAGGIO

Data inizio lavoro   Data fine lavoro   Montatori }

OSSERVAZIONI

Data   Il Capo Reparto

RELAZIONE SALA PROVA

Motore tipo **128/LM** N. interno **5/GES** Matricola N. **0728/**   Data **13/6/58**

PRIMA PROVA AL BANCO

Pressione barometrica   Temperatura   Umidità r.   Coefficiente di corr.

Ora	GIRI	Kg.	POTENZA		NOTE
			Letta	Corr.	

Carburante   Carburatore   Lubrificante

Candele   Accensione   Ant. fisso   Ant. aut.   Ant. tot.

Pressione olio   Temp. olio

Rodaggio ore

Note di funzionamento

Motoristi :

SECONDA PROVA AL BANCO   Data

Pressione barometrica   Temperatura   Umidità r.   Coefficiente di corr.

Ora	GIRI	Kg.	POTENZA		NOTE
			Letta	Corr.	
	7.400.				

Carburante **98/100. NO**   Carburatore **6.WEBER.38/DCN.3**   Lubrificante **X.100.SAE.40**

Candele **MARCHAL. 34.HFS**   Taratura: Diff. **33**   Getto **115**   Minimo **50**   Getto pompa **40X6**

Centratori **4.5**   Freno aria **140**   Tappo - Spillo **175**

Pozzetto   Consumo carburante = Gr./HP ora

Fori di progressione   Livello a m/m **6**   Consumo olio = gr.   in ore

Pressione olio   Temper. olio

Rodaggio ore

Note di funzion.

Motoristi {   Entrato in S.P. il   ore

Uscito di S.P. il   ore

Autotelaio tipo 526 B   Matricola N. 0710 TR

FOGLIO MONTAGGIO CAMBIO

Cambio tipo 526 B   Matricola   N. int. 4 LM

Scatola e coperchi 5080/54933/932

Marcie 4 con ingranaggi tipo 526

Sincronizzatore 513/53556 tipo PORSCHE

Ingr. prim. I 54944 2° III 54945 3° V 54930/508 ingr. rinvio I 54946 2° II 54946 3° V 53751

Albero rinvio 508B20/53904

Rinvio ad angolo per contachilometri NO   Rapporto 8x32

Pompa lubrificazione SI corpo pompa 342/53044

Comando marce centrale con leva piegata (non a disegno)

Giunto Fabbri ø 80

Prova al banco BUONA

NOTE

Ingranaggi con boccole in metallo bianco TRIONE.

Data 7/11/57   Montato da Beltrami N.   Il Capo Reparto Franchini

Autotelaio tipo 526 B   Matricola N. 0710 TR

FOGLIO MONTAGGIO PONTE

Ponte tipo 526 B   Matricola   N. int. 2 B

Coppia conica 8x52   Modulo corona

Planetari NO   Scatola differenz. 518/59113/117

Satelliti NO   Cuscinetti RIV

Autobloccante 518/59115/116   Ceppi 509/69123

Semiassi 518/61231   Portaceppi 526B/69374

Bracci laterali 518/61189   Cilindretti ø 25

Flange di attacco 518/61192   Guarnizioni freni Frendo 553

Scatola del ponte XXXXXXXX 518/61196   Tamburi 513/69161

NOTE

Giunto Fabbri ø 80.

Data 4/12/57   Montato da Giusti I.   Il Capo Reparto Franchini

Telaio tipo 532/D Chassis type	matricola serial No.	0766
Motore tipo 128/TR.59/R Engine type	matricola serial No.	0766
Cambio tipo Gearbox type	matricola serial No.	
Ponte tipo Rear axle type	matricola serial No.	
Collaudo il Tested on	Consegnato il Delivered on	

CLIENTE
CLIENT

Autotelaio Tipo 532/D Chassy type	Motore tipo 128/LM/59 Engine type	Matricola N. 0766/ Serial No.

FOGLIO MONTAGGIO MOTORE
ENGINE ASSEMBLING FORM

Basamento 128/LM/10612
Crankcase

Coppa olio 128/LM/111062 Elk.
Sump

Filtri Dinamo.DN.2/A.150/12/1400V
Filters

Albero motore 128/LM/12310
Crankshaft

Pistone BORGO.rif.3784/2   Rapp. 9.55 ∅ 73.20   Peso 249
Piston   Compression ratio   Weight

Anello tenuta 1.ACC + 1.ACT. ∅ 73.2X1.5X3.4   Raschiaolio 1.Rof/B. ∅ 73.3X4X3.4
Compression ring   Oil scraper ring

Bielle 128/14509   Peso 464   Pompa acqua 128/C/26449
Connecting rods   Weight   Water pump

Teste cilindri 128/LM/17457 condotti asp.29 -Scarico ∅30.   Coperchi 128/LM/17267
Cylinder heads.   Covers

Guarnizioni teste 128/LM/10622 Klingherite - Anelli rame amianto. 250/10420.
Head gaskets

Valvola asp. tipo 128/LM/17406   Valvola scarico tipo 128/LM/17267
Inlet valve type   Exhaust valve type

Molle valvola diam. 128/LM/17398   Alberi distr. 130/17229/230   Alzata 10
Valve spring diam. OCL/01665   Camshafts   Lift

Scatola distribuzione 128/22404 con valvola limitazione 128/D/24699
Distribution housing

Pompa mand. olio 128/B/24551   Pompa di ricupero 128/LM/24723/Ingr.24724/5
Oil pressure pump   Scavenging pump

Pompa benzina 1.FIMAC. 375/342225/D   Filtro benzina
Fuel pump   Fuel Filter

Carburatore tipo WEBER.38/DCN.   N.° 6 con celeren ∅ 12.mm.
Carburetor type   No.

Presa d'aria
Air intake

Accension con 2.Spinterogeni   Tipo ST.207/DTEM/A
Ignition by   Type

		Fase: R Timing: D	$=$	IO AA 42/72 CS 72/39 EC	L S	$=$	IO AA 43/75 CS 70/41 EC

Frizione tipo F.&S   Carico
Clutch type   Load

Giuochi albero-motore assiale 0.1 - Radiale 0.06   Punteria Asp. 02 - Scarico 0.25
Main bearings clearance   Tappet
                    bielle " 0.3   " 0.06

OSSERVAZIONI Cuscinetto di banco e biella normali.
NOTES
    Motorino avviamento. MT.21/F.18/12.D.9 - Collettore alimentazione 128/18770

    Bilancieri con rulli con aghi. 128/17243/44 esp. 1. - Canne cilindri 128/C/10604.

Carburante 98/100 NO   Carburatore 6.WEBER.38/DCN   Lubrificante X.100.SAE.40
Fuel   Carburetor   Lubricant

Candele Marchal. 34.HF.   Taratura: Diff. 33   Getto 120   Minimo 50   Getto pompa 40
Spark plugs   Tuning: Choke   Main jet   Idling jet   Pump jet
                                                                                CORSA 6 m/m

Centratori 4.5   Freno aria 140   Tappo-Spillo 175
Starting air screw   Air adjusting screw   Needle seat

Pozzetto F.14
Bowl

Fori di progressione   Livello a m/m. 6.
Progression ports   Level at m/m.

Pressione olio   Temper. olio
Oil pressure   Oil temp.

Rodaggio ore
Running in hours

NOTE   *giri motore 7.500 frenato.*
NOTES

FOGLIO MONTAGGIO CAMBIO
GEARBOX ASSEMBLING FORM

Cambio tipo 532/D   Matricola N. 2
Gearbox type   Serial No.

Scatola e coperchi in Atesia
Gearbox housing and covers

Marce 5 + RM.
Speeds

Sincronizzatore no
Sinchronyzer

Albero rinvio inr. 1° 17/34 e 4° 23/26
Layshaft

Rinvio ad angolo per contachilometri   Rapporto
Speedometer drive gear   Ratio

Pompa lubrificazione 532/D/55450/451/452
Lubrication pump

Comando marce con selettore 532/D/55299
Gear lever

Giunto FABBRI. ∅ 70
Universal joint

Prova al banco
Bench test

NOTE
NOTES

FOGLIO MONTAGGIO PONTE
REAR AXLE ASSEMBLING FORM

Ponte Tipo 532/D/con scatola in silumin   Matricola N. 12
Rear axle type   Serial No.

Coppia conica 9X38
Crownwheel and pinion

Planetari   Scatola differenziale 532/D/59381
Planet pinions   Differential housing

Satelliti Perno pert tassello 532/D/61910   Cuscinetti UE.RIV.6A
Sun gears   Bearings

Autobloccante 532/D/59378/379   Ceppi CHIAVETTE 532/D/59388
Limited slip   Shoes

Semiassi 532/B/61748   Portaceppi 532/C/69486/487
Halfshafts   Back plates

Bracci reaz Bussola cuscinetto 532/C/61861   Cilindretti ant.∅ 2"1/8 Post. ∅ 1"9/16
Reaction arms   Wheel cyl.

Guarnizioni freni Piste guide 508/D/61908   Guarnizioni MINTEX 2/875/A
Brake linings

Scatola ponte Tassello 532/D/61911   Tamburi
Axle casing   Drums

Giunto
Flexible joint

NOTE Assale DD. 532/D/61919 Camber negativo 1°30. Convergenza 0°30.
NOTES

Autotelaio tipo **525**   Matricola N. **0728/**

FOGLIO MONTAGGIO CAMBIO

Cambio tipo **520**   Matricola   N. int. **1**

Scatola e coperchi **Elektron**

Marcie **4**

Sincronizzatore

Ingr. prim.**520/53689**   2**ª 53691**   3**ª 53693**   ingr. rinvio 1**ª 53690**   2**ª 53692**   3**ª 53694**

Albero rinvio **520/53687- RM.fisso sul sec - Z-12 fisso sul prim.2-22 folle Z-12.**

Rinvio ad angolo per contachilometri   Rapporto

Pompa lubrificazione   **si**

Comando marce

Giunto **Fabbri Ø 80**

Prova al banco

NOTE

Data   Montato da   Il Capo Reparto

Autotelaio tipo   Matricola N.

FOGLIO MONTAGGIO PONTE

Ponte tipo   Matricola   N. int.

Coppia conica   Modulo corona

Planetari   Scatola differenz.

Satelliti   Cuscinetti

Autobloccante **519/C/59153/206 - 520/59165**   ~~546~~ **520/B/59207 chiavette mm.27.**

Semiassi **520 con sfere**   Portaceppi

Bracci laterali   Cilindretti

Flange di attacco   Guarnizioni freni

Scatola del ponte **519/C/59133/129**   Tamburi

NOTE

R = 11/42 - 15/16

Data   Montato da   Il Capo Reparto

Autotelaio tipo **525**   Motore matricola N. **0728**   Telaio matricola N. **0728**

FOGLIO MONTAGGIO AUTOTELAIO

Passo   **2320**   N. interno

Trasmissione **525/B. con giunto Saga e Fabbri - Albero lungo mm.464.**

Freni ant. **519/C/-400X55 - suole Fren-DO 553 Tamburi Alfin.**   cil. diametro **25**

Freni post. **508/C/548-con portaceppi 340/69083 forati per DD.**   cil. diametro **22**

Mozzi **166/70865/857 anteriori**   -   Post.**520/61283/284**

Pneumatici e ruote   ant. **RW.3112** - Post. **RW.3320.**

Ammortizzatori ant. **508/64457**   post. **520/B/61521.**

Sterzo **Errenraich 508C/76313/326**   **Scatola guida ZF. sinistra R- 1/17.**

Radiatore acqua e olio **526/81103**   -   **525/B/81117**

Serbatoio carburante tipo **525/820209**   capacitá lt. **164**

Indicatore di livello

Marmitta di scarico   Prolunghe diametro

Batteria   **Baroclem 28. Amp/h.**

Motore N.   **5.LM/Ges.**

Cambio N.   **1**

Ponte N.

Frizione   **Fichetel & Sachs con campana 525/B/50753**

Pedaliera   **520/B. Pompa freno° 1 Ø 32 tipo Locched.**

Sospens. anter. **526/con barra stabilizzatrice Ø 14 518/64524.**

Molle anter.   **525/64830 Carico 315 - Flessibilità 15.2%**

Balestre poster. dis. **525/61725**   Carico   **410**   N. foglie **7X4**   fless. **38.5 %**

Carrozzeria   **Scaglietti**

Strumenti di bordo

Quadretto

NOTE   **Assale D.D. tipo 520 .**

        Biscottini balestra mm.130.

        Filtro benzina MONA. Pompa benzina FISPA.

Inviato in carrozzeria il

Finito il   Il Capo Reparto

THE 330TR/LM: CHASSIS NO. 0808

Telaio tipo / Chassis type	568/TRI/330LM	matricola / serial No.	0808
Motore tipo / Engine type	163	matricola / serial No.	0808
Cambio tipo / Gearbox type		matricola / serial No.	
Ponte tipo / Rear axle type		matricola / serial No.	

Collaudo il / Tested on   Consegnato il / Delivered on

CLIENTE / CLIENT   *Crnetti*

4 e. Le MANS 1962

Telaio matricola N. / Chassis serial No.   0808

FOGLIO MONTAGGIO AUTOTELAIO
CHASSIS ASSEMBLING FORM

Passo / Wheelbase **2420**

Trasmissione / Transmission **568 CON 2 GIUNTONI SAGA 508E/57235**

Freni ant. / Front brakes **A DISCO DUNLOP ACCIAIO** Dischi / Discs **534B FORATI**   cil. diametro / Cyl. diameter

Portacaliper / Support plates   Pastiglie / Pad assy **FERODO DS 11**   Caliper / Caliper **VB 1084 – VB 1080**

Mozzi ant. / Front hubs **534/71002–03**   post. / Rear hubs **568/71080–81**

Pneumatici / Wheels and tires **DUNLOP ANT. 600x16 – POST. 700x16 – RUOTE ANT. RW3735 – POST. 3734 BORRANI**

Ammortizzatori ant. / Front shockabsorbers **KONI 82/1153 TARATURA 160/30**   post. / rear sh.

Sterzo / Steering mechanism **TIRANTERIA EHRENREICH – CON VERGENZA MM 3 SULLE RUOTE**   Scatola guida / Steering box **GEMMER FRANCE**

Radiatore acqua / Oil and water radiator **539/81243 – OLIO – 526B/81117 NORMALE**

Serbatoio carburante tipo / Fuel tank type **568/820405 – IN DURALLUMINIO CHIODATO**   capacità lt. / capacity l. **143**

Indicatore del livello / Level indicator

Marmitta di scarico / Muffler **COLLETTORI SDOPPIATI E PROLUNGHE CON SNAP**   Prolunghe diametro / Exhaust diameter

Batteria / Batte **N° 1 BAROCLEM E 1 MARELLI**

Filtro benzina / Fuel filter

Frizione / Clutch **FICHTEL & SACHS**

Pedaliera / Pedal system **547 CON DUE POMPE DUNLOP** ø **7/8"**   N. pompe / pumps No.   diam. / diam.   tipo / type

Sospensioni ant. / Front suspension **547**

Molle ant. / Front springs **547/65022**   Carico Kg. / Load Kg. **280**   fless. / flex. **18%**

Balestra post. dis. / Rear leaf springs   Carico Kg. / Load Kg.   N. foglie / Leaves No.   fless. / flex.

Carrozzeria / Body

Strumenti di bordo / Instruments

Servofreno / Brake Booster   Surpressore / Booster compressor

NOTE / NOTES

Finito il / Deliberated on

FOGLIO MONTAGGIO CAMBIO
GEARBOX ASSEMBLING FORM

Cambio tipo / Gearbox type **568**   Matricola N. / Serial No. **N° 5**

Scatola e coperchi / Gearbox housing and covers **532D/55397 ATESIA**

Marce / Speeds **5 PIÙ' RETROMARCIA**

Sincronizzatore / Sinchronyzer

Albero rinvio / Layshaft

Rinvio ad angolo per contachilometri / Speedometer drive gear **NO**   Rapporto / Ratio

Pompa lubrificazione / Lubrication pump **MAGGIORATA 532 D**   Overdrive tipo / Overdrive unit type

Comando marce / Gear lever **532 D**

Giunto / Universal joint **N° 2 SAGA 508E/57235**

Prova al banco / Bench test

NOTE / NOTES

FOGLIO MONTAGGIO PONTE
REAR AXLE ASSEMBLING FORM

Ponte Tipo / Rear axle type   Matricola N. / Serial No.

Coppia conica / Crownwheel and pinion

Planetari / Planet pinions   Scatola differenziale / Differential housing

Satelliti / Sun gears   Cuscinetti / Bearings

Autobloccante / Limited slip   Ceppi o dischi / Shoes or discs

Semiassi / Halfshafts   Portaceppi o portacaliper / Back plates or support plates

Bracci laterali / Reaction arms   Cilindretti o caliper / Wheel cylinders or calipers

Guarnizioni freni o pastiglie / Brake linings or pad assy

Scatola del ponte / Axle casing   Tamburi / Drums

Giunto / Flexible joint

NOTE / NOTES

Autotelaio Tipo
Chassy type

Motore tipo   163
Engine type

Matricola N.
Serial No.

FOGLIO MONTAGGIO MOTORE
ENGINE ASSEMBLING FORM

Basamento   163/10854   Coppa olio   163/111135   Dinamo   MARELLI SD 312 A
Crankcase   Sump   Generator

Albero motore 163/12334 ESP. 6 NORMALE
Crankshaft

Pistone 163/14649 RIF. 64736   Rap.   8,5   Peso   gr. 265 ESTRUSI
Piston   Compression ratio   Weight

Anello tenuta 1 ACT. 1 ACC Ø 77x1,5x3,6   Raschiaolio   1 ROF B Ø 77x5x3,6
Compression ring   Oil scraper ring

Bielle 163/14621   Peso   gr. 508   Pompa acqua   163/26514
Connecting rods   Weight   Water pump

Teste cilindri   163/17777 CONDOTTI ASP. Ø 29,5 - SCAR. Ø 38   Coperchi   163/17883
Cylinder heads   Covers

Guarnizioni teste   DIRING 163/10925
Head gaskets

Valvola asp. tipo   ZANZI 157/17534 SIOX   Valvola scarico tipo   ZANZI 157/17535 REEX
Inlet valve type   Exhaust valve type

Molle valvola interne 8c1/01665 esterne 128IM/17398 Alberi distr. 163/17587-88 Alzata   10
Valve spring inner   FRAM   exterior PER H=10 FRAM Camshafts   Lift

Scatola distribuzione   163/22560 - SUPPORTO SPINT. 128C/30585 E 128D/30610
Distribution housing

Pompa mand. olio   163/24271   Pompa di ricupero   128/IM/24723
Oil pressure pump   Scavenging pump

Pompa benzina   BENDIX   Filtro benzina
Fuel pump   Fuel Filter

Carburatore tipo   WEBER 42 DCN   N.   6
Carburetor type   No.

Presa d'aria   10   10
Air intake   Fase: R = AA 43/71 L = AA 43/73
                                    Timing: D   CS 73/40 S   CS 72/40
                                            EC   EC

Accensione con SPINTEROGENI   Tipo MARELLI S 85 A
Ignition by   Type

Frizione tipo   FICHTEL & SACHS Carico
Clutch type   Load

Giuochi albero-motore   ASS. 0,10 RAD. 0,06 + 0,07   Punteria   ASP. 0,20 SCAR. 0,25
Main bearings clearance   Tappet

OSSERVAZIONI
NOTES

Carburante   SHEL 98/100 NO   Carburatore   6 WEBER 42 DON   Lubrificante   SHELL
Fuel   Carburetor   Lubricant

Candele   MARCHAL 34 HF   Taratura: Diff. 35   Getto   130   Minimo   70   Getto pompa   50x4
Spark plugs   Tuning: Choke   Main jet   Idling jet   Pump jet

Centratori   5   Freno aria   160   Tappo-Spillo   200
Starting air screw   Air adjusting screw   Needle seat

Pozzetto   F 14
Bowl

Fori di progressione   3   Livello a m/m.   6
Progression ports   Level at m/m

Pressione olio   60 m   Temp. olio   120°
Oil pressure   Oil temp.

Rodaggio ore   9 PER TRASCINAMENTO + 3 A BENZINA
Running in hours

NOTE
NOTES

Championship Racing Summary

WORLD SPORTS CAR CHAMPIONSHIP

1957

CHASSIS NO.		EVENT
	Mille Miglia—May 11	
0677	3rd	Gendebien/Jacques Wascher #417 3.0-Liter Coupe
	Nürburgring—May 26	
0677	DNS	Mille Miglia Coupe—Crashed in practice by Von Trips
0666	10th	Masten Gregory/Carlo Marolli #7
	Le Mans—June 23/24	
0704	DNF	Gendebien/Trintignant #9
0666	DNS	First Prototype—Piston Failure Warming Up Before Practice
	Sweden—August 11	
0666	DNF	Gendebien/Trintignant #5
0704	DNF	Gregory/Seidel #6
	Venezuela—November 3	
0666	3rd	Von Trips/Seidel #16
0704	4th	Trintignant/Gendebien #18

1958

CHASSIS NO.		EVENT
	Argentina—January 26	
0704	1st	Hill/Collins #2—TR58
0666	2nd	Hawthorn/Von Trips #4—Prototype
0716	DNF	Musso/Gendebien #6—250 TR
0710	DNF	Von Neumann/Seidel #8—250 TR
0714	4th	Piero Drogo/Sergio Gonzalez #26—250TR
	Sebring—March 22	
0704	1st	Hill/Collins #14—TR58
0728	DNF	Hawthorn/Von Trips #15—TR58
0726	2nd	Musso/Gendebien #16—TR58
0710	DNF	Von Neumann/Ginther #17—250 TR
0732	DNF	Ed Hugus/John Fitch #19—250 TR
0730	DNF	E. D. Martin/Chet Flynn #23—250 TR
	Targa Florio—May 11	
0704	4th	Hill/Collins #98—TR58
0728	3rd	Hawthorn/Von Trips #102—TR58
0666	DNF	Gino Munaron/Seidel #104—TR58
0726	1st	Musso/Gendebien #106—Prototype
	Nürburgring—June 1	
0704	2nd	Hawthorn/Collins #4—TR58
0726	4th	Hill/Musso #5—TR58
0728	5th	Seidel/Munaron #6—TR58
0746 (0760)	3rd	Von Trips/Gendebien #7—TR58 Experimental
0736	DNF	Willy Mairesse/Alain DeChangy #11—250 TR
0748	10th	Gottfried Kochert/Erik Bauer #12—250 TR
0724	12th	Curt Lincoln/Pentti Keinanen #15—250 TR

The first disc brakes fitted to a Testa Rossa shown on the TR59 prototype (0726).

The TR59 and 60 disc brake showing the hand brake which was fitted only on the right rear.

1958

CHASSIS NO.		EVENT
		Le Mans—June 21/22
0704	DNF	Hawthorn/Collins #12—TR58
0728	1st	Hill/Gendebien #14—TR58
0726	DNF	Von Trips/Seidel #16—TR58
0722	DNF	Alfonso Gomez-Mena/Piero Drogo #17—250 TR
0666	DNF	Dan Gurney/Bruce Kessler #18—Prototype
0730	DNF	E. D. Martin/Fernand Tavano #19—250 TR
0754	DNF	Francois Picard/Jaroslav Juhan #20—250 TR
0736	6th	Alain DeChangy/"Beurlys" #21—250 TR
0732	7th	Ed Hugus/Ernie Erickson #22—250 TR
0718	DNF	Willy Mairesse/Lucien Bianchi #58—250 TR

1958 CHAMPIONSHIP POINTS

Make	Argentina	Sebring	Targa Florio	Nürburg-ring	Le Mans	Tourist Trophy	Total
FERRARI	8	8	8	6	8	—	38
ASTON-MARTIN	—	—	—	8	—	8	16
PORSCHE	4	—	—	—	—	—	4
MASERATI	2	—	—	—	—	—	2

1959 CHAMPIONSHIP POINTS

Make	Sebring	Targa Florio	Nürburg-ring	Le Mans	Tourist Trophy	Total
ASTON-MARTIN	—	—	8	8	8	24
FERRARI	8	—	6	4	4	22
PORSCHE	4	8	3	—	6	21

Note: Ferrari points at Le Mans were scored by 3rd place finish of "Beurlys"/Helde #11—250 GT Tour de France Coupe.

1959

CHASSIS NO.		EVENT
		Sebring—March 21
0766	1st	Gurney/Daigh/Hill/Gendebien #7—TR59
0770	DNF	Hill/Gendebien #8—TR59
0768	2nd	Behra/Allison #9—TR59
0666	DNF	Rod Carveth/Gil Geitner #10 Prototype
0728	DNF	Pedro Rodriguez/Paul O'Shea #11—TR58
0730	6th	Martin/Lance Reventlow #12—250 TR
0720	7th	Jim Johnston/Ebby Lunken/Augie Pabst #14—250 TR
0722	DNS	Lloyd Casner/Jim Hunt #19—250 TR
0724	DNS	Buck Fulp #82—250 TR
		Targa Florio—May 24
0768	DNF	Behra/Brooks #150—TR59
0766	DNF	Hill/Gendebien #152—TR59
0770	DNF	Gurney/Allison #154—TR59
		Nürburgring—June 7
0768	3rd	Behra/Brooks #3—TR59
0766	2nd	Hill/Gendebien #4—TR59
0770	5th	Gurney/Allison #5—TR59
0666	DNF	Carveth/Geitner #11—Prototype
		Le Mans—June 20/21
0736	DNF	Bianchi/DeChangy #10—250 TR
0774	DNF	Behra/Gurney #12—TR59
0766	DNF	Hill/Gendebien #14—TR59
0770	DNF	Allison/Fernando da Silva Ramos #15—TR59
0666	DNF	Carveth/Geitner #17—Prototype
0730	DNF	Martin/Kimberly #19—250 TR
		Tourist Trophy—September 5
0770	5th	Brooks/Gurney #9—TR59
0766	3rd	Allison/Hill/Brooks #10—TR59
0774	DNF	Hill/Gendebien #11—TR59

1960

CHASSIS NO.		EVENT
		Argentina—January 31
0770	2nd	Von Trips/Ginther #2—TR59/60
0774	1st	Hill/Allison #4—TR59/60
		Sebring—March 26
0774	DNF	Ginther/Daigh #7—TR59/60
0768	3rd	Nethercutt/Lovely #8—TR59
		Targa Florio—May 8
0780	DNS	Allison #196—TRI60
0772	DNF	Allison/Ginther #202—TR59/60
		Nürburgring—May 22
0782	DNF	Hill/Von Trips #1—TRI60
0770	3rd	Allison/Mairesse/Hill #2—TR59/60
		Le Mans—June 25/26
0770	DNF	Hill/Von Trips #9—TR59/60
0780	DNF	Mairesse/Ginther #10—TRi60
0772 (0774)	1st	Gendebien/Frere #11—TR59/60
0782	DNF	P. Rodriguez/Scarfiotti #12—TRI60
0766	2nd	R. Rodriguez/Andre Pilette #17—TR59

1960 CHAMPIONSHIP POINTS

Make	Argentina	Sebring	Targa Florio	Nürburgring	Le Mans	Total
FERRARI	8	4	6	4	8	30
PORSCHE	4	8	8	6	—	26
MASERATI	3	—	—	8	—	11

Note: Ferrari Targa Florio points scored by second place finish of Hill/Von Trips in a Dino 246.

1961

CHASSIS NO.		EVENT
		Sebring—March 25
0768	DNF	Nethercutt/Lovely #9—TR50
0766	4th	Sharp/Hissom #10—TR59
0792	1st	Hill/Gendebien #14—TR61
0780	2nd	Mairesse/Baghetti/Ginther/Von Trips #15—TR61 Prototype
0770	8th	Reed/Sturgis #16—TR59/60
0746	3rd	P. & R. Rodriguez #17—TR59/60
		Targa Florio—April 30
0780	DNF	P. Rodriguez/Mairesse #160—TR61 Prototype
		Nürburgring—May 28
0780	2nd	P. & R. Rodriguez #5—TR61 Prototype
0742	DNF	Georges Gachnang/Caillet #94—250 TR
		Le Mans—June 10/11
0794	1st	Hill/Gendebien #10—TR61
0780	2nd	Mairesse/Parkes #11—TR61 Prototype
0792	DNF	P. & R. Rodriguez #17—TR61
		Pescara—August 15
0780	1st	Bandini/Scarlatti #4—TR61 Prototype
0742	12th	Gachnang/Caillet #10—250 TR

1961 CHAMPIONSHIP POINTS

Make	Sebring	Targa Florio	Nürburgring	Le Mans	Pescara	Total
FERRARI	8	8	6	8	4	34
MASERATI	—	3	8	3	—	14
PORSCHE	2	6	—	2	2	12

Note: Ferrari points at the Targa Florio were scored by Von Trips/Gendebien with a 246 SP.

There should be no doubt that this is chassis 0770.

COMBINED RECORDS
FOR FACTORY ENTRIES 1958-1961

Races Started	19
Total # Entries	48
Victories	10
Total # Finishers	29
2nds	9
3rds	5
4ths	2
5ths	3
DNFS—Accidents	5
—Mechanical	12
—Other	2
Losses To:	
Aston Martin	4
Porsche	2
Maserati	2
Ferrari	1 (Rear engine)

INTERNATIONAL RACES

1962

CHASSIS NO.	EVENT
	Daytona—February 11
0746	5th Constantine #49—TR59/60
0794	15th R. Rodriguez/Peter Ryan #50—TR61
	Sebring—March 23
0746	DNF Constantine/Andrey #20—TR59/60
0792	1st Bianchi/Bonnier #23—TR61
0794	DSQ Ireland/Moss #26—TR61
	Nürburgring—May 27
0792	DNF Vaccarella/Carlo Abate #90—TR61
0742	17th Gachnang/Ernst Grog #94—250 TR
	Le Mans—June 23/24
0808 (0780)	1st Hill/Gendebien #6—330 TRI/LM
0792	DNF Bonnier/Gurney #15—TR61
0794	DNF Fulp/Ryan #18—TR61
	Bridgehampton—September 16
0808 (0780)	1st P. Rodriguez #8—330 TRI/LM

1963

CHASSIS NO.	EVENT
	Sebring—March 23
0808 (0780)	3rd P. Rodriguez/G. Hill #18—330 TRI/LM
	Nürburgring—May 19
0792	3rd Abate/Maglioli #112—TR61
	Le Mans—June 15/16
0808 (0780)	DNF P. Rodriguez/R. Penske #10—330 TRI/LM

TESTA ROSSA PRODUCTION SUMMARY

Chassis Number	Model Type	Year
0666	First Prototype	1957/58
0704	Second Prototype/TR58	1957/58
0710	250 TR	1957
0714	250 TR	1957
0716	250 TR	1957
0718	250 TR	1957
0720	250 TR	1958
0722	250 TR	1958
0724	250 TR	1958
0726	TR58/TR59 Prototype	1958
0728	TR58	1958
0730	250 TR	1958
0732	250 TR	1958
0734	250 TR	1958
0736	250 TR	1958
0738	250 TR	1958
0742	250 TR	1958
0746	TR58 Experimental—TR59/60	1958/60
0748	250 TR	1958
0750	250 TR	1958
0752	250 TR	1958
0754	250 TR	1958
0756	250 TR	1958
0758	250 TR	1958
0766	TR59	1959
0768	TR59	1959
0770	TR59/60	1959/60
0772	TR59/60	1959/60
0774	TR59/60	1959/60
0780	TRI60/TR61 Prototype	1960/61
0782	TRI60	1960
0792	TR61	1961
0794	TR61	1961
0808	330 TRI/LM	1962

Totals by Model Type

Prototypes—	2
TR58—	2
250 TR—	19
TR59—	2
TR59/60—	4
TRI60—	2
TR61—	2
330 TRI/LM—	1
Total—	**34**

APPENDIX III
Individual Testa Rossa Histories

INTRODUCTION

THIS APPENDIX CONSISTS OF detailed histories of each Testa Rossa constructed and includes their participation at major races, ownership changes during their active competition life, and current situation. Whenever possible, mechanical or bodily modifications are noted as well as unique components originally installed.

Bear in mind when reading these histories that changes in ownership were sometimes bewilderingly frequent; several examples were rebuilt from others; and in some cases it is very difficult to distinguish certain cars from identical brethren. Further compounding the identity problem is that substitutes may have replaced the specified by serial number race entrants on several occasions and fiddling of chassis numbers for customs and other purposes could have occurred.

It must be remembered that the Ferrari racing organization was primarily concerned with building and preparing the Testa Rossa to win races. The personnel were not overly concerned with exact chassis or engine numbers and did not make any particular effort to record such information in a definitive fashion.

Extensive research has gone into the preparation of the data presented here, but the author cautions readers that new and additional information may surface in the future significantly affecting our knowledge of certain examples. Whatever the case, the information shown is up to date as of the time published and is as accurate as possible considering the many difficulties involved in dealing with events that took place fifteen to twenty years ago.

-0666-

The first prototype. Based on an envelope-bodied 290 MM chassis with transverse-leaf, De Dion rear suspension and right-hand-drive. Completed in early May, 1957.

    1957 Nürburgring #7 Gregory/ Marolli—10th

    1957 Sweden #5 Gendebien/ Trintignant—DNF Blown Engine

Returned to the factory, converted to the final 1957 Testa Rossa engine/transmission combination. Rebodied by Scaglietti to the pontoon fender design and inside door hinges, with an air vent installed on the right side in the valley between the fender and hood.

    1957 Venezuela #16 Von Trips/ Seidel—3rd

    1958 Argentina #4 Hawthorn/Von Trips—2nd

    1958 Targa Florio #104 Munaron/ Seidel—DNF Broken Sump

Sold to Luigi Chinetti and delivered at Le Mans.

    1958 Le Mans #18 Gurney/ Kessler—DNF Crashed and Burned

Rebuilt at the factory with parts from 0760 and rebodied by Scaglietti. Sold by Chinetti to Rod Carveth of San Carlos, California, in February, 1959.

    1959 Sebring #10 Carveth/ Geitner—DNF Accident Ruined Lights

    1959 Nürburgring #11 Carveth/ Geitner—DNF Accident

    1959 Le Mans #17 Carveth/ Geitner—DNF Blown Engine

Rebuilt once again, sent to Australia and eventually to California where Carveth used it only occasionally.

    1960 Laguna Seca Examiner G.P. #154 Phil Hill—DNS could not qualify fast enough to make the grid

Later sold to Bev Spencer and a succession of other California owners in the early 1960s. The engine was blown up and the car was later burned in a garage fire. It is now owned and being restored by Chuck Betz of Manhattan Beach, California, who has acquired engine 0724 to install in the car.

-0704-

The second prototype. Built on a modified right hand drive 500 TRC chassis and the first Scaglietti pontoon fender body with outside door hinges. It had a live-axle-rear, 3.1-liter engine and was completed in June 1957.

    1957 Le Mans #9 Gendebien/ Trintignant—DNF Blown Piston

Revised at the factory to 3.0-liter engine and modified transmission.

    1957 Sweden #6 Gregory/Seidel— DNF Broken Transmission Shaft

    1957 Venezuela #18 Trintignant/ Gendebien—4th

    1958 Argentina #2 Hill/Collins—1st

    1958 Sebring #14 Hill/Collins—1st

    1958 Targa Florio #98 Hill/ Collins—4th

    1958 Nürburgring #4 Hawthorn/ Collins—2nd

Converted to a new four-speed transaxle and changed to the envelope body style with a rear carburetor air intake and became, for all intents and purposes, a TR58.

    1958 Le Mans #12 Hawthorn/ Collins—DNF Clutch

Sold to John Von Neumann in August 1958 and shipped to California.

    1958 Riverside Times G.P. #2 Richie Ginther—5th Overall and 1st in Class

    1958 Laguna Seca National #11 John Von Neumann—DNF

    1959 Riverside Times G.P. #112 Josie Von Neumann—11th

Sold to Jack Nethercutt of Los Angeles in late 1959 and resold in 1960 to Dick Hahn of Yakima, Washington.

    1960 Riverside Times G.P. #178 Jerry Grant—DNS Couldn't Qualify

Sold in 1961 to Art True of Seattle, Washington, who ran it often in Northwestern events for the next several years. It was eventually donated to the Henry Ford Museum in Dearborn, Michigan, where it continues to repose.

-0710-

The first customer's car with left hand drive, live axle, pontoon fenders, and inside door hinges. Unique to all the Testa Rossas, it has a detachable nose and angled cooling fins on the front brake drums. It was painted silver to the order of John Von Neumann, displayed at the pre-1958 press conference and shipped from the factory on November 25, 1957.

    1957 Nassau Trophy #50 Richie Ginther—DNS Brake Grabbing Problems

    1958 Argentina #8 John Von Neumann/Seidel—DNF Pinion Bearing

    1958 Sebring #17 Von Neumann/ Ginther—DNF Pinion Bearing

    1958 Laguna Seca National #211 Richie Ginther—3rd

The car was raced extensively by Richie Ginther and John and Josie Von Neumann in Southwestern races in 1958 and the first half of 1959. In the late fall of 1959 it was sold to Jack Nethercutt of Los Angeles as part of a package of racing Ferraris that also included 0704 and 0768. The car is believed to have been used only rarely afterwards, and eventually the original engine and transmission became separated. During the mid and late 1960s it passed through the hands of a number of California collectors, along the way acquiring the engine and transmission from 0750. It now belongs to a member of the author's family and has been completely restored to original condition, excepting color (now red), using an amalgam of engine parts from 0722 and 0710.

-0714-

The second customer's car and standard in every way with left-hand drive, live axle, pontoon fenders and inside door hinges. Sold to Piero Drogo, a Venezuelan, and delivered to him in Modena the first week of December, 1957. Drogo modified it almost immediately by installing rear brake cooling scoops underneath the doors. He secured an entry for the Argentine 1000 Kilometer race and his car was shipped to South America accompanying a factory machine.

1958 Argentina #26 Drogo/
Gonzalez—4th
1958 Cuban Grand Prix #30
Drogo—13th

It was returned to Europe and run in several minor events before being rebuilt over the summer and sold via Chinetti to Alan Connell of Fort Worth, Texas, in November 1958.

1959 Pensacola National #25 Alan Connell—3rd OA and 2nd in Class

1959 Virginia International Raceway National #24 Alan Connell—4th OA and 2nd in Class

1959 Cumberland National #21 Alan Connell—10th OA and 2nd in Class

1959 Bridgehampton National #124 Alan Connell—7th OA and 1st in Class

1959 Elkhart Lake June National #12 Alan Connell—5th OA and 1st in Class

1959 Buckley, Colorado, National #12 Alan Connell—4th OA and 2nd in Class

1959 Riverside National #12 Alan Connell—4th OA and 2nd in Class

1959 Riverside Kiwanis G.P. #12 Alan Connell—8th OA and 4th in Class

1959 Montgomery National #12 Alan Connell—6th OA and 1st in Class

Connell did not race the car after Montgomery and eventually it was taken to Chinetti's in New York, rebuilt and sold to Charlie Hayes of Washington, D.C.

1960 Thompson National #58 Charlie Hayes—DNF Dropped Valve

Hayes ran in a few other regional events in 1960, repainted the car white late in the year and sold it in February, 1961, to Carl Haas of Chicago who in turn disposed of it to Wayne Burnett in the same locale. Burnett repainted the car once again, now red, and took to the track.

1961 Meadowdale National #94 Wayne Burnett—16th
1961 Indianapolis Raceway Park National #94 Wayne Burnett—32nd
1961 Elkhart Lake June National #94 Wayne Burnett—17th
1961 Elkhart Lake 500 #94 Wayne Burnett/Charlie Hayes—DNF Bearings
1961 Nassau Trophy #94 Wayne Burnett—DNF
1962 Meadowdale National #94 Wayne Burnett—6th
1962 Elkhart Lake June National #94 Wayne Burnett—11th
1962 Elkhart Lake 500 #94 Wayne Burnett/Luke Stear—10th
1962 Nassau Trophy #94 Wayne Burnett—13th

At some point in 1961 or 1962 the original engine was removed and the dry sump unit from 0770 was installed along with a TR59 style clear carburetor cover and disk brakes.

1963 Elkhart Lake June National #94 Wayne Burnett—8th
1963 Elkhart Lake 500 #94 Wayne Burnett/Luke Stear—12th

The car was later sold to the St. Louis area with the original engine as a spare. It is now owned, restored, and re-engined back to original by Bob Dusek of Solebury, Pennsylvania. The car must be the most-raced customer's example ever, and one of the most extensively campaigned Ferraris of all time.

-0716-

A standard customer's car completed in December 1957 and used by the factory team for one race.

1958 Argentina #6 Musso/
Gendebien—DNF Accident

The car was sold in May 1958 to an Italian amateur driver, Celso Lara Barberis, who competed irregularly in minor races for several years. In the 1964-65 period it was purportedly re-engined and re-bodied as a street machine and later exported to the U.S. It has recently been re-imported back to Italy by Gulio Dubbini of Padova who also acquired engine 0748 to install in the chassis.

-0718-

A standard customer car completed in late 1957 and sold to Ecurie Belge.

1958 Goodwood #59 Lucien Bianchi—5th
1958 Silverstone #59 Bianchi—6th
1958 Le Mans #58 Bianchi/
Mairesse—DNF Clutch

Later in 1958 the car was sold to a Mexican, Julio Mariscal, painted white and shipped there. Upon arrival in Mexico the Testa Rossa was slapped with an enormous customs duty and Mariscal elected not to import it into his homeland. He had it reshipped to Los Angeles where John Von Neumann agreed to dispose of it for him. Before being disposed it was raced at least once while in Von Neumann's care.

1959 Riverside National #5 Ricardo Rodriguez—DNF Ignition

Von Neumann sold the car shortly thereafter to Gordon Glyer of Sacramento, California.

1959 Riverside Times G.P. #126 Gordon Glyer—8th

Glyer irregularly ran the car for the next several years until an accident damaged the front suspension. He removed the engine and transmission and later sold the car which acquired a Chevrolet drivetrain. It now belongs to and is being restored by Bill Chizar of San Francisco who has acquired the car's original transmission and the engine from 0750 to complete the package.

—0720—

A standard customer's car with left-hand drive, live axle, pontoon fenders, and inside door hinges. Ordered by Luigi Chinetti for Jim Johnston of Cincinnati, Ohio, and completed in January 1958. In 1958 Johnston ran the car extensively at S.C.C.A. National events and won the Class "D" Modified Championship.

1958 Marlboro National #15 Jim Johnston—7th OA (5th in C. Mod)
1958 Elkhart Lake June National #15 Jim Johnston—5th and 2nd in Class
1958 Lime Rock National #15 Jim Johnston—11th OA (3rd in C. Mod)
1958 Milwaukee National #15 Jim Johnston—5th OA (3rd in C. Mod)
1958 Elkhart Lake 500 #15 Jim Johnston/Eb Lunken/Bud Sea-verns—2nd OA and 1st in Class
1959 Sebring #14 Jim Johnston/Eb Lunken/Augie Pabst—7th

He continued to run the car in 1959, primarily at minor regional events and only competed in one National that year.

1959 Cumberland National #15 Jim Johnston—9th OA and 1st in Class

In August 1959 he sold the Testa Rossa to Dave Biggs of Clarksville, Missouri.

1959 Elkhart Lake 500 #16 Dave Biggs/Martin Baione—17th OA and 6th in Class
1960 Elkhart Lake June National #15 Dave Biggs—15th OA and 4th in Class
1960 Meadowdale National #15 Dave Biggs—10th OA and 3rd in Class
1960 Elkhart Lake 500 #52 Dave Biggs/Fred Van Beuren—24th OA
1962 Stuttgart, Arkansas National #65 Dave Biggs—8th
1962 Elkhart Lake June National #65 Dave Biggs—14th

Afterwards the car saw sporadic use. In the later 1960s, the Testa Rossa was totally destroyed in a fire in the building where it was stored and only the frame and some suspension components remain.

-0722-

A standard customer car with left-hand drive, live-axle rear, pontoon fenders and inside door hinges. Sold new to Alfonso Gomez-Mena of Havana, Cuba, and delivered to him there the third week of February 1958.

1958 Cuban Grand Prix #32 Gomez-Mena—DNS Accident in Practice

The car was quite extensively damaged in the accident and Gomez-Mena shipped it back to Modena for repairs and then entered it at Le Mans.

1958 Le Mans #17 Gomez-Mena/ Drogo—DNF Clutch

Gomez-Mena decided to concentrate on Gran Turismo racing later in 1958, selling the Testa Rossa to Chinetti, who in turn disposed of it to Jim Hunt of Fort Lauderdale, Florida. Hunt was prompted to take the action by Lloyd "Lucky" Casner who worked for him. They secured a reserve entry for Sebring in 1959, but Chinetti, feeling that Hunt lacked the necessary experience to handle such a powerful machine, made them switch to a 2.0-liter Testa Rossa for the race.

1959 Sebring #19 Hunt/Casner— DNS—Used Only in Practice

The Testa Rossa had been painted black by that stage, and was run only infrequently in 1959 before being sold to Dr. David Lane of Miami.

1959 Daytona National #90 David Lane—6th OA and 1st in Class
1959 Nassau Tourist Trophy #90 David Lane—DNF Pinion Bearing

The unhappy Dr. Lane persuaded Lucky Casner to buy the car back from him at the end of 1959.

1960 Cuban Grand Prix #40 Ward/ Gurney—13th

It was run rarely afterwards and stayed in the Southeast until 1969 when the engine, previously separated from the chassis, was sold as a spare for another Testa Rossa. Shortly afterwards the chassis was sold and, after passing through several owners, now belongs to and has been restored for Jim Rogers of Franklin, Kentucky. It is now fitted with engine 0758. The original engine has been split up, some parts going into 0710 and the balance into 0718.

-0724-

A standard left-hand-drive customer car sold new to the Scuderia Finlandia of Carl-Johann Askolin.

1958 Nürburgring #15 Curt Lincoln/Pentti Keinanen—12th

Chinetti purchased the car in late 1958 and shipped it to New York. He sold it in February 1959 to John "Buck" Fulp of Anderson, South Carolina, who ran the car very rarely.

1959 Sebring #82 Fulp—DNS Used Only in Practice
1960 Elkhart Lake USAC Pro Race #24 Skip Hudson—5th

The Testa Rossa was traded back to Chinetti in early 1961 and resold in August of that year to Alan Connell, Fort Worth, Texas. Connell removed the engine to install in a Maserati Birdcage and sold the chassis to Willis Murphey, Jr., also of Fort Worth. He fitted a Chevrolet engine and raced it for several years in that form. Murphey still owns the car and has plans to restore it to original condition. The Testa Rossa engine now belongs to Chuck Betz of Manhattan Beach, California.

—0726—

One of a pair of left-hand-drive, transaxle, pontoon fender TR58s completed in March 1958.

1958 Sebring #16 Musso/ Gendebien—2nd

Rebodied with enveloping front fenders and fitted with Solex carburetors.

1958 Targa Florio #106 Musso/ Gendebien—1st
1958 Nürburgring #5 Musso/Hill— 4th
1958 Le Mans #16 Von Trips/ Seidel—DNF Stuck in Ditch

Later the car became the TR59 prototype fitted with a clear carburetor cover and other TR59 like accoutrements. The body on this car is reported to have been constructed by Touring, and if so, it would be the last one done by that concern for Ferrari. It was sold via Carlos Kauffman to Escuderia Lagartixa in Brazil and ran in a number of Brazilian races in the 1959-62 period. Later it was rebodied and is believed to still reside in Brazil.

-0728-

A TR58 team car with left-hand drive, four-speed transaxle, rear carburetor air intake and pontoon fenders. The mate to 0726.

> *1958* Sebring #15 Hawthorn/Von Trips—DNF Transaxle and Clutch
> *1958* Targa Florio #102 Hawthorn/Von Trips—3rd

Converted to envelope body style, and rear carburetor air intake.

> *1958* Nürburgring #6 Seidel/
> *1958* Le Mans #14 Hill/Gendebien—1st

Sold to Luigi Chinetti and resold to Don Pedro Rodriguez in September 1958 to be entered for the Rodriguez brothers by NART, The rear carburetor air intake was removed and replaced by a front air scoop and the car was repainted gray and black.

> *1958* Nassau #10 Pedro Rodriguez—2nd
> *1959* Sebring #11 Pedro Rodriguez/Paul O'Shea—DNF Engine Blow up

The engine was rebuilt and the car did not see much further action during 1959. It was sold to George Reed of Midlothian, Illinois, in October 1959. He ran the Testa Rossa hardly at all and sold it in late 1960 to Owen Coon of Chicago, after purchasing a TR59. Coon ran the car quite extensively in 1961 at both Regional and National events.

> *1961* Elkhart Lake June National #8 Owen Coon—8th
> *1961* Meadowdale National #81 Owen Coon—13th
> *1961* Indianapolis Raceway Park National #6 Owen Coon—31st
> *1961* Elkhart Lake 500 #8 Owen Coon/Bob Major—DNF Engine Blow up
> *1961* Nassau Trophy #8 Owen Coon—DNF

The original engine was removed and replaced with a Chevrolet and run in that form for several years until the transaxle fell to pieces. The chassis currently belongs to Dick Merritt of Washington, D.C., who has not as yet restored it, lacking transaxle internals.

-0730-

A standard customer car sold new to E.D. Martin of Columbus, Georgia, and delivered to him in early March 1958.

> *1958* Sebring #23 Martin/Flynn—DNF Accident
> *1958* Le Mans #19 Martin/Tavano—DNF Blown Engine
> *1958* Elkhart Lake 500 #43 Martin/Flynn—DNF Pinion Bearing
> *1958* Watkins Glen National #64 Martin—10th OA and 5th in Class (C Mod)
> *1958* Nassau Trophy #46 Martin—3rd
> *1959* Sebring #12 Martin/Reventlow—6th
> *1959* Le Mans #19 Martin/Kimberly—DNF Engine

Martin brought the Testa Rossa back to the U.S. after a factory rebuild and sold it in September 1959 to Pete Harrison of Atlanta, Georgia. Harrison had continual engine problems in 1959 and 1960 and finally gave up on the car and sold it to Spencer Litchie of Fort Lauderdale, Florida. Litchie rebuilt the car from stem to stern and ran it on a number of occasions in 1961 and 62.

> *1961* Nassau Trophy #41 Litchie—12th

The engine again went sour in 1962 and was removed from the car and a 250 GT unit was installed in its place. The car was retired from racing at that point and after lying around for some years was exported to England. It has been recently sold to Beppe Lucchini of Brescia, Italy.

-0732-

A standard customer's car with left hand drive, live-axle, pontoon fenders and inside door hinges. Built for J. Edward Hugus of Pittsburgh, Pennsylvania, painted white with blue stripes to his order and delivered in early March 1958.

> *1958* Sebring #19 Hugus/Fitch—DNF
> *1958* Le Mans #22 Hugus/Erickson—7th
> *1958* Watkins Glen National #22 Ed Hugus—6th OA and 4th in Class (C Mod)

Used sparingly afterwards and sold in 1959 to Russell Cowles of Minneapolis, Minnesota, who ran it in several 1959 Regional events while living in the Southwest and then repainted dark blue.

> *1960* Riverside Examiner G.P. #24 Russell Cowles—5th

Cowles sold the car later in 1960 via Harry Woodnorth to Dave Deuble of Glenview, Illinois.

> *1961* Elkhart Lake June National #71 Ted Baumgartner—DNF Engine
> *1961* Elkhart Lake 500 #71 Ted Baumgartner/Buzz Hahn—DNF Accident

Deuble had the car rebuilt and then sold it to Tom Schelbe and Dick Candee in Milwaukee. Eventually it went to Omaha and stayed there until purchased in 1973 by Harley Cluxton of Phoenix, Arizona, and restored in his shop. Now belongs to Robert Bodin of Minnetonka, Minnesota.

-0734-

A standard customer car with left-hand drive, live axle and pontoon fenders. This car was purchased new by Frederick Gibbs of New York and was never raced at all. Gibbs kept it until he died in 1978. The literally new TR now belongs to Paul Pappalardo of Greenwich, Connecticut.

-0736-

A standard customer car, built and delivered to Jacques Swaters of Ecurie Belge in late March 1958, who already owned 0718. These two examples present a number of identification problems and some swapping of engines and chassis numbers may have taken place.

> *1958* Goodwood #58 Mairesse—
> DNF Ignition
> *1958* Nürburgring #11 Mairesse/
> DeChangy—DNF Pinion Bearing
> *1958* Le Mans #21 DeChangy/
> "Beurlys"—6th

The car is believed to have been run at a number of other minor races in 1958 and early 1959 before being rebodied to look similar to a TR59. The original engine was replaced with a 250 GT based unit for street usage and the car was exported to England. It now belongs to John and Edward Harrison of Sheffield, England.

-0738-

A standard customer car, excepting right-hand drive and a clear plastic cover over the carburetors. Sold new to Escuderia Lagartixa, a Brazilian racing team. The car remained in Brazil after its racing days were over, and during the mid-1960's it was shipped to Modena where Drogo fitted a GTO-like body for its owner, who brought it back to Brazil. The car remains in that form to this time.

-0742-

A standard customer car delivered in May 1958 to Peter Monteverdi in Zurich, Switzerland, and run infrequently for several years, primarily at hill climbs. Resold in 1960 to Georges Gachnang who rebodied it to look more like a TR61 and installed an independent rear suspension of his own design.

> *1961* Nürburgring #94 Gachnang/
> Caillet—DNF Broken Halfshaft
> *1961* Pescara #10 Gachnang/
> Caillet—12th
> *1962* Nürburgring #94 Gachnang/
> Grog—17th

The car was not used much subsequently and was eventually acquired by Pierre Bardinon of Aubusson, France, who has had it rebuilt to the original pontoon fender configuration.

-0746-

Originally a 3.0-liter V-6 Dino constructed in early 1958 and driven by Hawthorn at Silverstone on May 4. It was re-engined with a V-12 (0760) just afterward, becoming a Testa Rossa. It is believed to have run at the 1958 Nürburgring 1000 kilometers race as number 0760.

> *1958* Nürburgring #7 Von Trips/
> Gendebien—3rd

It lay at the factory in an inoperative state for the next several years. Chinetti purchased the car in the summer of 1960 and commissioned it to be rebuilt as a Testa Rossa "special" with a TR60 like body and right-hand drive for the Rodriguez family.

The car was delivered to the U.S. in November 1960.

> *1960* Nassau Trophy #57 P. & R.
> Rodriguez—2nd
> *1961* Sebring #17 P. & R.
> Rodriguez—3rd

Sold to John Bunch of New Canaan, Connecticut.

> *1961* Bridgehampton National #49
> George Constantine—4th
> *1961* Thompson National #49
> George Constantine—2nd
> *1961* Watkins Glen #20 George
> Constantine—1st
> *1961* Mosport Canadian Grand Prix
> #20 George Constantine—4th
> *1961* Riverside Times G.P. #49
> George Constantine—15th
> *1961* Nassau Tourist Trophy #49
> George Constantine—6th
> *1962* Daytona #49 George
> Constantine—5th
> *1962* Sebring #20 Constantine/
> Andrey—DNF Broken Halfshaft

The car was retired after Sebring and after passing through several owners now belongs to Pierre Bardinon of Aubusson, France.

-0748-

A standard customer car delivered to Gottfried Kochert of Vienna, Austria, in May 1958.

> *1958* Nürburgring #12 Gottfried
> Kochert/Erik Bauer—10th

After the fatal accident to Bauer, the car remained unrepaired at Modena well into the Fall. Chinetti purchased the car and commissioned a full rebuild, and sold it to Gary Laughlin of Ft. Worth, Texas, in April 1959, and the car arrived in the U.S. in July. Laughlin ran it at only a few minor events over the next several years, before disposing of it to Alan Connell, who removed the engine and sold the remainder to another local Texan.

The car suffered through various indignities over the next few years, acquiring a faired in windshield, modified exhaust pipes, clear carburetor cover and a 250GT based six-carburetor engine. In recent times the car has been restored and belongs to Bob Fergus of Columbus, Ohio. The original engine, somewhat damaged, is with Gulio Dubbini of Padova, Italy, to be installed in chassis 0716.

-0750-

A standard customer car, but having a particularly murky history. It is purported to have been originally owned by an Italian club racer. In 1959, though possibly earlier, it was sold to Ettore Chimeri of Caracas, Venezuela. During practice before the Cuban Grand Prix at Havana in February 1960, he crashed the car, and was killed. The TR was badly burned and stripped for parts. The engine found its way to California and became installed in 0710 and is currently fitted to 0718, the remains of the chassis were recently imported to France.

-0752-

One of the last batch of customer cars constructed, all featuring higher intake manifolds, a larger bulge over the carburetors and outside door hinges. It was sold new to Charles Hughes of Denver, Colorado, by Chinetti and painted blue to his order. The car was air freighted from Italy to Chicago in the last week of May 1958 to enable it to be prepared and tested to run at the Elkhart Lake races on June 21/22.

> *1958* Elkhart Lake June National #21 Dan Collins—3rd OA and 1st in Class

Hughes, unhappy with the color painted by the factory, had the car redone in a different shade of blue later in 1958. The car was run primarily (and very successfully) at events in the Denver area in 1958/59 as any non-local race venues were a long way off.

> *1959* Buckley Field National #21 Dan Collins—2nd OA and 1st in Class

Later in 1959 during the process of a divorce, Hughes sold the car to Alex Budurin of Tucson, Arizona, who had a generally desultory racing career with it. Later the original engine was removed and components from it were wedded to a 250 GT unit and reinstalled in the car which passed through a number of owners. It now belongs to Anthony Bamford of Stoke-on-Trent, England.

-0754-

A customer car sold new to Jaroslav Juhan of Guatemala and delivered to Paris in early June, 1958, where it would be prepared for Le Mans by Charles Pozzi.

> *1958* Le Mans #20 Picard/Juhan—DNF Accident

The car is purported to have run at several other minor races in 1958. It was sold to Stan Sugarman of Phoenix, Arizona, in early 1959, and resold that summer to George Keck of Vancouver, British Columbia, Canada.

> *1959* Elkhart Lake 500 #24 George Keck/Frank Beck—10th OA and 3rd in Class

Keck sold the car in early 1960 to Jack Graham of San Jose, California, who ran it in a number of events that year.

> *1960* Riverside Times G.P. #4 Jack Graham—DNS Accident
> *1960* Laguna Seca Examiner G.P. #4 Jack Graham—DNS Accident

The Laguna Seca accident quite thoroughly destroyed the body and a new one was built for it, though not totally identical to the original. The car is now owned by David Love of Berkeley, California.

-0756-

A standard customer car completed in late June 1958 to the order of Dick Morgensen of Phoenix, Arizona. The car was shipped by boat from Italy to California and delivered to Morgensen by Von Neumann in late August. Morgensen started racing rather cautiously but began to really hit his stride in 1959, racking up numerous successes over the next few years before retiring the car. Generally he campaigned the Testa Rossa in California Sports Car Club Races, but additionally ran at many other events.

> *1959* Riverside National #46 Dick Morgensen—2nd OA and 1st in Class
> *1959* Riverside Times G.P. #46 Dick Morgensen—4th
> *1960* Riverside Examiner G.P. #46 Dick Morgensen—4th

Morgensen retired the car after the 1960 season and it stayed in Phoenix for many years before being acquired by Harley Cluxton, also of Phoenix. The car now belongs to Dr. Lou Sellyei of Reno, Nevada, and has been restored to top-notch condition.

-0758-

A standard customer car completed in July 1958 and shipped to Caracas, Venezuela, for Carlos Kauffman. It was sold to Jose Miguel Galia who raced it on a number of occasions. The chassis is now in Holland, but has been so extensively modified over the years that hardly anything Testa Rossa remains. The original engine has been separated from the chassis for many years and in recent times was brought to the U.S. and is now installed in chassis 0722.

The Keck/Beck 250TR displays its chassis number at Elkhart Lake on September 13, 1959.

-0766-

The first of a trio of TR59s to be built carrying the Pininfarina-designed, Fantuzzi-built bodies. This car is very distinctive as it has a bump in the hood by the carburetor air intake to clear the fuel line.

> *1959* Sebring #7 Hill/Gendebien/
> Daigh/Gurney—1st

Changed from single to dual-pipe exhaust system.

> *1959* Targa Florio #152 Hill/
> Gendebien—DNF Ring and Pinion

Converted back to single pipe exhaust system.

> *1959* Nürburgring #4 Hill/
> Gendebien—2nd
> *1959* Le Mans #14 Hill/
> Gendebien—DNF Head Gasket

Converted to dry sump oiling system.

> *1959* Tourist Trophy #10 Brooks/
> Hill/Allison—3rd

Rebuilt at the factory. Sold to Luigi Chinetti for the Rodriguez family and delivered to the U.S. in November 1959.

> *1959* Nassau—Ferrari Only Race
> #10 Pedro Rodriguez—2nd
> *1959* Nassau Trophy #10 Pedro
> Rodriguez—12th
> *1960* Cuban Grand Prix #10 Pedro
> Rodriguez—2nd
> *1960* Le Mans #17 Ricardo
> Rodriguez/Andre Pilette—2nd

Sold to Hap Sharp of Midland, Texas, in November 1960.

> *1960* Nassau Trophy #95 Hap
> Sharp—6th
> *1961* Palm Springs #10 Ron
> Hissom—2nd
> *1961* Sebring #10 Sharp/Hissom—
> 4th

Sold to Bob Hurt, Bethesda, Maryland.

> *1961* Watkins Glen National #310
> Bob Hurt—11th
> *1961* Riverside Times G.P. #36 Bob
> Hurt—Did Not Qualify
> *1961* Laguna Seca Examiner G.P.
> #36 Bob Hurt—15th & 16th (Two
> Heat Race)
> *1961* Nassau Governor's Trophy #58
> Bob Hurt—3rd
> *1961* Nassau Trophy #58 Bob
> Hurt—DNF Broken Halfshaft
> *1962* Bossier City, Louisiana, Formula Libre #36 Bob Hurt—4th
> *1962* Meadowdale National #36
> Bob Hurt—DNF Food Poisoning
> *1962* Canadian G.P. #36 Bob
> Hurt—8th
> *1962* Riverside Times G.P. #36 Bob
> Hurt—Did Not Qualify
> *1962* Laguna Seca Examiner G.P.
> Bob Hurt—15th
> *1963* Elkhart Lake June National #36
> Bob Hurt—DNF

Later sold to Hurt's mechanic, Gordon Tatum, of Washington, D.C., who removed the engine/transmission. Disposed of to Bill Webber of St. Louis from whom a member of the author's family acquired it, purchasing at the same time the original engine and transmission. Now restored.

-0768-

A TR59 completed in January 1959.

> *1959* Sebring #9 Behra/Allison—
> 2nd
> *1959* Targa Florio #150 Behra/
> Brooks—DNF Ring & Pinion
> *1959* Nürburgring #3 Behra/
> Brooks—3rd

Converted to dry sump system and sold to John Von Neumann. Shipped to Los Angeles in late September, 1959.

> *1959* Riverside Times G.P. #2 Phil
> Hill—1st
> *1959* Nassau Trophy #4 Phil Hill—
> 2nd

Sold to Jack Nethercutt of Los Angeles in mid-December 1959

> *1960* Sebring #8 Nethercutt/
> Lovely—3rd
> *1960* Riverside Examiner G.P. #102
> Pete Lovely—3rd
> *1961* Sebring #9 Nethercutt/
> Lovely—DNF Broken Oil Pump

Sold to Dick Hahn of Yakima, Washington, in August 1961.

> *1962* Mosport Players 200 #78 Jerry
> Grant—9th

Sold to Bob Lampman of Seattle, Washington, in December 1962 and later resold to Pete Lovely, Tacoma, Washington, who still owns it.

Augie Pabst all wound up at Elkhart Lake on September 10, 1960.

-0770-

A TR59 completed in February 1959.
> *1959* Sebring #8 Hill/Gendebien—
> DNF Ring and Pinion

Modified to larger carburetors and revised camshaft timing.
> *1959* Targa Florio #154 Gurney/
> Allison—DNF Ring & Pinion
> *1959* Nürburgring #5 Gurney/
> Allison—5th
> *1959* Le Mans #15 Allison/Da Silva
> Ramos—DNF Engine Blown up

Modified to dry sump system.
> *1959* Tourist Trophy #9 Brooks/
> Gurney—5th

Rebuilt at the factory and modified to TR59/60.
> *1960* Argentina #2 Von Trips/
> Ginther—2nd
> *1960* Nürburgring #2 Allison/
> Mairesse/Hill—3rd
> *1960* Le Mans #9 Hill/Von Trips—
> DNF Out of Gas

Sold to Chinetti for the Rodriguez family.
> *1960* Nassau Governor's Trophy #28
> Pedro Rodriguez—DNF Accident

Resold in January 1961 to George Reed of Midlothian, Illinois.
> *1961* Sebring #16 Reed/Bill
> Sturgis—8th
> *1961* Meadowdale National #95
> George Reed—7th
> *1961* Elkhart Lake 500 #95 George
> Reed/Ed Hugus—2nd
> *1961* Watkins Glen National #63
> George Reed—7th
> *1961* Canadian G.P. #63 George
> Reed—5th

The Testa engine was replaced by a 3.5-liter 290 MM engine about this time. The original engine was sold to Wayne Burnett.
> *1961* Nassau Governor's Trophy #93
> George Reed—2nd
> *1961* Nassau Tourist Trophy #93
> George Reed—8th
> *1962* Mosport Players 200 #63
> George Reed—8th

In 1962 the 290 MM engine was replaced by a 4.5-liter 375 MM Ferrari unit.
> *1962* Elkhart Lake 500 #93 Bob
> Hurt/Alan Ross—DNF Differential
> Input Shaft
> *1962* Nassau Trophy #95 George
> Reed—10th

The 4.5-liter Ferrari engine was taken out and a Ford stock car engine fitted. In this guise it ran a number of races before being retired permanently. The chassis later went to England and is now owned by James Allington in Hitchin, Hertfordshire. The original engine is with Bob Dusek, Solebury, Pennsylvania.

-0772-

One of a pair of TR59s completed in April 1959 and utilized that year for various experiments. Rebuilt in the fall of 1959 as a TR59/60.
> *1960* Targa Florio #202 Ginther/
> Allison—DNF Accident

Subsequent to the Targa Florio accident it is reputed to have been stripped and scrapped with the chassis number applied to 0774 for the 1960 Le Mans race.

-0774-

Built in conjunction with 0772 and identical to it.
> *1959* Le Mans #12 Behra/Gurney—
> DNF Engine

Modified to dry sump oiling system.
> *1959* Tourist Trophy #11 Hill—DNF
> Dropped Valve

Rebuilt to TR59/60 form.
> *1960* Argentina #4 Hill/Allison—1st
> *1960* Sebring #7 Ginther/Daigh—
> DNF Seized Engine
> *1960* Le Mans #11 Gendebien/
> Frere—1st (Ran as 0772)

Sold to Eleanor Von Neumann of Los Angeles, California.
> *1960* Riverside Times G.P. #2 Phil
> Hill—7th

The clutch failed during that race and the car was not run again. Eventually it was sold to the Rosebud Racing Team in Victoria, Texas, who wanted the engine to install in a Lotus. Later, the chassis was given to Innes Ireland who drove for Rosebud, and he took it to England. Eventually Colin Crabbe of Baston, England, purchased the chassis, fitted it with a 3.3-liter 275 P based engine and larger brakes and went vintage racing. The car now belongs to Paul Pappalardo of Greenwich, Connecticut who has recently acquired the original engine.

George Reed waits for the start of the Canadian Grand Prix at Mosport on September 30, 1961.

-0780-

One of a pair of TRI60s constructed in March 1960 featuring an independent rear suspension and further rearward placement of the engine, but otherwise basically similar to the TR59/60.

1960 Targa Florio #196 Allison—DNS Wrecked in Practice
Believed rebuilt with parts from 0772 and entered for Le Mans.

1960 Le Mans #10 Mairesse/Ginther—DNF Broken Driveshaft
Kept at the factory as a test vehicle for 1961 and rebuilt late in 1960 with a TR61 rear body shape and retaining the 1960 style front end.

1961 Sebring #15 Mairesse/Baghetti/Ginther/Von Trips—2nd
1961 Targa Florio #160 P. Rodriguez/Mairesse—DNF Accident
Converted to TR61 nose.
1961 Nürburgring #5 P. and R. Rodriguez—2nd
1961 Le Mans #11 Mairesse/Parkes—2nd
1961 Pescara #4 Bandini/Scarlatti—1st

This chassis became the basis for 0808 and its history terminates at that point.

-0782-

The second TRI60 also completed in March 1960.

1960 Nürburgring #1 Hill/Von Trips—DNF Blown Gasket
1960 Le Mans #12 P. Rodriquez/Scarfiotti—DNF Out of Gas

There seem to be several different versions of the car's subsequent history. The most believable of them is that it was retained as a test vehicle for some years, sold in Italy where it was rebodied to coupe form and later to a 250 P-like shape. Another story has the car in Australia, but the author is unable to confirm this either as fact or fiction.

-0792-

A TR61 with nostril nose and squared-off back completed in January 1961.

1961 Sebring #14 Hill/Gendebien—1st
1961 Le Mans #17 P. and R. Rodriguez—DNF Blown Engine
Sold to Count Giovanni Volpi for Scuderia Serenissima of Venice in September 1961.

1961 Nassau Trophy #5 Graham Hill—5th
1962 Sebring #23 Bonnier/Bianchi—1st
1962 Nürburgring #90 Abate/Vaccarella—DNF Accident
1962 Le Mans #15 Bonnier/Gurney—DNF Rear Hub Carrier
Volpi had the car rebodied with a horizontal air spoiler just behind the cockpit, lowered the tail profile along with other changes which resulted in an altogether different looking car.

1963 Nürburgring #112 Maglioli/Abate—3rd
1963 Reims #30 Abate—1st
1963 Auvergne #59 Bandini—1st
The car was raced on a few other occasions before being retired for good. It is still owned by Count Volpi and he is known to sometimes use it on the road.

-0794-

The second and last TR61 to be constructed, also completed in January 1961. It had some handling ailments that prevented immediate competition use and did not see any action until Le Mans.

1961 Le Mans #10 Hill/Gendebien—1st
It was rebuilt after Le Mans as it had been sold to Luigi Chinetti and he wanted it for the 1961 Fall U.S. races.

1961 Mosport Canadian G.P. #2 P. Rodriguez—2nd
1961 Riverside Times G.P. #68 R. Rodriguez—Did Not Qualify
1961 Nassau Governor's Trophy #2 P. Rodriguez—1st
1961 Nassau Trophy #2 P. Rodriguez—3rd
1962 Daytona #50 R. Rodriguez/Ryan—15th
1962 Sebring #26 Moss/Ireland—Disqualified
1962 Le Mans #18 Fulp/Ryan—DNF Accident
Sold to Dick Hahn of Yakima, Washington, in the Fall of 1962.

1963 Westwood, B.C., Players 200 Stan Burnett—6th and 5th in Heats
1963 Kent, Wash., Northwest G.P. Stan Burnett—3rd
Later the car was acquired by Bev Spencer and has recently become the property of Anthony Bamford, Stoke-on-Trent, England.

-0808-

The 4.0-liter 330 TR/LM "Experimental" built on a lengthened TR61 chassis (0780) specifically for the 1962 Le Mans race.

1962 Le Mans #6 Hill/Gendebien—
1st

Sold during the summer to Luigi Chinetti for the Rodriguez family.

1962 Bridgehampton Double 500 #8
P. Rodriguez—1st
1962 Mosport Canadian G.P. #8
P. Rodriguez—2nd
1962 Nassau Trophy #7 Masten
Gregory—4th
1963 Sebring #18 G. Hill/
P. Rodriguez—3rd
1963 Le Mans #10 R. Penske/
P. Rodriguez—DNF Accident

Subsequent to Le Mans the car was sent to Modena, rebodied in coupe form and sent back to the U.S. It is now the property of Pierre Bardinon of Aubusson, France, who has restored it to the 1962 Le Mans roadster configuration.

0732 after flipping at Elkhart Lake on September 9, 1961.

Gendebien pays a good will call on the mechanics preparing his car the night before Le Mans in 1961.